THE 'COMPLETE' STORIES

Carole Malkin

Introduction

Earlier this year, 2015, I was going through Carole's papers and computers, and I kept finding stories that she had written over the years, with some going as far back to when she was a graduate student in Creative Writing at San Francisco State. Many of the stories were in a finished state, some were rough drafts in a few pages, and some were much longer and were later developed into full novels. I also found a type-written copy of *Moshe the Magician*, a complete novel finished in the 1990s which she had finished, attempted to publish and finally gave it a resting place in a desk drawer. This novel joined three other novels, now listed on Amazon's Create Space that I have self-published in her name over the past year. But what to do with these newly found stories?

I decided to put these into another volume with the above title. I am not sure there are not more storied hiding away in some file cabinet or in desk drawers and this is why I am tentative with the "complete" title. Much of the work was done on an IBM electric typewriter, and this necessitated having these digitized and then converted into usable computer files. There may be errors, etc., but this is not the original author's problem but rather those of a poor editor.

I have tried to give the stories some organization. One group, which I call *The Cancer Stories*, were written over a ten year period when Carole was fighting breast cancer. Several of the cancer stories were also written when our son, Daniel, was dealing with melanoma. The other larger group I have simply called *Family and Friends* because they deal with what Carole new best, her everyday friends and her memories of her youth and its many personal complications.

Dick Malkin
Colorado Springs
October 21, 2015

Table of Contents

Family and Friends

Cancer

The Search for Serenity

"How's my boy, huh? How's my girl?" were the first words out of Marv's mouth when he came home. He threw down his sample case, kissed his wife Linda and baby Amy, and three year old Julian, scampered up in his arms. His shoulders ached from so much driving, his head throbbed and he was bitter from a day of insinuating himself into the little shops where he sold his kitchen magnets, hooks and hot plates, but even so he infused his voice with enthusiasm. "How's my big boy? What? Are you playing with blocks?" and he got down on the floor to build a tower and give Julian a piggyback ride.

Their rent-controlled lower East Side apartment had been inherited when Linda's Aunt died six years ago. This was shortly before Linda and Marv were married, and the Aunt's son said, "Well, Linda has the same last name. Just move in, give the super a few hundred under the table and a bottle at Christmas, and I don't think there will be problems."

There was a minuscule kitchen and a living room and bedroom. Marv had painted the high ceilings and dingy walls himself, although he never intended to stay there long. By New York standards the living room was large, but that wasn't really large at all, not with the four of them and the apartment filled up like a junk shop. Even Linda's compulsive straightening never relieved the chaos.

For two years they had been house hunting, and although they diligently followed the leads of their realtor and scoured Long Island and Westchester, Marv could never bring himself to the point of signing a contract. His heart sank when he saw the slap-dash ordinariness of what they could afford on his salary as a 'sales rep,' and he kept searching, wishing to find something more substantial, a place worthy of his family.

"What in God's name are you looking for?" Linda asked with exasperation. She was thirty-nine, two years older than him. She had changed little despite the two pregnancies. Her figure was still trim, her movements brisk. Her dark hair framed a thin, foxlike face with faintly protuberant eyes. She had been jilted in her early twenties and by the time Marv met her, she accepted him because he was 'serious.' Marv, rounder, even pot bellied, with thinning hair, no longer had the good looks which had attracted the string of secretaries and typists he dated in his twenties and early thirties. His short temper ravaged each of those relationships. He was grateful for Linda, someone who kept out of his way when he was moody. He'd heard her boast, "I can handle Marv." Marv answered her question about what he was waiting for, "When I see the right house, I'll know it."

In high school a friend had invited him along on a trip to rich relatives in Westchester. Two decades later, he still thought of that sky-filled living room, the blues and whites of rug, walls and delicate furniture. On his salesman's route, as he steered his Plymouth along the fumed freeways with car horns honking on every side, he imagined the glass paned French doors open to the green lawn. At night he dreamt of the private dock and the bay of rippling waves and bobbing sailboats. The alarm clock would scream, and he'd stir for a moment, but the house and its beauty called him back to its ethereal rooms and manicured grounds. Not that he expected to find an identical house, but he wanted one that gave him the same light, cleansed feeling.

They took the children along house hunting. Julian came to hate being trapped in the back of the car and screamed during the long rides. For Amy's sake, they had to stop at gas stations to warm bottles under bathroom taps and dispose of diapers. The situation grew more urgent after a notice arrived announcing the apartments in their building were to be converted to condominiums. Linda snapped, "You better pick something before we're out on our asses."

He pleaded for patience. "Trust me," he said. When they found the right house, he would spend each weekend, mowing the lawn, painting fences or sanding cabinets. He often imagined himself performing these reassuring and pleasing chores with Julian and Amy beside him, looking up, grateful for the beauty in which he had placed them. Marv told her, "All week I'm selling my balls, trying to get the money together so we can get something better."

"Well, what do you think-I'm taking it easy working with my twelve year old hoodlums?"

Linda had a part-time job teaching art in a junior high school and he often tried to get her to see how different it was, that he felt degraded by the salesman flattery he oozed and the insults he took with a broad smile. He drove from one shopping mall to another to solicit orders for his kitchen sundries if he was in the area and dropped into one of the upscale boutiques, which carried his merchandise, he might be told, "Why didn't you phone for an appointment?" If he phoned, he was just as likely to hear, "Look I'm not going to tie myself up just so you can write an order. Take your chances and stop by when you're out this way." Linda sympathized with such frustrations, would soothe him, but he felt she never quite understood the pain he went through ever day.

One of the few customers he could count on for a warm welcome was Joanna. In her fifties, she dressed in tight dresses, spike heels and wore heavy make-up. False eyelashes framed her green eyes, and blonde streaks flashed through her wavy gray hair. Her mouth was soft and large. When he walked into the store she managed in the Long Island shopping mall, her eyes lit up. "Marv! How are you?

It was one of those hole-in-the-wall places with dainty dishtowels, bath salts and greeting cards. He knew that even if not a single one of his tiny ceramic sushi or croissant refrigerator magnets had sold since he'd come around three months before, she would order more. Her husband Ray had been an old friend.

Marv always liked the way they lived high, as if the party would never end. When Ray died, though, everything fell to pieces. Joanna might have starved if Marv hadn't helped out with a few bucks and used his contacts to get her job. It always gratified him to see her because she wasn't one of those people who used you and then moved on.

When he came in, she thanked him again and he told her, "Don't thank me. You can't trust anybody, not even me."

She would reply, "You. I'd trust you with my life."

The last time, he'd spilled out his guts to her and told her, "Mon--ney!" I'm being crucified by money."

She grew alarmed, and for the first time confided how Ray had borrowed from thugs from Carnasie and lived in terror he couldn't pay them back. Tension had brought on the heart attack. Marv wanted to know all the details. Perceiving his eagerness, she cried, "Keep away from them Marv. What are you crazy?"

"I'm not that crazy," he told her.

A few hours later, he was driving on the Belt Parkway in a rush hour jam. The traffic was moving slowly and there was a new blue Mercedes behind him. It would be a pleasure to be rear-ended. Although he didn't think he'd be hurt at all, he would claim whiplash and receive an out-of-court settlement of thousands. He often thought such thoughts, but this was the first time--as if in a dream--he slammed down on the brake The Mercedes swerved into the next lane, almost side-swiping another car. The driver cocked his finger as he drove by, and Marv cursed to himself as he watched the car drive past, a potential fortune out of reach.

At home, Marv lit a match to test the kitchen's smoke detector, hoping for defect, for a fire and the opportunity to threaten a lawsuit. When he confided his plan to Linda, she sneered, "This is planet earth, Marv."

My ace in the hole is Lou Gold," Marv explained to Linda. "The man is a legend in the industry. One word from him and people pay attention." Lou was in his seventies, silver haired, quick witted and Marv deeply respected his accomplishments and his graciousness. A Polish holocaust survivor, he had designed and manufactured all those useless store-away-in-a-high-cabinet items a bride receives, bun warmers, electric kettles and sandwich toasters, and become a millionaire. Their friendship was so precious to Marv that he hated to endanger it by asking a favor. But if Lou made the contact for him and Simons Mail Order carried Marv's sundries, he would write an order for thousands.

When Lou said, "I'm glad you asked. I'll see what I can do," Marv felt like he'd like to lay down his life for the man by the end of the week a buyer from Simons phoned and agreed to go to dinner. "Lou and I are like this," Marv told Linda, holding up two touching fingers. "He's like a father to me."

Marv planned his seduction carefully, taking the Simons representative to an expensive seafood restaurant overlooking the Hudson River. The headlights of passing cars twinkled like stars on the George Washington Bridge. The river shimmered. Lights sparkled on the Palisades, cliffs. Marv ordered salmon. It arrived, all pink and succulent scored by the grill. He intended to court the man with amusing jokes. But his pitch was off. With his delicate gagging, afraid he had swallowed a fish bone. Even at dessert he felt as if that tiny, dangerous bone was still lodged in his throat. He coughed. His napkin to his mouth, he spit out a mouthful of chocolate cake. Across the table, the small bespectacled man, looked away into the night. He told Marv, "I'll let you know."

But he didn't and when Marv phoned he couldn't get by the secretary.

"I'm sorry Marv," Lou Gold told him. "I really had to twist his arm and I don't think he was interested in the first place. I can bring the horse to water, but I can't make him drink."

"Yeah," Marv muttered, but he felt a sting of hurt. Lou had leverage, he hadn't used. All he had had to do was hint at withdrawing from his own contract with Simons for them to strike a deal with Marv. But perhaps he was mistaken. Perhaps Lou had tried his best.

Just as if he could read Marv's mind, Lou said, "I did my best." Marv just couldn't get angry or hold a grudge against this man whom he admired so much. "I know you did," he said, and inwardly, the salesman to the core, he started selling himself with a million excuses for Lou. It was a relief to resume the old, warm feeling between them and bury the incident. "I understand," he assured him as they said goodbye.

What he understood was there would be no coming home triumphant, crowing to Linda, "I did it!" He brooded over every mistake at the seafood restaurant. He'd had his chance and it slipped through his fingers like water.

Resigned, days later, he put in a bid for a home in Hicksville. It was a tract house, close to the street, abrupt and rawly efficient.

The bid was accepted on a Friday and on the following Sunday they were going to drive out to a family party in Blue Harbor, New Jersey. In the summers Marv's cousins brought Aunt Martha up from Miami. There was always a party for the old lady. His cousins who were in their forties and fifties, invited Marv and Linda, but when the two of them got there, they found themselves ignored or at best on the periphery of conversations.

Linda asked, "Why do you bother?" Many times she told him to just forget about them, that contact with his relations only reminded him of the homeless, shiftless life he had had—first his father had taken off when he was three and then when he was thirteen his mother died, and they'd passed him around, all of them throwing up their hands at his truancy and rebellion, not wanting anything to do with him and finally sending him to a State orphanage. But even though he despised these gatherings, he never could resist the compulsion to be included.

"What the heck? We'll go. Why not?" he said off-handedly, as if the whole thing amused him. "For Aunt Martha's sake. What is she two hundred years old now?"

"All right," she said. "But don't come crying to me. I'm not the one getting an ulcer."

They didn't get the children to bed until late. As usual, he bathed Julian. The boy was being toilet trained and they peed together. Julian was almost too small to reach and stood totteringly on tiptoes to get his small cock over the toilet's rim. He reached up for Marv's hand for balance while they sprayed their yellow arcs. "Old Man River, just keeps rolling," Marv warbled, pausing to cough, to take a drag from his cigarette. "You and me, we work and pee." Julian giggled with appreciation. "Old man river, just keeps flowing." He had a special voice he used, a "daddy-voice," Linda called it. "Marv," she'd tell people, "used to be devil may care, but he changed the second Julian came out of my vagina."

Even as he was reading Julian Dr. Seuss, Marv was adding up 'the numbers' in his head, the mortgage down payment, the closing costs for a house he didn't really want. "Hop on pop. Pop. Hop." Yes, that was him, a Pop hopping and hopping. Linda who grew up in a ranch house in the suburbs just couldn't understand what getting the right house meant to him, a house like the one he remembered with plenty of space so he didn't feel trapped. Tears filled his eyes as he read and Julian touched his arm and asked, "What's the matter, Daddy?"

It was eleven thirty and Marv had slipped out to an all night drug store to buy a pint of ice cream. When he returned he found Linda curled up on the couch in a zippered housedress, talking on the phone. "My mother," she mouthed.

Marv slapped his forehead and asked, "Does she know what time it is?"

She tried to continue her conversation but Marv couldn't contain himself, "Give me the receiver." There was a struggle with Linda holding on saying, "Ma, all right. I hear what you're saying, but I can't talk now. Let's talk tomorrow. Alllllright."

"What did she want?" Marv barked.

"She wanted to know when we're going to go see them."

"Are they going to pay for the gas and tolls?" Reaching for his pack of Luckies, he took out a fag, lit it and inhaled.

"What do you have against my parents?" She'd found a spot on the mauve carpet now and was working rubbing it out.

"What do they have against me? They never liked me." Linda shrugged. "They don't like anyone."

With difficulty he said, "They think you married down." It was Dave, Linda's father, he detested. He remembered the first visits when Dave would dig at him and

15

humiliate him. The man was a car salesman. He was an idiot but he had some business sense and he was always rubbing it in because Marv wasn't as successful as him. "Well, if they had their way I'd still be a virgin waiting for the Prince. What are you complaining about? My father paid for the wedding. Marvin, they're *mesuganah* old people, but they want to see their grandchildren."

"So? That's their problem," he said stubbornly, wondering at Linda's loyalty. While she was single her parents had taunted her for being an old maid, but when she met Marv, they didn't think he was good enough. Besides, they fussed over and spoiled Linda's brother and she was shunted into the background.

"You know what your problem is? You're too damn sensitive!"

The phone rang again and he grabbed the receiver before Linda could get to it. Certain it was her mother again, he said, "So Solly, Chinese Laundry, Long number," and slammed it down.

Linda shook her head, "What if it wasn't her?" Then she started to giggle. His outrageousness amused her.

He slept lightly, dreamlessly and then woke. The room was rank with the breath of the four of them, noisy with Julian's snores and whimpers, baby Amy's adenoidal breathing. A street lamp shone in the window and Linda's skin looked raw and pitted without makeup. The two cribs crowded beside the double bed. On a night stand the clock read four thirty two. Its glowing digits illuminated a five-year-old wedding photograph, Marv with a jocular expression, boyish with his blond hair and snub nose. A white rose and sprig of baby's breath was pinned to his lapel. Linda wore a beige suit and looked frightened behind a fixed smile. He had wanted her to wear a wedding gown, but she said she wouldn't make a fuss as if she were a young girl, and anyway, "Why waste money?"

Ambulances and police cars screamed in the streets. He could hear them over the whir of the noisy air conditioner. Never mind. Soon he and Linda would be moving. Today the Hicksville house would give his cousins something to gossip about at the reunion. Last year, he'd told them he was earning about twice as much as he actually made and Sol and Herman had looked at him with respect. But when they would hear "Hicksville," they'd know he lied or think he was timid and cheap. It would be a two-hour drive to Sol's country house and when they arrived he'd find the same old crap. But the moment he decided not to go, he regretted it. Maybe he would enjoy himself despite everything. He didn't have to tell them about the Hicksville house just yet. "What do they have to know?" he'd say to Linda. She and the kids would have an outing and he might find himself amused by all the usual goings-on.

He had to thread around the cribs to tiptoe out of the crowded bedroom, then down the hall where he half-tripped on Julian's tricycle. As he jutted his arm out to steady himself, pain shot through his back. He thought, 'this is it,' like Ray,' but in a moment the pain was gone.

At the first flicker of the fluorescent light, the kitchen cockroaches skittered back into the walls. Every day Linda warred against them with spray and cleansers, even though he'd told her, "The cockroaches came over with the pilgrims. They're God damned immortal." Everything was so facocktah old in the apartment, the veined sink, the bulky cabinets, and the claw foot bathtub. Hicksville would be better. He ran water into a coffee maker Lou Gold had given him at their last meeting. "Take it. Take it. I won't let you leave empty handed."

He sat at a small Formica table arrayed with chairs and two high chairs and cradled his calculator in his hand, punching in the numbers of his bank and checking accounts, his stock, and then subtracting running deficits like the remaining car and television payments. All these calculations had already been gone through in his head, but he had to do them again, praying they would change. If only miraculously several extra thousand showed up, he could pull off a better deal than the Hicksville house.

His fingertips were yellow with nicotine. He lit a Lucky. Goddamn, he'd been smoking since he was thirteen when his mother died and he just couldn't stop. One of these days he'd walk into one of the shopping mall stores and drop dead on the spot. Yeah, he really was a goddamn masochist, he thought to himself as he made himself count every dollar in his bill fold. The bit of paper with his father's phone number slipped out. He'd scribbled it down the previous winter when he got that unexpected call from Mrs. Fleischer.

"Your poor father's a sick man," she had told him in a whiny voice. The bastard hadn't even had the guts to phone himself. No, he left it to some busybody old harpy who wanted to see a sentimental reunion of seventy-two year old Daddy and little 'Mar-vie.' His father couldn't have come more than a half-dozen times after the divorce, and he hadn't even shown up for Marv's mother's funeral. After that, he disappeared from Marv's life.

"He remembers your blond curls," Mrs. Fleischer had said, and Marv had retorted, "Tell him I'm losing my hair."

Later, Linda had asked, "Now, what in the world does he want?

19

Sure that's what the bastard wants." Marv was glad she'd found some way of summing it up, enclosing a nebulous danger, which made his heart thump.

At least, Marv wasn't going to phone and beg him for anything. That gave him a lot of satisfaction "A swift strike, " Marv said as he steered the car along the turnpike passing green fields and weathered barns. They had left the New York apartment with an intention of arriving late and leaving early He sang out,"Hellooooo Aunt Martha, hellooo cousin Ceila, cousin Herman." Julian took up the chant. As a treat, he'd let him sit beside him in the front and promised that he could have a ride in Sol's motorboat. Linda sat in the backseat with Amy. Dressed up in her black, sleeveless shift, she looked smart in an angular way. The baby wore a pink, ruffled dress and Linda kept 'gilding the lily,' brushing Amy's dark curls or rewashing her face with a damp cloth. "Mommy's girl's going to look beautiful, isn't she? Isn't she?" she crooned.

Sol and Thea bought the New Jersey place for the "boating waters." It wasn't a rustic country home, but a brick suburban row house. As Marv came out of the air conditioned car into a blast of summer heat and up the walkway, he couldn't help but note that even though it was only a second home, Sol's house looked newer and costlier than the Hicksville place. Thea, tall and thin, dressed in a tailored skirt and shirt, threw open the door and cried, "Well look who's here." She drew them inside, down a hall, past a blown-up photograph of Sol and herself in their speedboat.

The living room was filled with Marv's relations, drinking scotch and soda, smoking. They were for the most part short and stocky, the men in the garment trade, cutters or owners of small factories-except for Sol who had gone to college and gotten an engineering degree and then become a manufacturer of generators and precision electrical equipment. Thea, a devotee of classic styles, dressed simply but the other women wore glittering, bright materials. They talked loudly, a rat-tat-tat of questions, but didn't wait for answers. "So how's business, Marv? What have you been doing with yourself?"

"Marvin," Aunt Martha cried. The shriveled, gray haired octogenarian widow, hobbled over to embrace him. "I can't believe it. I can't believe I'm seeing you." He was touched. The old woman had softened from what she'd been years earlier when she ordered him out of her house and had her son Ben drive him to the orphanage. She had been hysterical the months he lived with her, always nagging at him until he exploded and called her the devil. Still, he was grateful that later, she let him come and stay with her for vacations. No one else would have him. Now it was she who was alone and needy and she clung to him. He pulled her aside and gave her a ten-dollar bill. "I don't need," she protested. He insisted, "Give it to the *shul*. Make a contribution in my name."

Linda, carrying Amy on her hip and dragging a shy Julian along made a beeline for Sol to ask about the promised boat ride. Sol culled the most respect because of his greater financial success. Although the youngest of Martha's children, he assumed the role of patriarch. "Who wants to go on the boat?" he sang out. He wore a yachting cap perched on his frizzy hair. The room was bedecked with photographs of lighthouses, sea gulls and sailboats. Sol was the captain of both land and water. "Be sure you get a life jacket on him," Linda warned as she handed Julian over. Sol shrugged with genial mockery. The bad luck and disasters always present in Linda's imagination, didn't trouble him.

In the drift of the afternoon, Marv found himself talking with Herman, another cousin, this one with a close-cropped crew cut, intense blue eyes and a bulbous nose. His wife, an elaborate bleached blonde, famous for her migraines, had stayed home. In her presence, Herman was strident. But this afternoon, he stood in the light streaming through the big window, which overlooked a bay, and acted in a softened, friendly manner. Marv began to tell him about his friend Lou Gold. "Like this," he said holding up the two fused fingers. The others started listening too. They had read the name in the newspapers. "A legend in the industry....made millions....a prince of a man."

As he was basking in their attention, he noticed Julian come running in, crying, "Mommy, I had fun, " and he was glad he came. He continuing addressing his small audience, telling how a few years before Lou Gold had left his wife and married a young secretary, and had two children with her. It amused him to shock them, and he said, "I have to hand it to him, how many men in their seventies would have the balls to do that? He's a real prince, an aristocrat. He does what he wants. And he's like a father to me. He told me, 'Come work for me any time." "Why didn't you?" Herman asked. "Because," Marv answered, "I don't like to depend on friends. Ours is a friendship, not a business relation." He remembered, the time, he and Lou had a few drinks and Lou had made the offer but when Marv followed through the next day and said, 'yes,' he was interested, Lou grew distant. "I'll get back to you," he'd told Marv and Marv never brought the subject up again. Marv would have pressed someone else, but not Lou.

Thea called out that it was time for dinner. She was an excellent cook and he looked forward to the meal. The aroma of roasted turkey and mashed potatoes wafted from the kitchen. He whirled a finger, a sign that he'd continue his stories about Lou Gold later. The cousins rose and strolled into the dining room.

An extra table was set-up in the kitchen to accommodate a few teen-age children and grandchildren. Julian was perched on a phone book with a napkin already tucked into his collar. Marv's strategy was to linger about until nearly everyone was seated. That way he could choose whom he wanted to be near at the dining room table. Last year he'd been stuck beside Celia whose idea of wit was to point at a bowl of pesto, roll her eyes and repeat several times, "Now what in the world is that green stuff?" He'd had a few moments with her already this afternoon, and she'd discussed a tortuous six months of selling off a collection of radio and bicycle parts her father left when he died. Anyone else would have given it all to the junk man, but she'd found a way of calling in advertisements to radio shows and was nickel and diming it away.

To his surprise, Sol stayed behind with him. Marv felt flattered "Nice spread you put on for your mother" he remarked, adding, "After all you have to give some attention to the old folks. I've got to get around to taking the kids out to Linda's parents." Hi mood was expansive, one of brotherhood with Sol. The others like Herman or Ben, came and ate the food and went home, but he and Sol, well, they were the ones who took charge and gave a center to others couldn't have afforded to help, particularly Ben who was married to a wealthy woman.

"Look Marv, Thea and I need a favor."

"Sure, anything. Anything. Just ask. Glad to help," he said enthusiastically wanting to demonstrate he was on the same high plane.

"We thought you'd like to eat with the young people. Linda can keep an eye on the baby more easily."

He smiled but a queasy feeling was forming in his gut.

Encouraged, Sol smiled back. "It will be much livelier with the young people. Look, there aren't enough places around the dining room table. We didn't expect Ben to bring his in-laws..."

"You want us to sit at the children's table?" Sol wasn't treating him as an equal, far from it. He felt stiff, could barely get the words out. "You've got to be kidding? Right?"

"Don't get excited. Pretend I never asked. You and Linda can sit in the dining room. Thea and I will sit in the kitchen with the kids."

"Oh no, don't trouble yourself. Linda and I will leave and then there won't be any problem."

"There isn't any problem."

Everything was swimming around, and there was a loud shouting, and it was his voice. "I had to come out here to be insulted."

"Nobody's insulting you, Marv."

"Linda! Linda!" She was already at his side." She raised her wispy eyebrows and her mouth made an 'o' of surprise. But even so-- and despite his rage, he had to notice and admire this--she was unruffled.

"They don't want us here. Come on, come on." Calmly she gathered up the children and Amy's diaper bag, bottles and toys, and he felt her hand on his arm, steering him out of the room and down the hall. Where did she get so many arms to do everything at once? The door slammed shut behind him. He knew the others were gleefully discussing him, saying, "What do you expect? Marv is Marv. He's always the same." A sour fluid rose in his throat.

"I'll sit in the back with both the kids," Linda said. He didn't argue, although Julian protested, "Why are we going? I'm hungry? Why can't I sit in front again? I want to go on the boat one more time."

"Your father's upset," Linda told him.

"I don't want to ride in the car."

"Shut up," Marv yelled and pulled the car out of the parking spot. He wanted to hit Julian. It took all his strength to keep from striking him.

Linda was whispering promises in Julian's ears and that quieted him. Soon they were on the mesmerizing highway, the endless fields on either side. Amy whimpered a bit, then sucked on her thumb and fell asleep.

26

Marv said, "What really gets me is how they show off with that boat." It was hard to speak. As he drove, he brooded about the Hicksville house. He wanted a house he could be proud of. His fantasy was to invite Sol, Herman, Thea, all of the Resnicks to see his house, one so grand that it proved to them that he never needed them. He drove quickly, barely aware of the traffic. Horns bleated as he passed.

"Just slow down. Watch what you're doing," Linda warned. "How about it, Marv?"

"You know what? We're not going to take the Hicksville place."

"Really? We put in a bid."

"I can back out."

She was silent for a while, and then she said, "I can back out too, Marv."

"What do you mean by that?" he asked, but he knew. The long and short of it was she had done her part of the deal, presented him with the children, and now he had to do his. Give her a house. A deal was a deal.

"I'm not asking for the impossible, Marv."

No. She would settle for the Hicksville house. She had settled for him. But he wanted it to be completely different, to find a way of lifting all of them into a higher realm. If only he could.

They argued that night. Her face looked pinched.

"Don't worry he shouted, "We'll move, we'll get a house. A great house."

"How?" she smirked.

"I'm working on something."

"Why don't you ask Lou Gold? What are friends for? Right?"

"I don't have to bother him."

She was silent for a while, and then she looked at him hard and said, "So ask your father. Those city workers get a packet when they retire. Ask for an interest-free loan." She told him the old man was probably like her parents, just wanted to see his grandchildren. If he didn't want to go, she'd take the kids and visit him herself.

Furiously, he broke into her stream of speech. "Never! Don't you dare! You're not taking my kids there. He's not a father."

"I can take the kids anywhere I want. I could take the kids away."

His hands tingled and he was afraid of himself. He ran out of the room to the bathroom. The memory came to him of his father grabbing his yellow bathrobe off a hook, rolling it up and using it to beat him. When his mother tried to stop him, he turned on her, whipping the terry cloth robe at her as well. He was still afraid of him. Why didn't Linda understand

28

how it would rip him apart to ask him for help? A real father
would offer. The best thing would be if the old man died and
left him money, but his father wouldn't be so accommodating.
The old man would outlive him.

Glancing in the mirror above the sink, he saw how
flushed he was. He was going to die, drop dead, just like Ray.
He remembered how after Ray's funeral, he rushed out and
bought a new stereo system and then he took Julian to the
circus. He'd laughed at the clowns and looked with awe at the
high rope artists. Why did Linda have to say that to him about
taking the kids away?

The realtor entrusted him with the key to the house in
Monsey. From the moment he stepped over the lintel, he felt
as if he was in a dream. "This is it," kept ringing in his head.
Ping. The thing he had been looking for his whole life. He
floated through the rooms. He'd be safe here. His children
would be safe. Linda would be safe. They could put black and
white tile down in the entrance hall and hang a gold-framed
mirror. Simple, not too ornate. Nothing at all would have to be
done to the spacious living room with its marble fireplace. He
could just imagine the quiet lick of the flames in the hearth.
One thing he knew, he was going to buy a leather couch. Soft,
black leather was the only thing worthy of the room. The

kitchen--well, that wasn't so important. That's not where he'd take his guests. They'd eat in the chandeliered dining room.

He dropped the keys back at the realtor's and drove the quiet streets, admiring houses set back far from the street. So different than the Hicksville tracts. The house he would buy also had a long walkway leading to the entrance.

A few days later he led Linda through its rooms. Before she could even say, "How are you going to pay for it?" he told her, "Just trust me. We're going to get this house. Do you trust me?" His will prevailed. She said, "Yes, Marv I trust you," and her voice had a softness and love he had never heard before. "It's beautiful. It's perfect. It's like a dream. I feel like a fairy princess."

He drove her to see the Yeshiva, the one peculiarity of the neighborhood. "Strange having it out here in the suburbs," Linda commented. They saw Hassidic students with side locks and skullcaps on their heads walking about the building. "Does it bother you, Marv?"

Nothing to do with us," he said. "Not that I'm crazy about living next door. They're like hillbillies, aren't they? The way they all intermarry. The women have a dozen kids, half of them retarded."

"Will they throw rocks if I drive on Saturday?".

"Well, better a Yeshiva than a monastery. At least they won't be burning a cross on the lawn."

For a house like that I could put up with living with my crazy landsman. I still can't believe about the house. I was always afraid I'd land up stuck in that apartment, or worse, some little squalid studio." She snuggled next to him clinging to him as a bulwark and saved from some fate he didn't even understand. All he wished was that she had trusted him all along.

"Marvin, you finally came. What took you so long? She called you last February. I've been waiting for you"

Marv's father, Max Jaffe, sat in a wheel chair. One foot had been amputated because of diabetic infection, but a plaid blanket across his lap concealed Max's loss. He was still a powerful looking man, broad shouldered, with a large head and thick mane of gray hair. Wire rimmed glasses glittered on shrewd blue eyes. His lips were thin.

"I've been busy," Marv answered. The resentment was there, but he didn't want it to show Standing in the house in Monsey, he had imagined coming across town to the red brick cooperatives, taking the elevator up to twelfth floor, entering and finding Max's wallet lying on a dresser, and the old man averting his face while Marv just reached in and got what he needed. All a fantasy, of course. He'd have to work for that money, harder than he ever worked for anything.

"What happened to your blond curls?"

"I lost them. I had a hard life." It had always irked him that his father was more educated than himself. Max, the son of a Hungarian immigrant, had worked his way through college. Granted he had been unable to find a job in his field during the depression, but after a few years it was smooth sailing. He finally got a civil service position as city engineer and kept it until his retirement a few years before. But if he'd been a professional, what good had it done him? The yellow bathrobe was more threadbare and faded, but Marvin was sure it was the same one. Everything in the small apartment overlooking the Hudson River, the red couch with cigarette burns, the rows of bookcases, the water stained coffee table, looked dusty and old and further bespoke his cheapness. "He lives like an animal," he would tell Linda later.

Mrs. Fleischer, small but chesty with a beak nose, had rushed into the kitchen to get refreshments. "Marvin, come and help me," she sang out. In the midst of dishing out tutti fruiti ice cream into small pink plastic bowls, she intimated that Max had a lot of money and that he, Marv ought to be grateful to her because she'd almost persuaded him to rewrite his will. "I said to him who are you leaving your money to? He said, 'The boys in the office.' I told him, 'It's not right when you have a son.'" She winked and he understood her meaning that she'd help him carve the carcass up when the time came-- and she expected him to be generous, to not challenge any bequests to herself she'd inveigle into the will as well. "Tutti-fruiti, Marv," she cooed. "You like tutti-fruiti, don't you?" Costume jewelry rings flashed on almost every one of her fingers. His mother, he recalled, never wore makeup or jewelry. For a moment, he felt sorry for Max.

They carried the ice cream and cups of decaffeinated coffee back into the living room. Mrs. Fleischer told how she had met Max two years before. He had been sitting alone in the lobby of the YMHA on 92nd Street. When she struck up a conversation, she understood at once that he was a gentleman. His travels impressed her. He had gone to Canada and even to Russia on a B'nai B'rith tour. Marv pushed the spoon around his bowl. His stomach was delicate and there was something about the room, which suggested decay, Mrs. Fleischer's cheap perfume, his father's amputated foot, he didn't know what it was. God help him if he ended up like Max.

In a lull in the conversation, he took out the photographs and passed them around. "This your wife? Your children?" Max's voice was gruff, but Marvin saw the tears gleaming in his eyes. He felt a flash of triumph. It was going well. "They're great kids."

"Look, the girl's a beauty Max. You have gorgeous grandchildren. And with you for a grandfather, I bet they're smart too," Mrs. Fleischer enthused.

Marv flashed her a smile, handed her his empty cup and said, "Be a sweetheart and get me some more?" Then he winked. "I want a little time alone with Max." "Sure, sure. I understand," she responded.

When she left the room, he turned to his father and said, "The problem is..." He paused a moment, nearly choking on the word, but forced himself to say 'Dad.' "The problem is, well we're living in it's worse yet, they're converting the apartments to condominiums at the end of the month."

"Are you going to buy in?"

"No, we're trying to buy some place in the suburbs." It was nothing fancy, he emphasized. He didn't want his father to think he was extravagant, and he wanted to evoke his pity as well. To his cousins he had pretended he earned more than he did, but to his father he confided a lower figure to show him how he could ill afford any expense. Sadly, he concluded, "It would be nice if the kids had a little yard to play in."

"Where will you buy?" Max asked, his face impassive.

"We've only got a few weeks to get a house and to move out. I came to you because you're my father. Why don't I just get to the point? I have a little proposition for you."

"And what is that?" Max spoke precisely, a small frozen smile on his lips."

"I need a loan to make the down payment."

"How much do you need?"

34

Marv decided to make it more, to say twenty thousand when he needed fifteen. Then they could bargain.

"I can't afford it."

"It's just a loan. I can give you better interest than the bank. It would be worth your while."

"I can't afford it."

"How about nineteen thousand?"

"No."

"Eighteen? Seventeen? I figure you owe it to me. What did you ever do for me?"

Max stared at him, a pained look on his face. "I wasn't as good a father as I should have been, but I sent support for you. Every week I paid. First to your mother and then I sent money to your Aunt Martha for your expenses. I never forgot you Marvin, but I was having trouble. I wish I had been able to do better."

"What kind of trouble?"

"I was sick."

"Diabetes, because you needed a shot of insulin, you couldn't..." "Not the diabetes. Something else. Something mental. I can't talk about it."

Marv didn't want to get sucked in to hearing his problems and feeling sorry for him. His father wasn't going to turn everything around, so he had him on his back too. "Look do you want to see your grandchildren?" he said impatiently.

"I thought you said you came here because I'm your father. Well, now I know you're here with a reason." Max sighed. "I could give you a thousand. Then let's get to know each other. See how everything goes."

"A thousand is toilet paper."

"Maybe two thousand."

"Keep it," Marv cried and reached out and snatched the photographs off Max's lap.

The old man twitched. For a moment he looked lost and pathetic. Then he said coldly, "What do I need more? A chance to see my grandchildren? Or do I need to have a maniac for a son?" At this moment Mrs. Fleischer came with Marv's coffee, and Max turned to her, "Why did I let you interfere?"

"If I walk out now, you'll never see them," Marv taunted while Mrs. Fleishcer uttered chirps of alarm.

"What are they to me? I don't know them," Max said.

"At least buy yourself a new bathrobe," Marv responded and with this parting shot rushed out.

Riding down in the elevator, Marv decided he'd ask Lou Gold for the loan. Linda had been right all along that Lou was the one he could rely on. Lou wouldn't turn him down. He couldn't even wait until he got home. It was important to get this settled immediately. He needed to hear Lou's kindly voice. 'Like a father to me,' he told people, but only now did he know the depth of meaning those words held.

On the hot, humid street, he searched for a public phone. His hands were trembling and he could barely insert the change and then he saw the phone was out of order. His shirt stuck to his back. The street was deserted. His heart pounded He should really get back in his car and drive home. It wasn't safe on the streets at night. The bastard had insulted his children. The bastard. Across the street was a bar. He went inside, his eyes blinking from the darkness, and bought a beer. The beer tasted cold and delicious. He had a second and carried a third with him to the phone in the rear, which he placed on a small shelf while he fumbled for change. Lou lived in a large duplex on Central Park West.

"Hello," came a small child's voice. Lou's daughter was Julian's age and she kept saying, "Who is this?" "Please put your daddy on," Marv pleaded, but in a maddening way, even when he answered, "This is Marv," she kept up her refrain. Finally, Lou got on the phone. They conversed for a while about a scandal in the industry, price fixing for food processors, about their families and even about the hot weather.

Lou asked, "What's up? Why are you calling?"

"Did I ever ask you for money, Lou?" Marv said in a joking tone.

"You're not going to, are you?"

"Yeah, I am Lou."

"That's too bad. Times are hard "

"I'm serious, Lou. Can you give me a loan?"

"Business is business and friendship is friendship and I never mix the two. It's against my policy. I can't make exceptions, not even for you."

"I never asked you before."

"That's right. You never asked me for money before Marv. I always respected you because you never asked me for money".

"Lou, I'm desperate, I'm begging you."

"Don't do that Marv. Keep your self-respect."

"I don't have any self respect. I'm begging. Do you want me to cry? I'm crying."

"Enough of this Marv, I'm hanging up."

He'd been to the Monsey house again to look it over one last time before he signed the papers. Once again, it reassured him. The same 'ping' of rightness. He rushed away, wanted that feeling to still surround him when he arrived at the agent's office. He was going to swing it with the bank, and with Vince, from Carnasie whose name he had squeezed out of Joanna. "Vince's a thug," she'd said, but he'd been surprised that he was a salesman like himself, all smiles and smoothness. Well, he knew his business. No sense scaring him to begin with. Marv would pay out of his ass for the rest of his life.

It was worth it, he thought as he drove through the street past the large houses and beneath a canopy of trees. Were they elms? Julian would learn the names. He drove by the Yeshiva. A few yards down the road, a skull capped young man heard his car, stopped walking and put his thumb out. Marv slowed down and drifted to a stop about twenty-five yards ahead of the Hassid. In his rear view window he watched the man running, the flaps of his coat flying in the air. He tossed a cigarette into the road. Coming up to the car, he reached his hand out for the door handle.

Just at that instant, Marv put his foot on the gas and zoomed ahead. Glancing again in the rear window, he could see the pale, startled face with mouth opening and closing like a fish. What had he expected? A free ride? Marv could scarcely stop laughing as he drove away. Although later, as he drove home on the highway, he felt ashamed, a feeling soon lost in his swirling thoughts.

Enchained

Betty Durling phoned to tell me that six year old Gloria
Fry had died of leukemia. I scarcely knew the child's parents,
a poet-painter and writer who like my husband Jerry and me
were in in their mid-twenties, but for the last two years Betty
had been broadcasting rhapsodic reports of Dianne and
Lloyd's talents to me.

Betty was a friend from our student years in the 1960's
when Jerry and I had lived in a stretch along College Avenue
where all the big, old houses were honeycombed into tiny
flats. She and her son, Karl, rented two rooms in the house
next to ours. A decade older than I, she had granted me
neophyte status as a student of life. I used to set aside my
college books in order to sit and drink tea with her while she
talked about her travels, her marriage to a lunatic German
artist and the time she tended apple and plum trees on
Timothy Leary's upstate New York commune just before she
came to Berkeley. Betty was the first outsider I told that my
parents were survivors of Dachau. She urged me to write
about them and about my childhood. In this way, I stumbled
upon my vocation, dedicating myself in a way she could not.
When I first met Betty she threw pots. Eventually, she took up
the flute, and then painting. By the seventh year of our
friendship, she was taking Lloyd's classes and considered

herself a poet. With more in mind than poetry, she progressed from being Lloyd's student, to becoming an intimate to both him and Dianne.

When the Frys arrived from Atlanta to San Francisco, they had lived among the flower children in the Haight-Ashbury. Then Lloyd got a job at Hayward State and they decided to appear more respectable and moved to a glass and stucco apartment building, not far from the house Jerry and I bought just after Peter was born. So even before Betty's foray into poetry I saw them around Berkeley, and we had given each other   passing nods of recognition. Gloria had not yet gotten ill and since she was near the same age as Peter, they played together at the   park.

But it was only through Betty's toil that a invitation to a 'literary party' arrived. I was thrilled to be included because I had only begun writing a few years before and scarcely considered myself a writer. Any sign of acceptance helped me to accept myself, and I looked up to Dianne who had already published several short stories and was working on a novel. Moreover, I was intrigued by Betty's descriptions of the Frys. Her romantic imagination found hints of the grand and tragic in the way they drove about in a red sports car, drank and spent money recklessly. For her they were the sparkling Zelda and F. Scott Fitzgerald.

The night of the party Jerry and I walked over to the

Fry's. Their ground floor apartment was furnished with a thick rug, Danish modern couch, coffee table and overflowing bookcases. Everywhere I looked I saw Lloyd's murals, gigantic canvases of fat naked women with minuscule heads, expanses of flesh that made me think of a brothel. A blue-green parrot in a large cage in the center of the living room, screeched and hopped about. The wall opposite the couch bore a large mirror with an ornate gold painted frame.

Taller than anyone else, fair and sinuous,

Lloyd was the peacock of the family in a silk shirt a la Lord Byron. He flicked ashes from a thin, gold tipped cigar while proclaiming how modern physics and in particular, Einstein's theory of relativity, had shaped his poetry and enriched his language. He spoke of "quarks" and "black holes," and I was impressed. I wasn't alone either. A whole flotilla of his female poetry students, bobbed after him like sailboats.

Meanwhile, Dianne had settled into a corner. Looking about, smiling faintly, she sipped a beer and watched Lloyd flirt with the student naiads. She dressed more reticently than Lloyd, her Catholic school training still compelling a high neck, wrist-length sleeves and long skirt whose full folds partly concealed her thick figure. Her black hair fell across her brow and down her shoulders, framing a smooth, round, face, pale as the moon. Her body's secretive, powerful fleshiness, had not altered her delicate features, and in this disconnection I found a touching vulnerability. People approached her and occasionally I heard her voice rise in the heat of discussion, a musical, throaty voice, almost as deep as a man's.

Lloyd passed Jerry a roach clip with a joint of marijuana. The style of the two men couldn't have been more different. This was obvious even in the way they dressed. Lloyd's flamboyance contrasted with Jerry's unassuming white shirt and khaki trousers, the same outfit he wore to work at his engineering firm. The only thing missing was his worn briefcase. His mother had sent him a shiny new one that he promptly stowed in the closet. Lloyd's long locks were styled and blown dry, while I was Jerry's barber. His last hair-cut, my clippers had slipped and I had left a bald spot on the side of his head, but Jerry had laughed good humoredly and said, "What difference does it make? I don't have to look at myself." I knew he hated the noisy crowd and would rather have been home listening to his beloved Schubert than Lloyd's pounding rock and country music. Abstaining, he passed the roach clip on.

It went around the room to Betty who received it with an ecstatic smile as if it were the sacrament. She was so at ease with drugs. Years before, like Odysseus returning from foreign lands, she had described the gorgeous worlds of colors and feelings she discovered through L.S.D. She promised it would transform my writing and urged me to join her. I was tempted, but the thought of losing control during a bad 'trip' was too frightening and I demurred. Now, for reasons I could never get her to explain, Betty had retired from her vast explorations to the minor jaunts of 'grass.' Smiling, she extended her hand and she and Lloyd joined other fused together dancing couples, swaying in a sexual trance.   Jerry and I were accustomed to more staid gatherings, and the air of possibility both excited and disturbed me. Indeed, one man began shoving another and the second punched him back. As Lloyd expelled these drunken guests, Jerry told me he wanted to leave. It was late and I went to say goodbye to Dianne. Most of the evening she had been surrounded by her friends talking reverently about "Art," but now, I was able to seize a moment alone with her. She was in an exhilarated mood, her cheeks flushed and eyes shining. "Why don't you come visit me?" she asked in   her velvet voice. "Why haven't you shown me your writing? I want to know you better." Her warmth broke down my usual reserve, and I grew animated too and began telling her about the story I was writing.

"What did you think of the people?" I asked Jerry as we left the party.

"Oh, you know me. I don't care for parties," he said

mildly, but a few moments later he blurted out, "I thought they were phonies."

"Like who?"

"O.K. here's an example, Lloyd talking about how Einstein's affected his life. That's a bunch of hooey!"

"I guess so," I said, deflated.   We walked along in an uncomfortable silence, the sounds of the party growing fainter. Jerry never more than tolerated Betty and now he had turned against the Frys. Our disagreement upset me.   I counted on his affability and steadiness, so different from my parents' unpredictable moods, and when he drew his arm through mine, I felt reassured.

While rummaging in my refrigerator for a snack, Betty suggested, "Why don't you phone Dianne?"

"I don't do that."

"As you wish," she laughed. At Bryn Mawr, she had played Hamlet for the dramatic society, and now with a chicken drumstick aloft in one hand,   she opened her blue eyes wide, composed her pretty face into a tragic mask and strode across my linoleum like a stage. "Whatever you wish, my dear! Hide your light under a bushel.   You're getting as sensitive as my friend Jenny. She was a writer too, but she had to wear white gloves as she typed."

I did   telephone Dianne. I got as far as listening to her

phone ringing. Then a memory   flicked through my mind of
an evening I darted into the Durant hotel to use one of their
pay phones. The hotel's bar was across from the bank of
telephones and glancing into it, I saw the Frys with little
Gloria perched on a stool beside them. I was surprised to see
their daughter in the dark, mirrored room, inhaling cigarette
smoke and   listening to boozy conversation, a child more
knowing than myself. Uneasy, I put the receiver back in its
cradle.

A few days later, however, I   completed the call,
thrilled to hear that sensual voice again, "Yes?   What can I do
for you?" The ordinary words had little connection with the
magic of her throaty voice. I asked if I might drop off one of
my short stories for her to critique and was jubilant when she
agreed. That afternoon I left a manuscript in her mailbox.

Then weeks passed and I heard nothing and my pride
was wounded. Every time I thought of my short story cast
away in her desk drawer, forgotten or maybe discarded, I
burned with humiliation. My resentment dissolved, though,
when   Betty phoned to tell me Gloria had leukemia.

The news astounded me. I had just seen Gloria at a
child's birthday party. I remembered her making her
entrance like an infant actress in a ruffled dress billowed out
by crinolines and tied up with a huge bow at the waist. She

had worn shiny, patent leather shoes and her blonde hair was twisted into corkscrew curls. I had half expected her to tap dance and burst into song. It was hard to imagine her ill when I thought of the authoritative way she walked past Peter and the other children, but turned to me and said, "Hello, Rhoda Green. Where are you going Rhoda Green? I'll come too. It's boring being with babies." She had put her hand in mine and dragged me along, making me an accessory to her independence. Outside, she looked at me with the same shrewd eyes as her mother's and announced, "I didn't want to come, but my parents wanted to get rid of me."

To her credit, Betty was a stalwart friend to the Frys during their months of crisis. She kept me abreast of Gloria's radiation and chemotherapy treatments, and her stays at Alta Bates hospital. I saw Lloyd wheeling a lethargic Gloria along in a stroller, and at five she appeared abnormally large in it. Her wig lay on her lap and with her bare skull and darkly circled eyes, her head looked Humpty Dumpty huge. The change was so profound that I had to wrench myself away to keep from staring.

The afternoon I heard of Gloria's death, I hovered over Peter and finally got my courage up to tell him. He astonished me by saying, "She said she was gonna." When Jerry came home I told him too. He looked bruised and was particularly tender to Peter and myself. After dinner, he and

Peter trotted out to water the lettuces, dark green chard and yellow flowered tomato plants. I stood on the porch watching them aim the hose in a silver arc. Overhead a sliver of moon appeared. In the next yard, my neighbors barbecued steaks and the smoke drifted into my garden like incense. I felt so fragile and so sad for the Frys that my hesitations about them disappeared. Betty had invited me to the next day's funeral on their behalf, and I decided I would go.

Many of the mourners at Gloria's funeral wore black. Conscious of my tenuous connection to the family, I dared not claim a grief equal to theirs. I dressed in brown, a lighter shade of mourning, and sat in the back of the hall. From that vantage point, I recognized a few of the mourners. Several were neighbors. One was an esteemed woman poet in a wheelchair and another, a former convict turned poet, a short bantam cock of a man who tastelessly brought his German Shepherd along. The dog barked until everyone sat down and only then was quiet. I expected a priest to perform the ceremony and was surprised to see a Unitarian minister, a middle-aged redheaded woman dressed in black and purple robes.

Later, at the El Sobrante cemetery, the glaring summer sun beat down on Gloria's white coffin. Grave diggers in overalls lowered it into the tiny ditch. Sweat streaked the minister's make-up as she read from her bible. From her position alongside Dianne and Lloyd, Betty beckoned me to join her, but I ignored her and kept my place at the edge of the crowd.   The lush cemetery grass was still damp from the sprinklers. I looked at the crowded parking lot, across to the freeway, and out beyond to the shopping mall and the suburban housing tracts dotting the parched hills. A golden necklace glinted on the neck of a nearby woman. I inhaled her gardenia perfume and the scent brought back memories of my mother.

Tears filled my eyes, not for Gloria but for myself. I remembered coming home, excited, I was going to skip a grade. "Why are you hopping around like a crazy?" my mother demanded disdainfully and put a hand to her head, which, as I remember, always ached. Only days later, some fragment of my joy worked its way into her consciousness and she asked, "What were you saying about school the other day?" "Nothing," I replied. I wanted her to beg me to tell her but she only shrugged as if to say, 'What difference does it make? It can't be important. Nothing is.' I did not even consider telling my father. Not that I wouldn't have liked to make him proud. But I wasn't going to risk a smack for "trying to act like a big-shot." As the minister intoned her concluding words, I hurried out to the parking lot. Betty caught up with me to say that the Frys had invited me to the wake.   From the road below came the roar of traffic like blood pounding in my ears.

"I couldn't do that." I said.

"Dianne especially asked you to come."

"All right," I agreed. "But I can only stay a little while."

The vinyl-covered car seat scorched the back of my thighs; the steering wheel burned. I glanced at the back seat where I had put the cooler which held a lentil casserole, and funeral meats I'd intended to have Betty give to the Frys along with a note. Now I would drop it by myself. Starting my engine, I joined the cars snaking down the curving road to the freeway.

The Frys reminded me of high wire artists as they gaily greeted their guests, directing them to a table of food and drinks. 'Death defying smiles,' I thought, astonished at their transformation. Their friends too set aside their mournful expressions and devoured great quantities of ham and potato salad. Betty Durling waltzed gracefully from one cluster of people to another, sipping a goblet of white wine. The bantam cock poet pulled on a joint of marijuana and shouted across the room to a man with waist length hair. His dog, tied up on the patio, howled. Lloyd flicked on the radio and danced with a young, blonde woman, while Dianne sat drinking a beer. Beside her, the parrot squawked frantically. Answering an insistently ringing phone, a red faced Lloyd screamed into the receiver, "What do you mean we're making too much noise? Don't you know we buried Gloria today?"

Betty waved to me carelessly. I stood gazing at the whirling reflections in the large gilt edged mirror. The mirror would have been draped in black in a Jewish home. The mourners would have been in stockinged feet and sat on wooden boxes, all with grim faces. I found the press of people sickening and slipped down the hall to find the bathroom but mistakenly opened the door to Gloria's room.

The canopied four poster bed, shapely white furniture and filmy curtains reflected the China doll way Dianne had dressed the little girl. I glided into Gloria's bower. As a child, I had made forays into my parents' bedroom to discover their secrets. What first sparked my detecting was an argument I overheard. My father had screamed at my mother, "Nazi whore." I imagined the soldiers lined up to have sex with my mother and it excited me. I searched through their drawers to find out more, but no Nazis, Jews or Kapos lurked among my father's frayed underpants or my mother's slips and stockings. Unbeknownst to me, my father was home sick from his furrier's job one afternoon, and he caught me in my rummaging. "What are you doing?" he cried. He stood there, short, powerful, his bulldog face contorted. I expected a blow, but to my amazement he let me off, saying hoarsely,

"Are you a rag picker too? Do you go through the garbage pails searching for food? Don't shame me. Don't shame yourself." Gloria's death had brought back this thread of memory as well as my old convulsed curiosity, although now I justified my peering about the room as "writer's curiosity."

Thrust into one corner was a pair of high heels. For a second, I thought them an old pair of Dianne's, but they looked unusually large for a woman's foot. They might have been an adult size ten or eleven, big enough for Gloria to clump about in with her own shoes on and room to spare. The closet door stood half open, revealing not only Gloria's ruffled dresses but also several long gowns to match the dress-up shoes, one covered with shiny black sequins. At the French provincial dresser I took up Gloria's brush. It still held a few blonde vestiges of her curls. A photograph showed a grinning Gloria in a felt hat with mouse ears.

A hand tapped my shoulder. I was absorbed, I hadn't noticed anyone slip into the room. Looking up, I saw Dianne's image beside mine in the mirror and my heart pounded like that time my father caught me.

"We took her to Disneyland while she was still well enough to go."

"I shouldn't have come in here."

She studied me, and with an odd smile, said, "I don't mind." Her response confused me as much as my father's had years before. I felt she understood and that I had even become more interesting to her. "I haven't forgotten about your manuscript," she told me.

"Don't worry about it. Don't think about it now."

"Why shouldn't I think of it?" she declared passionately. "Literature is my reason for staying alive."

Footsteps sounded in the hall and Lloyd put his head in, raised his eyebrows, and demanded, "What's going on in here?"

"I have to go," I said.

"Don't leave," Dianne appealed. "If people go, Lloyd and I will have to be alone with each other."

"I'm so touched by your consideration," Dianne told me on the telephone.

"You didn't have to call. I didn't mean to put any obligation on you."

"But your casserole was so thoughtful. We appreciated it. I wouldn't dream of not thanking you. I'd like to see you. Do you think you could come over today?"

Late in the afternoon I found Dianne still wearing her bathrobe. The disordered rooms smelled of stale food, beer, mildew, and dirty laundry. The large parrot cage stood empty. "I forgot to feed the bird and it died," Dianne explained. "Everything dies on me." The radio and the television were blaring. "To scare away rapists and murderers," she explained as she went from one room to the other, snapping them off. "I get frantic when I'm alone. I think someone will break in and attack."

I had grown up with such dirt and smells and with my parents' conviction that at any moment Anti-Semites would break into the house. My fingers itched to straighten, to vacuum, to wash. I wanted to draw the blinds and throw open the windows to sun and air. All at once I wanted to be the magical healer.

"I look terrible, don't I?" Dianne inquired as I trailed after her to the tiny kitchen. "At the hospital I stood next to Gloria's bed wishing she'd die. So it'd be all over and I could go home and sleep. 'Why doesn't she die?' I kept saying to myself. Then the nurse came in to take her pulse and told me, 'I'm sorry, she's gone.' 'Gone? That's all?' 'Yes, go home and get some rest.' So I went home but I couldn't sleep. Not that night, and no night since. I wander about this apartment and occasionally I collapse in exhaustion. But never for more than an hour at a time."

Dianne got a soda for me and a fresh beer for herself. "Would you like to see Gloria's photographs?" She had taken down Lloyd's paintings and hung up dozens of pictures of Gloria instead. I moved around the rooms, respectfully studying them. Dianne told me, "I wanted her to have ballet

lessons. I had a lot of dreams for her. But no. Do you think
I'm morbid? Lloyd says I'm turning the apartment into a
shrine. Look, I want you to listen to something. Now where
is it? Everything gets lost. Ah, here!" She set up a tape
recorder on the low coffee table. "Lloyd's always taping
himself and luckily he taped a few conversations with her."

The cassette rewound with a whirring sound. Dianne
fast-forwarded Lloyd's parts on the tape so he sounded like
Bugs Bunny. A blissful expression came over her face as she
listened to Gloria's thin voice talking about the trip to
Disneyland, how she liked the airplane, the motel and the
scary rides. Dianne mouthed her words along with her,
laughing when an exasperated Gloria rebuked Lloyd, "Oh,
shut up. Don't talk like an idiot."

When the tape ended, she asked, "Do you want
something to eat? Not that there's anything in the house. All
I've had today is ice cream with chocolate sauce. What do you
want to drink? Beer? Another Coke?"

"Nothing. I'm fine."

Returning from the kitchen, she slipped off her
slippers and sat cross legged like a school girl and snapped
open the can. "Did Betty tell you I'm an alcoholic? You don't
have to look alarmed. It's a family tradition. I'm the fourth
generation. What do you think of that for ancestral loyalty?"

The bells at the nearby Catholic church tolled and

Dianne went on, "The Church doesn't exist for me anymore. It doesn't exist, except as a retrograde symbol in my writing. I didn't summon a priest for last rites for Gloria. I chose a Unitarian minister from the Yellow Pages for the funeral. She dressed herself up like a bishop though, didn't she? The last time I attended a Catholic funeral I was twelve and stood holding the hands of my three and two year old sisters, Tessa and Susan. We mourned our mother who drank herself to death. Did you notice Tessa and Susan at the funeral? The girls in the Catholic School uniforms? Lloyd and I wired money for them to come out for the funeral. They went back to Atlanta a few days later. They're charity girls at a Catholic boarding school like I was. Susan, my youngest sister, was born with no thumbs and blurred features. She was pickled in my mother's alcohol birth waters. Mother was too far gone by the time she was carrying her. Did I tell you my mother was buried in Atlanta? One day I'll move Gloria's remains next to hers and build a monument. When I die, I'll be buried with them. In the end I'll go back to the South. Have you been to the South?"

"No."

"It's not so much American as European. Your parents were European, weren't they?"

"Yes," I said, uncomfortable at the question.

"I know about your childhood. Betty told me about

your mother and father and how they were in a concentration camp. Are you upset that she told me?"

"I didn't tell it to her as a story to tell other people."

"If she'd told me you'd grown up in the suburbs in an average family I wouldn't have wanted to meet you."

"There are plenty of holocaust survivors who live in the suburbs. They want to conform and be like everyone else so they can pretend nothing bad ever happened to them. They can hide behind banal clothes and banal furnishings. The suburbs are   great big sponges to absorb everyone who wants to be inconspicuous."

"But you're not like everyone else, are you? It's because of what she said about your parents that you're interesting to me."

She spoke non-stop, flitting from the war going on in Vietnam, to open marriage, back to Gloria and then returning to what linked us, to writing. This barrage might have made me restless, except I found her to be a brilliant talker. I was moved when she told me, "I saw War and Peace on television last week. For the first time since Gloria died, I wanted to live. I thought if something so beautiful exists, then I want to stay alive."

She shook her beer can. "Empty. "Won't you have one? Can't I corrupt you? You'll succumb in the end." She got up and went first to the toilet to pee and then to the kitchen.

When she returned she switched on a lamp and I blinked from the sudden light. I heard a baby bawling in another apartment. Cars swished by along the street. The afternoon had passed quickly.

Peter loved Ginny, the fifteen-year-old baby sitter from next door, but I could never be away from him for more than a few hours without getting uneasy. When I glanced at my watch, Dianne pleaded, "Please, don't go. Not yet. Just a little more...We haven't even discussed your manuscript...I wanted to read it, but..." She rummaged through her stack of tapes and put one in the tape recorder. "Do you like the Beatles?" The croon of Paul McCartney's, "Michelle....my belle," filled the room and Dianne rose and twirled about with her eyes closed. Her hands reached out for me. "You too, Rhoda. Come on." We danced with Dianne leading. When we bumped into furniture we giggled. "I can't forget a girl I met...Ooooh ooooh." I coiled into Dianne's arms and then uncoiled. She turned up the volume and grabbed me around the waist, whirling me round and round until I was breathless.

The phone's burr startled us. "The neighbors," she grimaced. "Let it ring." It stopped but in a few minutes it rang again. Dianne grabbed the receiver and said abruptly, "Yes, what do you want?" She handed the phone to me.

Jerry had relieved Ginny. "What's going on?" he asked.

I tittered into the phone, "Sorry, I just lost track."

"When are you coming home?"

"Well, soon," I answered, suddenly irritated with him for breaking the spell. When I set down the receiver, I told Dianne, "I really have to go," and gathered up my purse.

"I wish you didn't have to," she began pleading again. "Do you really have to? We were having so much fun. We have a lot more to talk about. I feel like you've just arrived."

"I have to make dinner."

"Dinner?" she asked as if puzzled at the meaning of the word. "Can't Jerry manage to make dinner?"

The sounds of keys turning in the door's multiple locks made her freeze. Her eyes widened and she looked terrified. "It's me," Lloyd called. Dianne relaxed.
Dressed this time in a turtle neck and all in black, he loped drowsily down the long entrance hall and stopped when he saw us. "You remember...," Dianne began and he finished her sentence. "Rhoda Green," he said nodding vaguely at me.

"How was..."

"The class was all right..." He moved lazily about the room, taking up a cigarette, striking a match and slowly inhaling. "Any mail?"

"Only bills."

"By the way, Tannenbaum came up to me as I was walking across campus and told me he just heard about Gloria."

"What did he say?"

"He said I should have let him know earlier and he would have arranged a leave of absence for me."

Nearly an entire wall of the living room was given over to the sliding glass door that led out to the patio. Because of the darkness outside, the glass became Lloyd's mirror. "He's always admiring himself," Dianne said, grinning. "With a few strategically placed mirrors, Lloyd would be caught here forever."

Dianne's cutting remark made me alert and waiting for something to happen. I remembered my parents circling each other, working themselves up to rages; they would ignore me--the way the Frys ignored me now--yet I was the audience to whom they played.

Lloyd turned to Dianne with a cold smile. "I got another parking ticket today," he said, his voice a drone. "That makes about forty. If they pull me into court, I'll bring the pile in, dump it on the judge's desk and tell him about Gloria. That will get...." Unable to control the impulse, he returned to his reflection, this time though, he positioned himself to glance in the plate glass and the gold framed mirror as well. As Lloyd studied his reflection, I could not take my eyes off the original. Perhaps it was because he was dressed entirely in black and throughout my childhood, I had been forbidden to wear either black or brown. I was astonished at how much he repelled me; he reminded me of an S.S. officer. My mother once told me about the S.S., "They were play acting and they didn't know what they were doing was real."

"It will get you off." Now it was Dianne finishing Lloyd's sentence. "And for another year at least Gloria will be a good excuse for whatever comes up."

"Yes. That's right. People respond," he answered, matching her cynical tone. "Like Tannenbaum. He said I could get a leave now if I needed it. Why shouldn't I use the excuse 'for another year' or however long it's good for? I wouldn't mind getting some time off."

I was scarcely surprised when he turned on me. He had noted the reflection of my red skirt and checked blouse and said, "Where'd you get that outfit? Dianne, don't you like that outfit?" "Lloyd," Dianne warned, but he plunged ahead, "I'm sure Rhoda wouldn't mind telling us. Why I bet it's from Sear's catalog. Do you mail order all your clothes?"

It turned out I didn't need to defend myself because Dianne squelched him, saying, "Leave her alone Lloyd. We're not going to start on her."

He wilted. His face took on an expression of injured

innocence. "I just wanted to let her know how much I admired her outfit," he said and slunk off to the kitchen. Then I was leaving again with Dianne pleading with me to return soon with that flattering attachment, that disturbing desperation, that meant, all at once, I had become her life preserver on a sea of grief, just the way I had been for my parents. Not that I didn't want to come back, but the afternoon had exhausted me, and I was reluctant to visit in only two days when Lloyd was away teaching his poetry class again.

"Isn't there someone else like Betty?" I asked

"I want you."

"I'll try to get a babysitter," I said and finally left to return to the my immaculate house, to order and sanity and Bach on the phonograph. Peter had had dinner and Jerry was kneeling on the bathroom tile bathing him in the tub. Tiny soap bubbles floated in the steamy air.

"I'm sorry I'm late," I said.

"Did you have a nice time?" he asked.

"Where were you, Mommy?"

"I told you. At Gloria's mother."

Jerry held open a towel and expertly enfolded a clean, pink Peter.

"Gloria's dead," Peter pronounced.

"Come on, big fella. How about a story?" Jerry said quickly. I trailed after them into Peter's bedroom. It was so different from Gloria's. There was just a mattress on the floor and books and toys scattered over the garage sale rug. In the mornings, Peter woke slowly and it was difficult to get him dressed. Jerry came up with the scheme of having him sleep in his trousers and t-shirt instead of pajamas. Putting on Peter's socks, he tickled each foot in turn. Peter pulled his feet back, joyful in the game.

I volunteered, "I'll read to him."

"That's all right," Jerry said kindly. He saw how the afternoon had tired me. I gave in to his willing competence, kissed Peter goodnight, and padded downstairs to prepare our meal.

In the weeks that followed, Dianne was all but helpless, an invalid locked in the stifling rooms. Unable to drive, she told me that she had Lloyd shop and do all their other errands while she remained home drinking and grieving. The only time she ventured out was to water the plants on her patio. She grew bloated. Her skin looked pasty and dead and her eyes dull. I thought she was dying.

Imagine how surprised I was on the evening she opened the door with a glowing face and greeted me excitedly, "I've got a surprise for you!" With a mysterious air, she led me down the hall and threw open the door to Gloria's room. She had turned it into a study. Proudly, she displayed the bookcases lining the walls and the electric typewriter on the enormous, sturdy desk that replaced the flounced fourposter. "What do you think? Do you like it?" she asked eagerly. I hugged her to me to express my delight. Her recently washed hair was damp and shone black. Her skin looked fresh. She had grown younger.

"I write in the evenings," Dianne said. "While everyone else's sleeping. By the light of day, I don't believe in what I've done. At night, I'm closer to my dreams. I've been working ten, even fifteen hour stretches. Afterwards, my back and neck ache. Lloyd massages my back for me. He brings my meals on a tray. He draws my bath for me, and lights candles. He's not working. Not painting. Not writing poems. He's letting his talents lie fallow for a few months.

He told me, 'Just let me know how I can help you.'"

I listened attentively. Lloyd with his goose stepping in front of mirrors, fascinated me, and now Dianne presented a facet of him, I couldn't fathom.

"I don't know what I'd do without him. He's my life-line," she told me.

The spartan study fought back the chaos of the other rooms. In it I experienced the order of disciplined work. We settled on chairs across from each other. Pulling heavily underlined books off the shelves, Dianne talked about the writers she admired; Leo Tolstoy, Ernest Hemingway, Flannery O'Connor. She spoke of the Teachings of Don Juan by Carlos Castanedas as a Catholic book, a vision of one individual guiding another, the way a parent guides a child. I took the book home to read. Like Dianne, the book's promise of an ideal parent enraptured me. We brought Castanedas' exquisite standard into our relationship, exchanging manuscripts with the pride and tenderness of new mothers. Anxiously, I watched the flicker of her eyes as she read, then returned to her crisp pages on my lap. I marveled that the creator sat across from me. I struggled to phrase my criticisms with a delicacy that matched hers. She looked up and listened so acutely that I felt relief when she wasn't offended.

There was a hard currency in this exchange of criticism. We both needed each other. She had folders and folders of stories and five drafts of her novel, and I read everything. We gave each other an audience to write towards. Not that we couldn't have found other people to read our work, but she told me, "No one has ever given me such good criticism," and I felt the same. I knew I was writing better.

Dianne was working on a novel about a handsome, intellectual homosexual, a young hustler who charmed rich old men. Possessing an x-ray vision into the innermost needs of his clients, he gradually dominated them completely. They relied on his subtle torments to stir them to life. He too required violence or sexual perversion to pierce his own benumbed senses.

After one of our sessions discussing her novel, Dianne joked, "I could be a sadist. There are so many masochists around. They'd probably pay a lot to find someone to whip them. Most people crave pain. Were your parents tortured?"

I stiffened at her crassness. There had been other pinpricks of pain from her, moments that scarcely seemed real because before I responded, she quickly moved on to some other subject. This time it was Hawthorne's Young Goodman Brown. ""I respect Hawthorne," she said, "because he knows innocence doesn't exist."

"In children?"

She laughed, "Are children innocent? I thought they were evil."

"What about Gloria?" was almost on my lips, but it was too cruel to put to her. When she spoke again, I saw it wasn't Gloria she had in mind.

"I must have been about six when I discovered my mother was a drunk. Before then, well, the old cliche, I

66

thought she took medicine. She started drinking first thing in the morning. By the afternoon she was strange. 'Come here baby,' she'd call to me. I was scared. 'What's the matter? Are you afraid of your own mommy? You come here or I'll spank you.' She'd pull me up on the bed and say, 'Are you a boy or a girl. I'll bet you're a boy.' 'I'm a girl,' I'd scream. 'No, you're not.' Then she'd pull my panties off. 'Little boy,' she kept saying as she stroked me. 'Little boy likes our game.' Finally, she got so excited she turned over and masturbated herself. When I started going to school, she stopped 'our game.' Probably she was frightened I'd tell the nuns. But there was no danger of that. I was scared my teachers would find out. The nuns taught us how to undress and how to bathe without ever looking at our bodies. They talked constantly about how Jesus died for our sins, and I knew exactly which sin they meant. Probably, as good Catholics, my parents didn't use contraceptives. My mother gave birth to Tessa and then Susan. The mystery was that there hadn't been more kids. As my mother drank more often and became more helpless than ever, the babies stayed with my aunt who already had a house full of children. A number of times my mother went into the hospital. Then one afternoon my aunt came to pick me up at school and she told me, 'Your mother's dead.' I burst out, 'Thank God.' I don't think I shocked her. She felt the same way."

"What happened after she died?" "I became a boarder at the school. The other boarding students were paupers and orphans like myself whom everyone looked down on. A few rich South American girls also boarded. They used to get huge boxes filled with delicacies. The rest of us flattered them so we could get a share. We hated the watery soups and the foul-tasting margarine sandwiches we got at the cafeteria. Once one of the girls threw her sandwich in the trash. A nun caught her and screamed, "That was good food! You're the one who belongs in the garbage!" She picked the girl up and stuffed her in the garbage can. You know what I felt as I watched?"

"You must have been so afraid."

"Yes, I was afraid. I knew the real reason she was being punished. My body told me. I was terribly aroused. To this day when I think back on that incident, it excites me. I was terrified someone would guess my feelings. When I was with the other girls, I pretended I knew nothing about sex. I forced myself to read the silly romance magazines the others secretly passed about. I mooned over teenage boys with acne and sang pop songs about loving them. I felt so isolated until I met Lloyd at college. He saw through me and for the first time I didn't have to put on an act. Nothing shocked Lloyd." I cherished my time in that small study which both resembled and differed from my parents' claustrophobic lives. After our talks, I danced home with excitement. Jerry looked at me sadly. He felt excluded, at sea in a world he didn't understand. "I feel like I'm losing you. Even when you're with me, you're thinking about Dianne," he said plaintively. I flashed a gay smile and tried to compensate, but he was right. I couldn't wait to be alone with my reveries.

More direct, Peter tugged on my skirt and shrieked, "Look at me."

Several months into our friendship, Dianne knocked at my door. I didn't hear her because I was vacuuming. She let herself in and stood watching me until I became aware of her presence. That moment of domesticity repelled her. "No, no," she said, "Now I see I'll have to stick with Lloyd. You and I can't live together."

"Were we going to?"

"Perhaps," she grinned. The thought chilled me. I wondered if she had had a fight with Lloyd and decided that if she left him, I would take over his role. But the sight of me doing my chores reminded her of my loyalty to my family. When we went to sit in my garden, she said, "I never thought of you as the little housewife." She wouldn't let the subject drop, not even when I got some wine for her. Usually I brought out a liter bottle but this time, all I had was a large jug. "The big green bottle," she called it, sitting with her legs drawn up beneath her, Japanese style, her black hair glistening in the sunlight.

In the course of a few hours she drained the 'big green bottle.' Drunker than I'd ever seen her, she kept taking my hand between hers. To begin with, I suspected it wasn't affection that prompted this display, but her annoyance at my conventionality and housewifeliness. She needed a sign that I would sacrifice everything for her if she wanted me to live with her. I don't think she even noticed Peter climbing the blue-barred jungle gym at the other end of the garden, even when I called to him and waved. A light breeze blew the leaves of the fig tree, the needles of the sequoia. Her pale gray jumper, drawn tightly across her chest, flattened her breasts. It occurred to me that most of her clothes, high necked, long-sleeved and voluminous, were like infants' christening gowns, and dressed like this, she reminded me of an imperious child.

"I never had a woman friend before," she said.

"Betty..."

"My relationship with Betty was never serious. You're the one who showed me I can really be friends with a woman. I want us to be closer. I'm so lonely."

Gently, I drew my hand back and tried to change the subject, only for her to take it again. "I long for sensuality," she told me. Dianne had to explore every nuance of feeling, the way she did in her writing. I envied her courage, even though I knew once she sobered up, I might have to hear a puritanical, 'How dare you try to seduce me into perversity!'

"You must drive men crazy with your beautiful body," she went on. As unnerving as her attentions were, I wasn't vigorous in stopping them. I was too curious at what would happen, too excited by such a conversation the like of which I'd never had before. It chipped at all those things frozen within me, fantasies of naked women at Dachau , stroking each other, begging for favors from their captors, as they're led into the gas chambers.

"What do you need Jerry for? He's holding you back," she said and my heart began to pound. I felt frightened and ashamed. Like the sirens, Dianne had lured me to her with her beautiful voice, her writing, her madness, but I could only enjoy her because I was bound to Jerry. To be without Jerry was to fall into chaos.

She lurched towards me and I asked in a cool voice, "Can you stand up? Do you want me to drive you home?"

"Get Lloyd," she told me, blinking her eyes as if she were awakening from a dream.

The next day she phoned and said, "I'm sorry for the way I behaved."

We'd talk for hours on the telephone so my neck and shoulder ached. My opportunity to stretch came only in the brief intervals she excused herself to use the bathroom and get a fresh beer. She was furious with Betty Durling for complaining about these long conversations, but now I felt collared by the receiver and leashed by the chord. When Jerry, Peter, and I returned from a camping vacation to Yosemite, as soon as we opened the door, the phone shrilly summoned me. Jerry rolled his eyes as I resumed my post. He went into the kitchen and with a clatter of dishes and pots started dinner.

After Dianne released me, he said, "She won't give you a moment, will she? Why don't you tell her you have to get off?"

"It's not easy."

"What's so hard? You say 'goodbye' and put the receiver down." He slammed a pot on the stove as if to show me. The dinner he had prepared was long cold, and he was heating up my share.

Once again I repeated how much she offered me as a writer. I reproached him with a litany of her sufferings: her daughter's death, her unrecognized talent, the lack of respect from others, Lloyd's infidelities and her alcoholism. Jerry looked hurt and I knew everything I said only separated us.

But I was addicted now to Dianne's Scheharazade stories.

As she spun them out on the phone, delivery men rang my doorbell, my cat clawed unpacked bags of groceries, saucepans of food burned and I made a frantic dumb show to Peter to avoid this mischief or that danger. Like my mother I was absorbed and unavailable. Dianne had brought chaos into my life. My husband and child resented me; my friends felt abandoned. I no longer had time for any of them. "She needs human sacrifices," Betty warned me, angry because Dianne had urged her to send truant Karl away to a military academy. Despite all this, Dianne's talk mesmerized me. I had to keep that receiver glued to my ear, listening to her stories.

"I sent Lloyd to the bath houses along with two of our homosexual friends," Dianne told me one night on the phone.

"Aren't you jealous?"

"Of men? Why should I be? It was my idea. I want to know all about it. As a writer."

"But what if it draws him away from you?"

"Turns him gay? You don't understand about Lloyd. Ours is a peculiar marriage...I can't act and he can't feel. Together we make a whole."

"I don't understand."

"I tell him who to sleep with. He's a zombie. He can

do anything; he could murder someone and not feel anything. He can be homosexual one day and heterosexual the next. I give him an identity. You know why he's always looking in the mirror? Not just to admire himself but to check to see if he exists. Do you think I'm a damn pervert like my mother? You don't really know me, Rhoda. I'm the devil. It would have been better if I never was born. Maybe it's better Gloria died. I would have turned her into a monster."

She waited for my absolution and I gave it willingly. Her confessions made me believe that she said the worst about herself and that she acted from pain. "Please don't talk that way about Gloria. You're so hard on yourself," I pleaded.

"You're not disgusted with me?"

"Of course not. What right do I have to judge you? Even it I had the right, I don't feel capable of judging. I haven't figured out the right way to live. I wouldn't presume to judge others. Not me."

"Neither of us learned 'the right way to live.' My mother didn't even teach me how to wash my underwear. I remember the shame I felt in the locker room when the other girls saw my makeshift safety pin holding my panties together. That little pin screamed, 'The secret's out. This girl is unloved. No one cares about her.'"

I danced towards her bright flame but always drew

74

back at the fatal moment. My resistance challenged Dianne. When I refused to speak about my parents' concentration camp experiences, she persisted in asking me questions. My protest, "I don't want to talk about it," made her all the more eager.

"I only thought it might bring you relief. I thought as a writer, you would find it important to talk about."

"It would be a betrayal to my parents."

"Is it a betrayal to bring something to light? You don't have to tell me, but you might think about this some more. Writing is like taking an x-ray. Nothing can be concealed. If there's something important you have inhibitions about, it will stymie all of your writing."

"Some kind of experiment was done on my mother. I don't know what. I've never seen her naked." I tried to say this as calmly as possible, although inwardly I shook. I'd fantasized so often that the 'experiment' was done on my body and in that way I merged with my mother.

"And your father?"

"My father? I don't know what happened to him. To this day he won't let anyone touch his head. I've inherited the same sensitivity. I don't like anyone to touch my head either." I didn't tell Dianne that my father had beaten me once on my head and shoulders.

The next day she offered to set my hair with her 'hot

rollers.' When I agreed she said, "Maybe, another time. I actually don't feel like it now." She let me off. Not just from the hair setting, but for the moment, she was sated with what I'd told her of my parents.

But she came up with another demand. "Why don't you write at my house? You could use Lloyd's typewriter while he's away at school. I swear I wouldn't disturb you."

I knew if I sat in her apartment with her hovering over every word, I would die creatively. "I can't," I said. "I know I wouldn't get anything done."

"Don't you want to try it? What can I say to convince you? It's so lonely here without Gloria."

"I can't."

"Well, maybe you'll change your mind," she concluded. I was relieved. It was so difficult to resist my own craving for her searchlight attention.

Dianne's doorbell rang and Betty Durling dropped by unexpectedly. She fluttered about Dianne's living room, telling anecdotes accompanied by her gasps and dramatic gestures, feverishly entertaining. As always, I was swept away.

Not Dianne. She sat practically frozen, steadily drinking beer after beer and tapping her foot in a nervous tattoo. The two of us had gossiped about Betty and that collusion made me guilty. Dianne had told me what Betty herself would never have confessed; that Lloyd had persuaded Betty to strip off her clothes so he could massage her. Dianne reveled in watching, but later she was overwhelmed by the feeling that compared to Betty's trim figure her body's fleshiness was grotesque.

Dianne kept tapping her foot, maintaining a beat which drove Betty to perform with even greater elan. She proceeded to tell us about the nanny who had cared for her during infancy, a Chinese woman whom she had loved dearly but who was dismissed after a few years. "I was heartbroken," Betty sighed. "To make matters worse, my cousin Francine was born. I couldn't stand it when all the relatives drew around Francine's bassinet to coo. To this day I have dreams that it's me in the bassinet, and the entire United States army has gathered to admire my charms."

"What's the point?" Dianne finally spoke, "that you're infantile?"

"Infantile," Betty echoed. She was obviously hurt but salvaged her pride by laughing. "Yes, of course, we're all children." Betty plopped down next to Dianne on the couch and made a sweeping gesture which included the two of them and me. "None of us are adults," she decreed airily. "That would be so boring."

"I'm afraid I don't agree." "Are you angry about

something?" Betty grinned. She was trying to lure Dianne into playfulness, and succeeded to the extent that an amused expression crossed Dianne's face.

"Yes! "Do you want to fight? Come on let's fight," Dianne cried, poking Betty first in her arm, and then in her neck, her thigh and her belly.

"Stop it!" an alarmed Betty cried, twisting around and trying to shove Dianne's hands away.

"Go a few rounds with the champ, baby-face," Dianne taunted.

"Stop it."

"Come on, hit me! Let's see if you've got the guts."

"I don't want to hit you. Just leave me alone!"

Betty half-rose and with surprising strength, Dianne pulled her back down next to her. In a gravely voice, she drawled, "Oh no, baby-face. You're not going to get off so easy. No way." She stroked Betty's hair, crooning, "What beautiful hair," and then yanked a handful of it. By now Betty had had enough. She whipped around and slapped Dianne hard across the face. "I'm leaving," she mumbled, surprised, I think, by her own violence. She ran out in a rush, leaving Dianne and me to the post-mortem.
A red streak stained Dianne's cheek. I offered to get ice.

"No, don't bother," she replied still excited. "You saw how she hit me! You witnessed it."

"She shouldn't have hit you," I said, grasping at something to say. After all, it was Dianne who had acted like a barroom bully. I was glad I wasn't the one she turned against, but I was ashamed that I hadn't intervened to help Betty. If I'd not been there, Dianne would never have orchestrated this scene.

"I don't regret it," Dianne reasoned. "I wanted to get rid of her. Now she's finished it herself. At first she fascinated Lloyd and me, but in the end we saw how superficial she was. Lloyd calls her Madama Butterfly. He says her poems show promise, but she'll never fulfill that promise. I just don't want to waste my time with that kind of person. You agree, she's a diletante?"

Just then we heard Lloyd's key at the door and I was glad his arrival saved me from answering. Dianne called out, "Betty slapped me in the face."

"Oh, did you enjoy it?"

In June, Dianne's middle sister, eighteen-year-old Tessa arrived from the Atlanta convent to live with the Frys. They squeezed a cot into the study for her. It was as if they had a new child. She brought a freshness with her that exhilarated Dianne. "Isn't she beautiful?" she whispered to me. Lloyd, too, became her devoted admirer. He took her to his classes, films, museums and Golden Gate Park.

Dianne took steps to make drastic changes in her life. She started using birth control pills and antibuse tablets to force her to stop drinking. She got a driving permit and began driving lessons. This was hardly the same woman frozen by a terror of murderers, rapists and invisible germs. This was not the Dianne who washed her hands compulsively and was frightened to cook for fear she would poison the food. "Tessa," Dianne explained, "is like a bright sun, shining innocence all around her. She's what I once was long ago. You know she arrived dressed in her convent jumper. She was carrying a cardboard suitcase. On her first night here, she wanted to impress us with her sophistication, so she lit a cigarette. She was so proud of her daring."

"What's she's going to do?" I asked.

"We're not rushing her," Diane said, fingering a strand of hair. It's too exciting just getting to know her. We want her to look around and develop." Just then Tessa entered the room and Dianne smiled broadly. "Why should such an angel do anything?" she asked. "We'll take care of her."

"My sister and Lloyd are so generous, but I'm not going to impose on them forever."

"Yes, forever!" Dianne took Tessa's hand between hers. "We're not going to let you go. What do you know about the real world? You've been secluded most of your life."

"I haven't been a real religious Catholic for the last two years."

"In other words, you occasionally skip confession."

"Don't tease me, please." A blush spread over Tessa's pale face and neck.

With Tessa around, I panicked as Dianne drifted away from me. Now she spent next to no time with me and when we did meet, she yawned. Tessa absorbed her completely. The few times I did see Dianne, she insisted that I admire Tessa's beauty. No one, I was told, possessed a more sterling character than this child. "She's more spontaneous than...well, you," Dianne crooned. "It's not surprising though; I mean with your background you would be controlled. The holocaust and being Jewish."

"Being Jewish?"

"Jews tend to be quite serious, don't they? You don't mind me saying that, do you?"

Dianne watched me closely, smiling. Once a necessary sounding board, I was now a nuisance. She made a slow, drawn-out game of getting rid of me. I kept pretending that if I ignored her barbs, my devotion could win her back. I pitied poor Betty Durling, ousted from the magic circle, but then Dianne amazed me, saying they were friends again. Betty, Dianne explained, was "fun." Trying to fathom exactly what was meant by "fun," I remembered that Betty had taken her clothes off.

As I lost favor with Dianne, an extraordinary thing happened. Lloyd grew congenial. "How yer doing?" he drawled when I visited. "How's your writing?" I even viewed him more sympathetically, cringing when Dianne jerked him around like a puppet. One moment she benevolently praised him, "You're just brilliant," or laughed at his cutting remarks, "Well, she deserved that!" The next, she spewed righteous anger, "I owe you for the little affair you had with that policeman's wife." I saw Lloyd never relaxed. If he played Narcissus in front of the mirror, I suspected it was because he was a conscientious actor checking his ever-changing roles. No wonder he was so interested in costume. I recalled those size eleven pumps in Gloria's room and wondered if it wasn't the child but Lloyd who had used them at Dianne's bidding.

One evening, I picked a bouquet of daisies and roses in my garden and presented them to Dianne. "Daisies and roses. Like sisters," Lloyd crowed. He clutched a beer in one hand. Then I noticed Dianne was drinking too.

"Don't look so shocked," she said. "I went off the antibuse two weeks ago. We're celebrating. Do you want one?"

"No."

"Tessa's having one. Look at Tessa, she's not going to let

the church's teachings stifle her life. The trouble with you, Rhoda, is you're so damn incorruptible. It's really boring. By the way, how's Peter and...oh, what's his name?"

I said nothing.

"What is his name?" she laughed. "I've really forgotten. Harvey?"

"Jerry," I corrected in a low voice. How far would she go?

"Some people just fade into the wall. Not that I mean that about...Jerry."

Tessa took my flowers, smiling uncomfortably. "Be careful of the thorns," I warned. From the kitchen I heard the whoosh of water as she filled a vase.

"Rhoda looks well tonight, doesn't she, Lloyd?"

He turned towards me   slowly and grinned.   "I swear, you'd just think she gets all her clothes from Paris. One stunning ensemble after another."

Girlish Tessa reappeared with the bouquet. She sniffed delicately at the red roses and handled the vase carefully.

"Too bad you haven't met little Peter," Dianne said to her sister.

"I'd like to," Tessa replied ingenuously.

"Now what is it," Lloyd mused, "that Gloria said about Peter? I just know it'll come back to me in a moment. Wasn't it that he looked dead? Like a mummy?" He crowed, "That's it! She called him the Green mummy!" Cackling with delight, he added, "Didn't she say he cheated during a game? Peter, Peter, little cheater."

It took these disgusting shots at my son to shock me out of my passivity. Bad enough for Lloyd to exploit his dead daughter, bad enough for Dianne to ridicule Jerry, and now Peter was attacked too. I fled the room, hurrying down the dark hallway and out the door to my car. I lay my head on the steering wheel. Suddenly, months of passionate friendship were in question, as if I'd done something vile. After arguing with myself for a half hour, I decided to go back inside and 'clear things up one way or another with Dianne.' When I left before, I neglected to pull the door completely shut and the lock hadn't caught. So when I rapped lightly with no answer, I simply pushed the door open and walked inside. In the dim hall, I paused to gather my courage. The living room was lit up like a diorama. From my position I couldn't see the three of them directly, but they were reflected in the large gold framed mirror. They were playing cards, Dianne and waif-like Tessa on the couch, and Lloyd sprawled nearby. They were playing strip poker. Fascinated, I didn't declare myself but stood concealed in the shadowy hall and watched.

"You lost again, Tessa," Lloyd cried jubilantly.

"I already gave you my shoes and socks and my

earrings."

"Well, now you have to give us something else. What will it be? shirt? or slacks?"

"Why is it that I'm the only one losing?" Tessa giggled. "Do you cheat when you deal? I want to deal. How come Lloyd always deals?"

"Would I cheat?"

"Yes, you would."

"You don't know me truly. I'm taking off my shirt. Do you see any cards up my sleeves?" He shook the shirt vigorously.   "Now you take off yours and we'll see if you cheated."

"I don't want to play any more." Tessa snatched the deck, tossed it in the air, and the cards fluttered over the rug.

"Oh no, once you started you have to finish," Dianne laughed.

Tessa ripped a button off her blouse and threw it at Lloyd.

"Does a button count, Dianne?" Lloyd asked.

"No Lloyd, a button doesn't count."

Tessa   undid the other buttons and pulled off her blouse revealing her brassiere. Throwing the blouse across the coffee table towards Lloyd's head, she pouted, "All right, here!" and grabbed a sofa pillow to put in front of her bosom like a shield.

The blouse landed over Lloyd's face. He rose zombie-like, waving his arms, and in a deep voice from beneath the blouse called, "There's a way...we could finish up the game...right now."

"What's that?"

"Just....take off...all your clothes...every stitch!"

"Why should I?"

"I'll take off my pants, if you take off yours." He balled the blouse up, thrust it back at Tessa and lunged towards her, tickling her sides and pulling the pillow away. Shrieking with laughter, she fell back onto the couch against Dianne. "Stop, stop," Tessa gasped.

"Why should I? Why should I?" he imitated her soprano with a falsetto.

She tried to push him away, but he fended her weak efforts off with one hand while tickling her with the other. I expected Dianne to make Lloyd stop, but instead she got up with her beer and walked over to seat herself in the easy chair. Lloyd kissed Tessa's lips. He pulled down her bra and sucked at her bare shoulders and nipples. With eyes shut tight, Tessa stiffened and tossed her head in ecstasy while Dianne looked on impassively. She glanced across the room and began to watch Lloyd and Tessa's gyrations in the mirror the way I did, growing absorbed as if watching a film. With this horrible connection between us, my chest constricted so I could barely breathe, but I managed to slip away. This time, I drove home.

"What's the matter?" Jerry demanded, but I only flung myself in his arms and wept.

"Calm down. You're choking yourself."

I scarcely heard his voice, only burrowed into his chest for refuge. When I'd stopped crying, I told him what had happened. What sickened me was how Dianne sat there watching. I knew her power over the two, that she directed and drove them on, that neither of them possessed a shred of independence. Only after telling Jerry, did it occur to me I might have acted more responsibly to Tessa. "I should have helped Tessa," I said.

"It sounds like she knew what she was doing."

"No, no she didn't! She's only a kid."

"She has Dianne to look after her," Jerry went on bitterly.

In a burning hot bath, I scrubbed my body with a wash cloth, then went to sleep and listened to Jerry's calm, even breathing in bed. I crept down the stairs, picked up the telephone and dialed Dianne's number. It rang four or five times and then I slammed the receiver down.

The Mathematician

When Robert Stern first received the invitation to the mathematical congress in Chicago, one of the reasons he accepted was to get away for a while from Louise. The arguments with his wife continued day after day, so he no longer felt the justice of her complaints, only that she was forcing him to the end of his strength. She was one of those who knew how to fight, whereas he did not. He floundered helplessly. Against his passive assistance she unloosed herself with real violence, throwing an iron that chipped the wall, deliberately becoming drunk, thrusting herself on him sexually..."God damn it make love to me"...and all this in the chaos of the house. She had never cared for keeping house and now it seemed that everything— high heels, toaster, lingerie and even his mathematics books and papers were mixed together in clumps on the counters and floors. When he came home from the university each day, even before he opened the door he knew that Louise was waiting, stiff with her loneliness and her demands.

She wanted a child. They were not too old. He was thirty-five and she three years younger. He had always felt detached from being any age, lifted up out of ordinary chronology when at twelve he had attended Harvard University as a mathematics prodigy. He explained to her that such a responsibility was impossible for him. He was dedicated to his work. That was the most important thing to him. "Yes, your true child" she said and burst into tears. He could not comfort her. Their lives in the ten years of their marriage seemed to work in some attrition of qualities, some bond of opposites. She became more "physical" and wore short clinging dresses and laughed loudly while he became more "cerebral." When she cried he pitied her, but he could not bring himself to put his arms about her. His thoughts that he could not share seemed to extend even to the nerve endings of his fingers.

The night he left for Chicago the crescendo of their arguments had finally reached a zenith. He was in a numb daze when he took the cab to the heliport, at the airport, all through the plane trip and when finally he was in the hotel room in the center of the city, He was too upset to unpack. He let his clothes fall from him in a heap on the floor and lay on the bed. His flaccid body was stiff against the mattress.

It was a luxuriously appointed and immaculate room with yellow satin drapes, armchairs and antique dresser. Faintly from the next room he could hear the sounds of a party. Staring into the darkness, he had an acute and painful vision of himself from the outside—he was tall and corpulent with a high nimbus of frizzy black hair and protruding eyes. As he lay there his belly made a white mound over which he could imagine small ants crawling.

The phone began to ring about three in the morning. He guessed it was Louise and did not answer. Finally in fury he stumbled from the bed over to the small table and picked up the receiver only to hear it click at the other end. He had a vision of Louise with a phone pinned to her ear. So many times he had come home to find her talking on the telephone, or in the middle of the night she had groped through the chasm of the house to find comfort from her patient friends who did not mind being awakened by the shrill ringing summons. He had no friends--to that extent of purity had he consecrated his life. Louise joined encounter groups with their formalized and guaranteed sympathy.

He glanced at his wristwatch. It was twenty after three. How would he sleep? He sat in the armchair awhile and felt calmer. Something in the black night had soothed him. He dialed the hotel desk and asked the clerk that he receive no more calls for the night... but then thinking of something else that was important to him, he mentioned he was expecting a telegram and gave detailed instructions he wanted relayed to the day clerk about where he would be the next morning and afternoon and that he wanted to be informed at once if a telegram came. "Yes Doctor Stern" the clerk said courteously. "Please..." Robert implored him. Slowly he put the receiver into its cradle and thought with wonder that he could concern himself at that moment with the Fisher Prize. It was the highest mathematical accolade and Robert knew it would be awarded sometime in the following days by telegram.

He lay down again and fell into a grey, restless sleep. He was asleep and yet he was aware that he "thought," he did not dream. He heard a murmuring in the hall and someone brushing against his door. He tried to remember the room number. He began to count. Numbers were magical, a separate language that few understood.

At dawn he awoke violently, a red light bursting in his head. He had, after all entered the death of the deepest sleep. He was confused by the strange room and then remembered the congress and became excited. He would have to give a speech. He would have to stand before a huge audience of his colleagues who would judge him. But had not that been the most important reason for coming? Reticent and shy as he was, he wanted to politic for the Fisher prize. Although he was an eminent mathematician and had published a paper five years before which was a major breakthrough in logical theory, he had been passed over to see lesser men receive it—one recipient had even built on Robert's work. It had embittered him and he was determined now his work would receive the credit it deserved.

He sat up, swinging his naked legs from beneath the twisted linen and went to the white tiled bathroom to shave. He did it carefully, wetting his face, lathering, scraping his skin of the dark growth. When he dressed, it disturbed him that his suit was crumpled. Anxiously he tried to smooth it out with slow, pressing motions of his palms as if to wipe away memories of the previous evening. He finished his morning toilette, locked the room and walked through the corridor, passing a maid wheeling a stainless steel cart materials and linens. At the elevator he realized how hungry he felt. He would get some breakfast at the hotel's coffee shop. Afterwards he would register for the Congress and go to the talks that were held in the grand ballroom.

He arrived outside the ballroom at nine. The hotel staff was still arranging the folding chairs and people waited in the hallway. At first there were not many, but shortly a sizable crowd formed. People were subdued, still dull with sleep. There were few women. The men wore dark suits generally and had plastic badges on their lapels that had been distributed at the registration table in the lobby.

Robert began to pace up and down. He recognized people in the crowd. He had worked at numerous universities. Following his success five years before he had been inundated with offers of jobs, and in a wild, unstable mood that possessed both Louise and himself they had uprooted themselves going from one prestigious academic setting to another. He felt himself in little mood for socializing, and he kept his eyes averted so that he could pretend that he had not noticed his acquaintances and would not seem rude. He fixed his eyes on the carpet and saw only a blur of the restroom doors opening and closing, the line at the water fountain, the iridescence of burning cigarettes in the dim light and the smoke from the white Styrofoam cups of hot coffee that people sipped. The leather attaché case Robert carried with his work and his speech was heavy and he switched it from one hand to the other. He thought how he could read his speech automatically later from the neat pages the department secretary had typed. At the last conference he had accidentally upset a pitcher of water and it had spilled all over his clothes. The dread of displaying himself, of doing something clumsy again made him nervous but allowed him to forget Louise.

He was aware of snatches of conversation about him, the usual small talk of foundation grants, who had switched jobs or been promoted, some technical discussions of mathematics...but also there was talk of the Fisher Prize. The suspense that would grow as the day progressed was almost palpable as were the currents of vanity, greed, and desire to secure a career, simple curiosity and even spite. Robert drifted over to the wall where he touched a flocked "*fleur de lys*" imprinted on the wallpaper. Why should he seek the prize he wondered when it seemed to him in many ways such a doubtful and ignoble goal? His greatest weakness was the need to be recognized for what he did. He could not escape such ambitions just as he failed to escape the needs of his body.

His reverie was broken by an unfamiliar voice. "Hello Doctor Stern." A hand was stretched out to him. You don't know me." "Yes?" He turned towards a young man of about twenty with long hair and thick glasses, obviously a graduate student. "I want to tell you how much I admire your work." He leaned forward eagerly, adulation blurring his eyes. Would Robert explain something to him? He had struggled with it but had never been bright enough to grasp it. "I'll try" Robert said. He was troubled that the boy had asked about the "breakthrough" and not about more recent work. Even so he was flattered. He began to deftly untangle the graceful, subtle propositions of the proof. Just as he finished his explanation, the buzzer sounded indicating the Congress would begin. "Thank you, you don't know how much this means to me," his companion said and backed away and then merged with the crowd that flowed through the double doors that had been opened.

Robert followed the others into the hall. How opulent, how dazzling it was. Their shoes made a low shuffling on the polished parquet and they passed slender marble pillars. The windows were high with brilliant red curtains and on the walls were hung gold framed paintings of nymphs and cherubs. Absently Robert took a program from an usher. His speech was later in the afternoon. At the tenth row from the back, he pushed though mumbling, "excuse me" and finally sank down into a chair. His attaché case he pushed underneath the seat. He saw that the first speaker was already at the podium standing beside Carter the organizer of the Congress. Their baldheads beneath the chandelier shone like billiards.

After a short introduction by Carter the speaker began. "Is there a non-trivial measure defined on all sets of real numbers?" The man to Robert's left was scribbling formulas in a leather covered notebook and to the right a second man had removed his glasses and was chewing on the plastic earpieces. He felt people pressing on him from all sides and he longed to stretch out his arms and legs that felt cramped in the small space. He closed his eyes in a kind of somnolence and then opened them and twisted about anxiously in his seat. The door in the back swung out and someone had left. "Did a hotel bellhop come in?

Do you know?" he whispered to his neighbor a sandy haired man with dense freckles. The man shrugged, Robert felt foolish. He must control himself. He must be patient.

After fifteen minutes the speaker folded the sheets of paper before him and smiled faintly. There were a few questions from the audience and then he stepped down from the stage to polite applause. The next speaker was called and the morning wore on in monotony until eleven thirty when the sound system broke.

It spluttered and squawked at first drowning, out the speaker's voice, and then failed altogether. From the back of the ballroom someone shouted, "We can't hear." People began to murmur and there was a confused rush of movement to the dais. Two mathematicians ascended appeared promptly with a tool case and Carter called a break for lunch. Everyone rose to escape from the tedium of the talks and began to retreat from the room. Many would use the opportunity to escape and go sightseeing out to the famous university at the south of the city, or Lincoln Park or "Old Town."

Robert felt his stomach knotted with nervousness and decided to stay behind. He did not want lunch. For a few moments he watched the workman who had pulled a thick cable onto the red carpet in front of the dais and seemed to be stripping its tip with a sharp tool. He stretched his arms and happened to look up and noticed for the first time a picture of a smiling milkmaid with pink cheeks and a large bosom over a corseted waist painted directly above on the vast vault of the ceiling. Something about her, the mixture of voluptuousness and vulgarity sickened him. He looked away abruptly.

He took his attaché case and put it on the seat beside him. The clicking sound of it opening was sharp in the huge, empty hall. He took out some paper and began to work. He was glad of the quiet, the reassurance of entering the mesh of his work. As frustrating as it could be, it could still bring forgetfulness and intimations of the ecstatic explosion of discovery. What had happened lately was that his insights were too shallow— a disaster for him, as impotence would be for another man. Still he persisted. How could he explain the joy of creating something from nothing, of finding order in chaos, of sitting at his desk but to feel as if he were flying through the air? And afterwards, days after he would walk about contented with all of life, seeing only beauty. Nothing was ugly and nothing, nothing could hurt him. There was nothing, not sex, not love of another human, not music or art, not food, not wealth, riot religion that could bring him this happiness. He wrote equations and proceeded through a problem. The secret was to look at something from an unusual angle. He must probe gently, gently.

He became aware of someone standing nearby. It flashed through him it was the messenger with the telegram about the Fisher Prize. He wanted the prize because he wanted full recognition of his work. He wanted the prize because he knew it would buoy him, would somehow give him an energy and patience to go further then he had before. He looked up and it was not.

He recognized Henry Lawson. "Robert." he said, "How are you?" The man had worked at The Institute of Advanced Studies when Robert was there, and they had been neighbors on Max Planck Drive, but Robert had barely known him. "How are you?" he repeated, "It's wonderful seeing you." "I'm fine" he said and studied Lawson's face curiously. The silken mustache curved down and there were slight lines about the mouth and on the broad forehead, and he had bright blue eyes. His shirt was made of soft striped linen and his shoes, loafers, were pointed. He was a large man and yet somehow he seemed to have a sinewy compactness. In a controlled, mellifluous voice he asked "How's your wife, how's Louise?" Robert winced. "Oh she's fine, No, not exactly." Lawson took the seat next to him. "How so?" His face became a study of sympathy and concern. "Louise. Not well?"

How it happened that he let Lawson draw him out, he did not know. Against the man's refined courtesy he was helpless. He had always been inept and innocent so that he could not understand or manage the common currency of deception, of polite conversation. Always a "mark" to a salesman, a landlord, a student who concocted a pathetic excuse and begged for a higher grade, he paid in cash or feeling, twice or three times the ordinary price. To this stranger who sat beside him, bent forward slightly his his legs planted apart, he told his innermost feelings and sacrificed his privacy.

He began to tell small parts of the story of the day before when he had told Louise about the small room he had rented and that when he returned from the Congress he would live there, that he had to have a spare life with no distractions. As he spoke or as he pressed his lips together and listened to Lawson's expressions of sympathy, the pain and guilt came back to him intensely of how Louise had sat at a small table in the bedroom and looked at him with disbelief. He remembered the uneasy sound of his voice, "Soooo....", as he waited for her to understand, and how frightened he was. She was a wild being. Her face was stamped with misery. He believed she worshipped him--and guiltily he knew if she was always resentful it was because she had ached so long for some sign of his love and he had failed her.

He tried to explain to her as gently as he could that despite their "disagreements" he knew what a good and generous woman she was. He would miss her compassion, her humor, her exuberances, and a thousand fine qualities... but he could not go on with the marriage. The intimacy distracted him from his work; it blurred his ability to think. Even if they could avoid fighting he could not go on with the marriage. The nature of the commitment to his work he had made prevented that.

Her manicured nails traced the design of a circle on the arm of the chair where she sat. She stood up and walked over to the glass doorthat led out to the patio. The frilly peignoir she had taken to wearing about the house made a static electric sound.

"It's another woman Robert, isn't it?"

"No, how could that be? Don't you see I never should have married! I should have been a celibate or a monk." It pained him to say this; it was a gift of his humiliation he gave her as fair compensation.

"There's something I've been wanting to tell you. I was waiting until we were really close...so you would understand. Now...I'm glad that I waited. Did you know I had lovers? There were three of them...only three! With a husband like you, I'm not sure why I practiced so much restraint."

He had felt then as if the breath was knocked out of him. His mind swam with anger, with what a fool he was, with "who," "when," "where," with agonizing memories of his own clumsiness during their lovemaking. He was impaled by his revulsion for this own body, his feeling that it was ugly in its size and clumsiness and no woman could desire it. If only she had spared him this. He did not want to hate her.

She was within moments repentant, crying, saying, "They meant nothing. It was experimental. It was because I had no child," but how could he believe in her love when he felt so empty himself. She saw his utter indifference, his contempt and first she tried to embrace him, but he took her by the wrists and put her away from him on the chair. He could hardly bear to touch her. She had said, "I can't go on if you leave me. Do you understand?" She had in a way killed him, so how could he understand or even hear? He was dead, unmoved. When he left the house that evening it was like some large animal that fled to nurse its wounds. It was not how he had imagined he would leave.

Robert became suddenly aware of his own voice in the vast hall. The workman had left, "People are coming back," Lawson said softly. "Yes," Robert answered. Lawson put his hand forward on Robert's arm. He was sorry about Louise, and he hoped it all came out all right. He got up to go back to where he had been sitting before. Robert watched him merge with the crowd of people who began to stream into the room. He was struck by the man's grace, his sensuous movement and he felt a sudden distrust of him. Why had he asked about Louise? It was strange that he had come back to the ballroom to seek him out.

He took the program out of his pocket and ran his finger down the thick white vellum. He would be the fourth speaker that afternoon. He removed his speech from his attaché case, folded the pages in thirds and slipped them into the inside pocket of his suit jacket. His throat felt dry.

People seated themselves. Carter ascended the dais once again and the meeting began. He could barely concentrate. He noted only that the talk being given concerned computers. The speaker had an irritating self-possession, and it seemed to Robert that the man was glossy, up-to-date like the subject he discussed. He had observed that people's work reflected their personalities. When Robert had tried to solve some facile problem, his mind closed against him. His thoughts drifted away from the objective reality. Irresistibly his eyes were drawn to the picture above and he saw that it was just necessary to squint slightly and the breasts of the milkmaid became comfortingly two ellipses—no confusion, desire, or hope, only a sense of being bereft.

There was a new speaker. Robert's turn would come two after him. A joke must have been made that Robert missed. The audience began to laugh. It drew them together and excluded him. He felt how alone he was among these people. He had made a conscious choice and cut himself off from everyone—friends, parents, the child he might have had and his wife. He yearned for solitude. He thought of Louise always pleading with him for less involvement with his work, hitting a table before her for emphasis, "Do you remember the child in the park?" and as she spoke it had come back, of walking through the grass with her one day, of lifting a small boy he had met and dancing with him like a giraffe in the light that broke through the trees. Then in that great dizziness the idea had come to him, the essential link necessary for his work. But it had to have been only an accident that it occurred just then and that Louise was wrong that creativity was connected to love of other people. He was wary. Contact with others wasted and drained him, and he wanted only to be alone.

Suddenly someone was tapping him on the shoulder. No, no, he could not stand to be touched, especially near the head. His head was exploding. It was as if a raw wound was pierced, the smoldering fire of his isolation. To come back to consciousness was to be caught unawares aid exposed.

The man behind him whispered, "I believe it's your turn." Robert was about to answer angrily "It can't be," when he realized that his name was being called. He had relied on the predicted sequence, just as when he walked down tie corridor in Evans Hall at the University he counted off the doors to the offices to come to his own. Somehow they had skipped the person before him. He rose unsteadily moving past the people in his row out to the aisle where he began to walk in an awkward, broken rhythm. He thought of Louise and of her threatening him with her desperation. It was as if she revenged herself by making him so nervous in this moment.

The audience applauded enthusiastically. They craned their heads to see the famous prodigy. Robert smiled weakly, piteously, looking about himself like a frightened child. They clapped louder and louder. He thought, I am falling. He felt a heavy weight implanted in his bowels. He distrusted this acclaim, and in his imagination there were people in the audience who heaped on him jealous malice and whispered--- "He has barely published anything for three years."

"Oh well. Mathematicians like ballerinas have short careers." "It burns out the brain."

The applause continued, reaching a crescendo as he came closer to the podium. It became a dissonant rhythm that set him on edge like the pounding beat of certain modern music. He felt them looking at his flaccid uncoordinated body, the result of a life-time of the most minimum movement beyond sitting at a desk-he could never balance on a bicycle, on ice skates, in an sport he was terrified of being injured. Just as Louise must, they were thinking he was grotesque. His body was moving apart from himself and although he struggled to make some connection with it, he could not. He noticed only too late that the workman had left a cable exposed and he stumbled on it. He felt the breathlessness of falling, his insides rising up in a sort of lost sickness. He was unable to recover himself before the tips of his fingers touched the velvet of the rug. He came up quickly, but not so fast that the audience had not noticed it, and their applause was replaced by a low murmur, and also Carter on the stage ahead, perhaps without understanding his cruelty was introducing Robert and making a quip about how perilous mathematics could be.

He tried to grin but the burning humiliation that swept through him left him helpless to do so. Nothing worse could happen he thought as he ascended the dais. The faces of the audience blurred. Something snapped. As if he had been strained to his utmost and his system took its own relief he began to feel a blank calm. He fumbled for the text of his speech, spread it before him on the stand and read. The words were memorized and passed his lips without him understanding them, yet he knew they represented months of the most difficult struggle. He glanced at the sun reflecting through the windows with the red velvet drapes. The sun was low and the day would be over soon. How numb he felt.

Then he saw the door to the side of the hall opening, a steward entering and proceeding down the aisle. There seemed to be a yellow scrap in his hand. The steward paused a few yards before the stage. It was an envelope in his hand, the telegram. He whispered something to a member of the audience who listened and then pointed at the stage. Robert felt a surge of exhilaration, the knowledge that the telegram would be for him. At last, before all of his colleagues he would be awarded the prize he had waited for so long. He could take this formalized sign of esteem with him, to comfort him in the isolation he had chosen. Louise had shattered his trust in all people but the prize would salve even the wound that she had inflicted.

He thought the steward, a young man in a blue blazer would rush forward but he stayed to one side waiting for Robert to finish the talk. He could not go on. He stopped reading and murmured, "Excuse me," and gestured towards the steward. He approached in long, loping steps and gave Robert the envelope. He tore it open. He clutched the thin paper and his eyes went over the typed words again and again, "I can't believe it, no, I can't," he muttered. Wearily he turned back to the table and riffled the paper of his speech and cleared his throat. Carter came over to him, put his face near Robert's and asked "Is anything wrong?" Robert glanced once again in disbelief at the message, "Wife attempted suicide. Critical condition. Come at once."

He said, "I was expecting a different message." In a halting flat voice he went on with the speech.

Later that evening he sat in the hotel room, the newspaper open on his lap. Johnson, a colleague at the University had received the Fisher Prize. The phone kept ringing and ringing.

Outpost of Civilization

The town with the University was fifty miles south of the
Arctic Circle. They offered him the professorship, so Lars went
there. It was unthinkable not to accept such a high honor, the
goal to which his whole career had been directed. Gertrud
accompanied him. That was five years ago. She had a job at first
with the Government Health Insurance program. Then the
economy went bad and she was one among several laid off in her
department. She wanted new work, but it was too isolated, too
frozen a place to have any jobs. All efforts were in vain. She saw
she would have to hibernate like a bear.

She began staying home all day and hoped several things
would occupy her—her poems, her embroidery, her houseplants
and housework. But they barely filled the emptiness of the day.
The emptiness outside, the emptiness inside. She spent the time
eating and filling the big hole up. Constantly. Shoveling things in,
sweet things with whipped cream and red current fillings. It
made her think of a time long ago when she had been happy. She
had been working at her father's bakery shop. How had the
dusty flour transformed to snow? She chewed slowly, licked the
last crumb off her lip. How sad it was over, and she had to look

and sigh over the folds of fat that now enveloped her. She had to use all her strength to heave herself up panting from the chair.

Six in the evening. Eighteen o'clock. She dragged her fat-column legs over to the window. Outside was the northern slope. It never melted, not even in summer. Beyond was the last lamppost of the town; always the light was shining because of the almost perpetual blackness. It cast its faint light into the wilderness of tundra beyond.

There was Lars sliding over the snow on his snow scooter, his body twisting, turning for warmth, a lone figure against the annihilating blankness. She could see his breath stiffen in the air. The thermometer at the window read thirty degrees below zero centigrade. She could imagine the sharp pain in the lungs he felt with every inhalation.

Shuffling steps. Click of key in door. Glittering glasses and frost covered black beard. "Good evening." "Good evening." Voices rang and were absorbed by the silence of the room and the greater stillness of the white snow covered plains that surrounded. He was there, but far from her, as if he had not come in and had not spoken. His arrivals home a long time ago had been like this too, but this far North everything crystallized, became a purer form of itself. She watched in fascination as his red fingers tugged with the fastenings of his coat. The tip of his nose was not red, but white, and she thought if he had not come at that moment it would have been frost bitten. He hung the coat in the warming closet with gloves stuffed in pocket, took off the Russian hat, the scarf and put the furry boots on the drain over the flat pan. He wiped his watery eyes with a handkerchief. Layer after layer he removed until he was ordinary in his plaid shirt. He seemed plucked and vulnerable.

Eight long hours alone when time was like cement pouring into her pores. Thighs trembling, stomach swaying, she grabbed his hand with an urgency that told her long loneliness. He said, don't suck me in with your mouth, don't swallow, don't drown me in your cunt-fat-disgusting belly. Except he did not say it, just held himself. But the room was so still, that she could hear thoughts. He was going to ask her for a divorce soon. She knew it. There was the little redhead at the office. The little Britt. His lips moved, "Is dinner ready?" But she heard, can I have a divorce? "Dinner?" she said in a daze. Panic. What would she do? She was too large and weighted now t o move without assistance. If he let go of her she would fall like a boulder to the bottom of a well right into the madhouse a kilometer away.

"Yes, dinner's ready."

"Come. Let's go in the kitchen," he said. I can't get my courage up to get rid of you because my pity stands in the way.

She served gruel for supper. All over the country, housewives were silently, bitterly dishing out their hearts— but she, witch—like had concocted an essence. You think I'm an ugly old woman, so here, eat this grey, ugly slop.

"I'm sorry, I was too lazy to prepare something else," she said as she poured it into his bowl.

They sat at the pine table with the light fixture dangling low between their faces. The shade had some forest fairies printed on it and was stained in a few spots with grease. She murmured something. "Ummmm" he replied buzzing like the summer mosquitoes. Three nice days after the frost went, then the mosquito eggs hatched and the gigantic monsters appeared with mouths to suck her blood and send her into rampages of clawing her flesh. The bites itched worse, bled, infected. "Ummmm.."

She shoveled in the gruel indifferently. It slid down her throat, the kind of food that never filled. But it was better to be eating than not eating, because of the hunger that gnawed all the time. Lars lifted the silver spoon with unfailing rhythm, its flash, the even motion, hypnotizing her. He was handsome, not even any grey hair—no, a thick, luxuriant head. His lips were red and full, wordless. He got up and carefully washed his dish. Then he left the room, and so meaningless was she to him, that he forgot her presence and closed the light after him. That's how it would be when he left her; death would be in total darkness. When would it happen? In a week, in a month. She hated the little Britt.

Shuddering, she went to the window to see the snow covering everything over and receive its cold, still calmness. It was snowing more, the flakes adding to the already enormous drifts. Soon the windows would be blocked. It was so cold, and she needed more food for the oven of her belly, but she was to slothful to prepare anything more.

She joined him in the living room, a spare room with an old couch whose springs were Broken and a few chairs, none of them comfortable. No comfort in the house. In one corner was a desk. Lars was there with a magnifying glass and tweezers, poring over his stamp collection. His glasses slipped to the tip of his nose and he pushed them back. She sat on the bumpy couch. They were drifting even further away from each other, ice ships on the tundra, with his stamps and she with her embroidery. She had sent to Stockholm for the exact pattern that was identical to one her mother had given her to do when she was a child. The silver needle flicked in and out and the thimble flashed. The white linen became alive with a dark leaf beneath her fingers. She could almost smell the branches of pine she would pick for her mother. Back with her mother, she had worn her yellow hair in silken braids. Her mother would play with them twisting them in her fingers. She broke the seal on a new skein of thread. She needed a lighter color to do the moss at the bottom of the design. Next she would work on the little mushrooms. She sewed; she smiled; her mother whispered sweet words in her ears.

"One day my darling, my fine little lady you'll be a famous doctor. The king will give you a beautiful medal on a red silk ribbon to wear about your neck, Men of all colors and all nationalities will beg you to marry them.

You'll have a yellow canary which sings thrillingly."

The sound of the metal tweezers coming down on the desk broke her train of thought. She struggled to go back to that ethereal forestland where her dead mother whimpered. "Why are you frowning; is something wrong?" The magnifying glass was held in front of one of Lars' eyes, enlarging it grotesquely.

No, nothing wrong."

All the clocks in the house had begun ticking very loudly, including her heart. Her thread knotted and with tears almost in her eyes, right on the brim, she folded the embroidery and put it away. Then she sat very still and imagined that Britt was sitting in the chair opposite her, lounging back, one slender stockinged leg crossing the other at the knee, the French lace of her slip showing enticingly. Gertrud began to tell her about a lover she had.

"That blonde boy on the canal. Gjert was his name... the white curtains blowing in, the big bed, the fan going around. He had a friend, another little garcon who wanted to play. The heat, the wonderful warmth. I find young boys so irresistible. Their lips are still wet with breast milk and they yearn for their mistress to be a mother too, to be large, very large... I've always found it...and they are fresh as the first violets."

The phone screamed taking her breath away. Lars answered, "Yes, she is." He handed it to her. She listened for a while to the news. It was her Aunt. "Yes," she said, "I'll come. But the planes don't fly this time of year up here. I'll have to come by train." She began writing the details she needed on the back of an envelope near at hand.

When she hung up, Lars was staring at her curiously. She said, "My father's dead. I have to go to the funeral. I have to pack."

"I see."

She tried to form plans in her head. She walked into the kitchen, threw open the refrigerator and by the tiny electric light began taking whatever came to hand, cheese, butter, a hardboiled egg and packing it into her mouth and choking it down. Her motions were so clumsy that she knocked over a bottle of lingonberry jelly, but even when it crashed to the floor she continued to rummage. The sound of the breaking glass

114

brought Lars to her. "What are you doing? Stop it. Pull yourself together." She grabbed a fjilm milk, ripped off the top of the pyramidal shaped carton, and dug her hand in, a white slime covering it. "Stop it," he screamed, clutched her shoulder and jerked her back.

She wheeled around and with a wolf-like lunge clamped a piece of his cheek between her teeth, bit down and pulled some off. He howled. His hand went to the raw place that was oozing blood. She fell back a little. Stunned, but she could not stop chewing. She chewed with all her might. Chewed, ground her teeth. It was the sweetest pleasure she had ever known. It was filling every hollow of her body. Later in tears, she told him "I was hungry." He didn't understand and his smile was like syrup. So odd he looked with the white bandage on his cheek, leaning over and patting her arm. He seemed to be listening to something, then she heard it too-the wailing of a siren. She braced herself in the chair. "Calm yourself," he kept saying as one would to a child.

The Gardener

Chung, chung, chung, sounds the spade against rocks, earth and roots. My neighbor Nadine digs constantly. She begins early when the grass is still wet with dew. "It's good for the earth to turn it over," she says. Anyway the garden is so over-tended that there is really little else for her to do. Around noon she disappears for awhile and it is this time, when the sun Is directly overhead that I go out with my blanket and suntan lotion, and dressed in my new turquois bikini, I lie on my back sensuously enjoying the heat, my skin open to it as I would be to a lover.

Chung, chung, chung. Soon the sound begins again with renewed vigor. Lazily I turn my head and glance to Nadine in her peddle pushers, her floppy hat and big military looking garden gloves. She is a large, sturdy woman, her face heavily lined. Even when she digs she has an excellent, stiff spined posture. With her left foot she stamps the top edge of the spade several times, driving it deep, deep down. Then with a jerk from her muscular arms she explosively drives up earth like a steam shovel.

The doves on the telephone line are cooing. About eight of the grey-brown creatures are strung out making a cacophonous chorus. Perhaps it is this that breaks Nadine's severe concentration. She leans on the spade, looks about shading her eyes with her gloved hand, taking in **EVERYTHING**.

"Your bamboo is getting out of hand," she calls into the air, with no preliminary greetings. I pretend not to understand she is addressing me. When she repeats herself, I obey the signal, rise slowly and go to the fence

"Oh, sorry, we'll see to the bamboo. Harvey will do it. You show him what you want done to it."

For a moment her grey eyes turn blank as if the sun blinds her. "Shouldn't let things get out of hand," she answers in a mollified voice, "No. Have to do them right away. I'm going to paint the den Friday. What a job!"

"What color?" I ask eagerly, not only liking color, but resisting some somberness in Nadine. I feel it emanating from her, blocking the sun and I shiver slightly in my bikini.

Dully she replies, "Beige," but then becomes immediately firm and energetic. "I'm doing it now! Who knows? In another year or two, I'll be too old to do a job like that, so I better do it now."

"You're not so old as you're making out."

"I'm not a newly-wed either." As she talks, she nervously snaps dead leaves off the "yellow broom," or breaks off small branches that deviate from the shape she desires the bush to be. She bends; she stretches. "I remember when I got married." Snap, snap. She moves a few steps to the rhododendron from which she takes a large, browning leaf, folds it on its center vein and presses it hard between her fingers. "Oh, my in-laws were horrible. They didn't want Ed to marry me, aid they wrote him this letter. He ripped it up in tiny, tiny pieces," She rips the leaf, pulverizing the pieces to a dry, brown dust, "He put the pieces in an envelope and mailed it to them,"

"Well good for him. They sound like they deserved it, lid they come around later? I bet they were sorry,"

"Them! Are you kidding? It was ME who went to see them, and they wouldn't even open the door!"

"I'm sorry. How terrible for you,"

"I never forgot that,"

"Yes, I can imagine,"

"Standing there like a fool, and then the landlord came out in the hall and said, "What's the matter? Aren't they in? Why do you keep pounding on the door?" I told him I was Ed's wife and talked him into giving me a key. I didn't use it that day, but went back the next day and surprised them,"

"What did they do?"

"Oh, they were so meek. You can't imagine. My father-in-law sat there all hunched over in his Morris chair while she rushed into the kitchen to get tea. She dropped the pot as she was carrying it in. You see she wasn't well then, and neither was he. He had had a stroke a few months before and never told us, and she was worn out from caring for him…the reason he was all hunched over was that he was still partly paralyzed. I saw I better take things in hand. They hadn't been very nice, but still, after all, it wouldn't look right, not to help.

The older they got, the weaker they got. My father-in-law never fully recovered…You see that's what I mean, why I want to paint the den…why I'm always careful to keep the garden up. You never know what your future health will be when you're getting on."

"Come, come. You're starting to sound like you're sewing your own shroud." I laugh and stretch my limbs ostentatiously. As it drifts overhead, a white cloud shaped like a fat man catches my attention.

Nadine bends down, crouches, her hands pick up a lump of earth and pulverize it. She takes off one glove and lightly explores the ground. It is rich with fertilizer, black. A worm shows its head,

"It didn't stop with just one stroke. He had a few more, and in the end he couldn't get out of bed. Her insides were rotting with cancer...Oh now they wanted me, they needed me. I went over daily." Her fingers probe the earth relentlessly as if looking for something. "One time I lost the key. She fell down on the way to answer the door and couldn't get up. Of course it wasn't possible for him to get out of bed. There was no way to get in to them without calling the fire department to come break the door down."

"The landlord...what about?"

"No..no…away,..not there...the firemen came....later when Ed came home from work, we went together and told his parents, 'This is the end; you have to go into a Home.' But what choice did we have, considering their condition? They couldn't live alone."

Nadine spies a weed, a tiny spot of green against the earth and pounces on it. She rips it up with a grimace of annoyance.

"Weak as they were, they struggled and they had to tie them down to take them there. Two hours after entering the Home, my father-in-law died of a hemorrhage, and then ten hours later my mother-in-law had a heart attack."

"That's an amazing story, amazing…it's as if their fates were hound together forever,."

I want to say more, but Nadine pulls on the glove again, waves me off and says, "You'll see to the bamboo." She walks off and stretches out on her lounge chair, a respite for a moment from her constant, hard digging. Within five minutes 1 hear the sound of the spade.

The Convert

The occasion was a circumcision. A tiny baby boy, eight days old as is the custom, was carried out before the congregation at the synagogue and placed on the lap of a *sandek*, the godfather. It was just three days after Passover and the spring sunshine flooded in the enormous stained glass windows. The cantor sang a Hebrew melody accompanied by the caterwauling of the infant.

The Rabbi said, "Circumcision is the most ancient Hebrew custom. A doctor emerged from a side door dressed in hospital gown and surgical gloves. He had a modem, antiseptic air except for the skullcap on his head and the worn down heels of his shoes peeping from beneath the gown. The godfather ran his finger over the child's mouth, somehow soothing it, while the doctor clipped the foreskin.

"It's over," the Rabbi said and the congregation broke into applause, surging up in a crowd, hugging the parents, greeting friends and crowding to a reception hall. A long buffet was set with a breakfast of herring, sweet rolls, bagels and cream cheese, and orange juice and coffee.

"Hurry up. What's holding up the line?" an impatient woman cried from the end. People piled food onto paper plates and made their way to the clusters of bridge tables set about the room. In the center of the room stood a carved wood rocking horse. The sisterhood president made an announcement that this was a gift to the new baby.

A woman of about 35 years of age, slender with blonde wavy hair and dressed in a cotton dress stood hesitantly with her plate of food and studied each of the tables, as if uncertain where to go. Finally she sat beside an elderly man in his sixties.

"Mind if I join you?" she asked and busied herself with spreading a napkin on her lap and beginning to eat. The food appeared to puzzle her as much as the seating arrangements. She poked at the herring with her fork and seemed to be steeled to take a bite, when her companion addressed her.

"And then the penny dropped, as we say in England," he said, leaning towards her. He was thin, his face almost gaunt with strong lines from his nose to the corners of his mouth. His long gray hair--a bohemian touch to his appearance--was slicked straight back aid from beneath the light summer suit and white shirt peeped the hint of a bright orange undershirt.

"Yes, while I was watching the ceremony, the penny dropped. I realized it was exactly 43 years ago today that my own circumcision took place!"

The woman who had lost heart over the herring and pushed it to the side of her plate, looked at him curiously, a little shocked by his comment.

Not gauging her response, he continued, "Really it is so extraordinary, this coincidence, I hope you don't mind listening to my story. Today's *briss* makes me think of it so vividly.

"Well, go on with your story," she said in the middle of a tiny, tentative bite of bagel. Across the table from herself and the man, three Russian women drank coffee and smoked. Each of the Russians had dyed hair, a heavy fullness to their figures and wore thick gold bracelets. At the adjacent table a very old man with two canes spoke in Yiddish.

"You see I'm a convert," the man said in his clipped British accent and introduced himself as Ernest Transmount. His voice was a bright English touch in this particular comer of the noisy synagogue reception hall. Across the room the Rabbi could be seen moving from table to table greeting people and a few women went about with carafes of hot coffee.

"Why did you convert?" the woman asked rather starkly.

Another man would have recoiled, but Ernest, sipping his coffee, simply accepted her sudden intent interest. The woman had turned all the way round towards him and drew her chair closer. Ernest expected her to introduce herself in return but when she did not, he went on in a cheerful tone, "You see, I never could accept the Trinity. It puzzled me terribly. How could there be three separate parts--all separate and yet indivisible? I just couldn't see going through life with the Trinity. And now Judaism. Judaism was just so utterly monotheistic."

"So you converted purely on intellectual grounds."

"Well," he gave a slight chuckle, "it wasn't just the three parts of the Trinity. There were also the six Rosenbaum girls."

"You had a fascination with numbers."

"Picture this if you can, a man in a tiny English village with six unmarried daughters. Just like a Jane Austen novel. Except the man was a Jewish tailor and they were the only Jews for miles around. Those girls certainly were striking. In the beginning I thought they were Spanish because they were swarthy. And they dressed so well. Of course their father was a tailor. It kind of advertised the business, if you see what I mean. But as far as I was concerned it just advertised those girls.

There they were, six nice looking girls in a dull, humdrum village--them the most exciting things about and no one dared to have anything to do with them. Socially they were taboo. You could bring disgrace on your whole family if you were seen with them."

"Yes, it can be a real social stigma to be Jewish," the woman muttered. "You have to feel it's really worth it,"

Ernest, warming to his story, went on, "Well, what can I say? I got introduced and started visiting the Rosenbaum house. My parents didn't like it. They suffered a lot of anguish because of me. The gossip was going day and night and I brought disgrace on them.

"What do you want to do this for Ernie?" they pleaded with me.

I just didn't listen. I got on my bicycle and rode off to the six daughters.

Then one day I was walking along the street and I met Mr. Rosenbaum and he said to me, "I think you'll understand what I'm talking about and why I'm asking when I say you shouldn't come to my house anymore." He was a short, barrel chested man. His parents had come over from Russia in the 1880's and lived in Whitechapel in London. In his home he and his family spoke Yiddish. In fact, at this point I had picked up a lot of Yiddish in his house and could always make out what was said. He knew that, but as we stood there in the main road in front of the baker's, he spoke to me in English like an Englishman. "You're not playing by your rules," he said.

I promised him I wouldn't come to his house. You see, I was cunning like Jacob, the one who put on hairy skins to seem like Esau. Gladys and I--she was the third from the eldest of the sisters--did not meet at his house. We met secretly outside his house. Forbidden fruit made us all the more keen.

It finally got back to Mr. Rosenbaum. The next time he saw me he grabbed my arm and pulled me along with him home. There he sat me down and boomed, "What exactly are your intentions?"

I didn't hesitate a moment, "I intend to become a member of the Jewish faith."

His face turned white and then red. He pulled on his ear lobe and bit his lips. Finally, all he said was, "It's not easy." By some mysterious signal, his wife appeared with a cup of tea and honey cake with raspberry jelly. "Eat, eat," Mr., Rosenbaum said. I knew the tide had turned. He was a practical man.
Gladys slipped into the room with a shy smile.

"Nu, there's the *collah*, the bride," the mother said.

"We'll see...we'll see," Mr. Rosenbaum said and turned on the radio to the B.B.C. news. This was in the late 1930's. The man I hoped to be my future father-in-law stared with merciless attention at me to see every tremor of feeling my face would record as we listened to the translation of one of Hitler's ranting speeches. Not for a moment did his eyes leave my face."

"What a thing to become a Jew at that time--of all times," the woman interrupted.

"Belief is a constant isn't it? One doesn't become a Jew because it's convenient."

"But Hitler must have had some affect on your feelings."

"I hate to admit he had any influence, but he did. He strengthened my feelings. I started to work hard at becoming a Jew. After some study on my part, Mr. Rosenbaum and I took the train to London and went to Whitechapel. There we made our way through narrow winding streets among hawkers selling herring, sour pickles, cloth, pots and pans. Religious women in matron's wigs and men in dark suits with long side locks passed us. There was a synagogue on every street. I remember being enchanted with it all, and yet a t the same time feeling terribly frightened. In those days you had to convert the hard way. Not reform but orthodox.

We went to a Jewish court, a *Bet Din* and had to wait for a long time in an anteroom. Finally the secretary led us into a room in which three Rabbis sat. My father-in-law and I stood before them with our knees trembling while they asked me questions. I don't know if they all had their doctors of Divinity from Oxford University but they were quite impressive and terrifying. I left them no better than I came in, still simply a Gentile civil service clerk from a small village in Kent. They had turned me down.

You see what I found out later was that's standard form. They never take you the first time. You have to persist and prove your mettle. But Mr., Rosenbaum and I didn't know that. By this time I had him on my side and we were both downcast. There he was an orthodox Jew his whole life and yet on the way back all he could do was mutter about how we were going to appeal to the liberal Jews. In a sense, he was ready to convert himself, to go from being orthodox to something that seemed to him a compromised religion.

The next week I got a registered letter from the *Bet Din* in which a teacher was proposed for me, a Rabbi in another town. Every Monday night I took a thirty-minute train ride and went to a tiny *shul*. A young Rabbi, a tall, fair-haired man with thick glasses would be waiting for me in the women's balcony of his synagogue. Together for three or four hours, he would tutor me and I would go home quite late at night. One time he met me with a smile and said, I think you're ready. I've written to the *Bet*

Din." He laughed, but with embarrassment when I said, "You mean I might be ready to go down to the men's section." We had become quite attached and before we parted he embraced me and wished me luck. I saw he felt his own worth as a teacher would be measured by my performance."

The woman asked, "Do you mind if I smoke?" She lit a cigarette, her hand trembling slightly.

"Funny I've never seen you here before?" Ernest commented.

Exhaling a cloud of smoke, she said, "I'm just visiting...but please, please do go on with your story." It was a weekday morning and people, anxious to get back to work, had begun to leave. Only the two of them remained at their table and the rest of the hall, almost devoid of people, had a kind of vacancy--an emptiness that comes only after a great crowd has left.

Ernest with an air of gallantry, a way of continuing the party for her sake, took up exactly where he had left off. "My teacher wished me luck. This time, to my astonishment, there was only one Rabbi to judge me at the Bet Din. He was an old time Jew, his face just shining with virtue. We were in a study with ancient books on the table and filling bookcases. In those days I could say the *Shmah* backwards and you can imagine my relief when he put some Hebrew in front of me to read aloud and it turned out to be the *Shmah*. There was no trickery in his questions. He asked about the holidays aid the observances and it was really a pleasure to converse with him. I remember feeling enthusiastic and excited about the things we were saying, as if it were a class and I was learning. I just completely forgot myself and talked freely.

Then he asked me, "Can you tell why Jews don't offer sacrifices any more?"

I thought and thought and began to squirm in my seat as I forced out an answer that even to my ears was twisted, "Well the fad passed, so to speak. It was no longer the trend."

My face burned and 1 could not bear to look at my examiner who said calmly, "We don't offer sacrifice. We give God our prayers."

"I see," I muttered. It was so beautifully simple. The room seemed dark and hot and I could not understand why the Rabbi was smiling. I was convinced I had been rejected again--and forever.

The Rabbi said to me, "1 think you'll be an excellent Jew."

I was ecstatic. I had become a Jew. He filled out a long document that was like my diploma. There was a formality or two left. As the Rabbi said today, "the most ancient of Hebrew customs," They put me to sleep, so I didn't really witness my *briss*. My father-in-law was next to me while they performed the circumcision--it cost 5 pounds for a *mohel* from Portsmith. And my father-in-law was standing nearby too when the Rabbi said a prayer over me and J stood stark naked in the ritual bath, I remember thinking that Mr. Rosenbaum looked a bit amused as if he wanted me to recall his words, "It won't be easy," In the end he put his arm about my shoulder and said, Now you're *glatt* kosher--pure as can be."

Well, that's the point about being a convert. You have to prove yourself. You're required to know more than the born Jews. In certain ways I appreciate the religion and admire it and the contributions Jews have made in all fields more fervently than your average Jew. And, oh, you want to know what happened to Gladys's sisters?"

Ernest took a sip of luke warm coffee as if to revive his now slightly hoarse voice and inclined his head to his attentive neighbor at the table.

"Three died spinsters. There was no one acceptable for them to marry as far as they were concerned. The two youngest married Christians and had their babies baptized in the church...Yes, I have a son. It was for me to carry on the Jewish birthright. He's not quite as zealous in his observance as I am, but still he's a Jew. Gladys and I named him Abraham Isaac Jacob Rosenbaum Transmount. What do you think of that?"

The woman was smiling warmly at him now. "You know," she said, "I'm very grateful to you for telling me your story. I'm not a Jew. I came today because I am seriously considering converting. You've given me more confidence."

"Whose to say?" Ernest remarked. "I think it all has to be preordained. It was in my case. You know my name is Transmount and 'trans' like in 'transportation' or 'transfer' means to change. And not only that but after I converted my mother said, "You know Ernie, when Dad and I first married, we lived in Holborn across from a synagogue. It must have cast its spell."

Music

The light faded from the room and Dorothy listened first to one son out in the street shouting to his friends as he played ball and then to the other son, the musician in the overhead bedroom playing the same difficult phrase on the cello over and over. She imagined Max with his erect posture, the cello held like a ballet dancer balanced on its pointed peg. Its sharp tip, and those of the two smaller cellos which Max outgrew, had pitted the wood floor of his room over the years. The damage irritated Dorothy when she first noticed. Then she came to think of it as a testimony to Max's labors, like the hardened callouses on the fingertips of his left hand. Occasionally, Max paused in his practicing and she was so connected to his starts and stops that she knew when he stared into space, leafed through music, paced, or applied rosin to his bow. When he put aside his restlessness and failures of concentration and resumed practicing, she felt relieved.

'Max's back,' she whispered dreamily, rejoicing over his return from the conservatory for the summer. Stretching sensuously on the striped cushioned couch, her long legs reaching beyond its opposite arm, she glanced about at the room with its dark redwood paneling, wainscoting, leaded windows and stone fireplace. On the walls hung her father's paintings of the mid-western landscapes of her childhood. Untouched since her husband Billy's death five years earlier, his grand piano gleamed in an alcove, contrasting with the Spartan rusticity of the redwood picnic bench against one wall, wooden lawn chairs and a lounge covered with a madras spread. The large house begged to be furnished grandly, but Dorothy's instincts recreated the casual style of the small cabins at her father's summer art school. Max's stuttering starts and stops, bursts of lyrical playing and his low humming, reminded her of the erratic current of the lake about which the cabins clustered. She felt herself a small girl again, drifting across the water's surface in her big, black inner tube.

Through the open window, she heard ten-year-old Jack among the neighborhood boys, his piping voice crying, "Get it, get the ball." Dorothy knew that Max, who had just ended his practicing, also separated Jack's cries from the others. In Max's fourteenth year, a hitchhiker had killed his father, and he hovered protectively over his younger brother. His attention followed Jack, even when she believed him absorbed in a conversation with her. Suddenly he'd pause and put his forefinger over his lip to signal her to silence. He wanted to watch Jack in the garden throwing a ball in the air, to observe him doing a puzzle or eavesdrop on his chatter with his friends. "He's smarter than the others," Max whispered admiringly.

When Max left Berkeley for New York the year before, Jack drooped about the house. He confided to her, "I want to be just like Max. He's my model," and pleaded to talk to him long distance on the phone. She tried to solace him by taking him out to a Chinese restaurant, but they scarcely conversed as they sat over Chow Mein and egg rolls. Jack loved comic books, television, electronic games and chess—Billy would have squelched all but the chess playing. "The trouble is," Jack told Dorothy, "you and I don't have anything in common." She knew what he meant, that no one understood or made him come alive like Max.

Nineteen-year-old Max came down the stairs in a child-like way, a few quick steps, pausing, then a few more. "How was the practicing?" Dorothy asked, feeling she had to modulate her voice and make it free from her hunger for him. "You'll be ready for the recital?"

He had phoned from New York to ask her to arrange for space at a church or a rented hall for him to perform, but not at his former cello teacher, Rosa's. The recital would be in another week and he answered, "I think I'll be ready, Mom," and settled in the armchair across from her.

"You look tired, Max."

"I am."

"You didn't get enough sleep."

"I didn't get enough sleep all year. I'm used to it."

The night before the old house's growling pipes had awakened her as   Max turned the tap on at two in the morning to fill the kettle. From her bed, she listened to his pacing back and forth in the kitchen. "You shouldn't drink coffee in the middle of the night."

"I'm an addict," he answered, smiling in a way that enchanted her, his head tilted, his dark curls falling over his forehead. She saw in that moment, not Max but Billy, that wild card whom she had married after an acquaintanceship of two weeks at Yale where she taught business English. Boyish, impulsive, fast talking and Jewish, he swept her up as he did others. Although he flunked most of his undergraduate courses at City College of New York, a professor at Yale fell under his spell too and welcomed the brilliant Billy as a graduate student in theoretical physics. Then the University of California hired him and he spent the mornings teaching and writing and the afternoons playing the Steinway. His sons inherited his dark coloring, slight figure and quickness, but no hint of the Swedish-Finnish ancestors on her side. She alone was blue eyed and by the time she met Billy, in her early twenties, her long, blonde hair had already changed to silvery white. He told her in those first infatuated weeks that she looked like a Norse goddess, that her hair shone like an angel's halo.

"Why is that?" she pressed Max about his coffee addiction.

He shrugged dismissively but then blurted, "Pressure. Nerves. Stress. Do you know what it's like at the conservatory?"

She leaned toward eagerly, encouraging his confidence. Since his arrival, she felt a barrier of polite reserve separating them, but so vague and uncertain that she kept telling herself she was mistaken.

"We're all pitted against one another. None of the violinists talk to each other. None of the cellists talk to each other. We'd like to slit each other's throats. It's a war zone and each person wants to be the only one surviving. Everyone has to be a soloist."

"Perhaps, Julliard isn't the right place."

"Leave Julliard?" Max shook his head.

No, she realized he couldn't, that he'd been consecrated for Julliard from the beginning. Billy had bought him the first small cello when he was eight because Billy loved the sound of the instrument. Max dutifully lugged it on the bus and to each class, desperate to please a father of effervescent moods. Billy could be as rigid as his contentious, communist relatives who cut each other off for the slightest deviation from doctrine. Once he yanked a comic book from Max's hand and ripped it to shreds because it 'wasted time and rotted the mind.' In high school Max found a deserted staircase landing a half flight below the school's roof where he practiced during his lunchtime. After Billy's death, she thought he might give up the cello, but he plunged into music more intensely, giving up his friends, filling the house with his practicing hour after hour, as if his playing replaced the sound of the piano.

Jack interrupted their conversation, racing up the outside stairs and ringing the bell in shrill blasts. She and Max exchanged looks, hers perturbed and his amused.

"It's not locked," she called out, but he still rang insistently and she got up to open the door.

"Why did you take so long?" Jack demanded angrily. She saw strained fatigue in his delicate features, his face paler than usual, his head looking large on the long, slender stem of his neck. Even more than Max, he resembled his high-strung father, but Dorothy always suspected his moodiness sprang from losing a parent at such a young age.

Max stood up. "Guess I better practice."

"Practice, practice," Jack mimicked it. "That's all you do. Come on Max," he wheedled, "let's wrestle."

"I don't want to."

"You don't play with me any more."

Max conceded, "All right, I'll wrestle with you, but just once. I don't do things like that any more."

In a moment, they rolled on the rug, embracing, grunting, and laughing. Then Max pulled away, saying, "That's enough."

"No, Max," Jack complained and butted Max in the belly.

Max shoved him away.

Laughing, pretending the match resumed, Jack butted him again. It took the wind from Max and he cuffed him hard on the side of the head Jack looked startled. His face turned paler and his mouth twisted, opening and closing like a fish's. "You...you," he howled, so convulsed that at first he couldn't get the words out. His hands clawed the air uncontrollably.

Max backed quickly away before Jack could lunge at him. "Jack," he began.

"I hate you," Jack screamed between choking coughs.

Dorothy reached out to him but he pushed roughly past her and up the stairs to his room where they heard him like a fly caught in a jar, racing about, overturning furniture and throwing books about. She knew the futility of trying to stop him, like trying to stop a hurricane. Max walked over to the phonograph and with trembling fingers selected a Mozart quartet and put it on the turntable. He turned the volume on loud and it filled the room, almost drowning out the crashes from overhead. He closed his eyes, bent his right arm and with his left hand played the cello fingering on it. Her heart ached, Jack's disappointment her own, that Max had changed and drawn away.

"Mom," he said and lowered the volume. "I'm sorry about Jack. I'll apologize when he calms down. I shouldn't have lost my temper. I can't be what he wants me to be. I can't be the old way." Her silence revealed her resentment, and he gave up the attempt to explain. "I need to practice."

Jack, tear stained and with hunched shoulders, passed him on the stairs. He whispered hoarsely to Dorothy as if each word hurt him, "Can I eat by myself?" Perched on a stool at the kitchen counter, he dangled his skinny legs and chewed slowly on a tuna fish sandwich, but jerked to attention when Max appeared in the doorway.

In an expressionless voice, Max said, "If you have something to say to me, Jack, you don't have to trash my room. Just tell me to my face. It will take me more than an hour to sort out the music you threw around." He turned and left, and in a few moments Dorothy heard the first notes of a Bach cello suite. She barely recognized one from the other, knew only that each night he ended his practicing by playing a movement or two from the suites, and that she looked toward to this conclusion. Other nights she sat on the stairs to hear him better, first tuning his instrument, a kind of clearing of the throat, and then playing this prayer.

"Aren't you going to see Rosa?" Dorothy inquired. The morning sun flooded the living room.

"Don't nag," Max snapped, but then seeing her hurt look, added more gently, "I'll go see her. I'm just not ready."

For years she had driven him to Rosa, to the small cottage in the Berkeley hills. Children sat around munching Rosa's licorice and chocolates, but none bold enough to whisper a word while tall, hawk nosed, Rosa boomed orders at the victim in the hot seat, the young cellist receiving instruction. On the rug at her feet an ancient dog snored, his large head balanced on his paws. In the kitchen, huge cauldrons simmered with food offerings for whoever wanted to eat. A bumper sticker plastered to the wall ordered, "Defy Authority," but Rosa didn't mean her own.

Dorothy remembered overhearing Rosa implore Max, "Sweetie, I just showed you how to play it. Why the hell aren't you doing it?"

Because I worked out my own way," Max responded. Fifteen then, pimples lightly dotted his forehead.

"Worked it out my own way,' she imitated. "You're too young to work out your own way."

"Couldn't you even listen?"

"Why do you have to be so arrogant? Why do you have to think you know more than your betters?"

"Just listen. Just once."

"I don't have to listen. I know what it will sound like. You'll sound ridiculous. Now do what I told you."

Angrily, Max followed her direction, his playing stiff.

In the car on the way home Dorothy asked, "Do you want to switch teachers?"

"No," he responded adamantly.

"The two of you don't seem to be getting along."

"You don't understand, Mom. Just let me work it out myself."

Rosa accompanied him to competitions, shooing him out on the stage and then catching him up in her arms as he stumbled back. "Sweetie, you did your best," she said, pressing his face into the softness of her large bosom. Sometimes, he wept. In a few weeks, chain-smoking her mentholated cigarettes, she started preparing him for another. "Max is going to win this next one," she announced and gave him free extra lessons.

He grew more defiant. She'd play what she wanted him to play on the piano. He'd give his own rendition. Then, angrily, she'd play what she wanted again. Again he'd repeat his interpretation.

"Dorothy," she inquired, "Have you considered taking him to a shrink?"

"But why?"

"Why? He cursed me. That's why! He called me a fucking bitch. Nobody cares about Max more than I do. He's so sweet to the other kids. He's talented. I worry about Max. Why does he practice so much?"

"Don't you want him to practice?"

"I want him to practice but not all the time. There's a point of diminishing returns. Look, I'll treat him to a session at my therapist. He's a terrific shrink. Do you want me to make an appointment? Max will get a lot out of it."

"I'll talk to Max about it."

"All right, you talk to him and you think about it," Rosa said and reached up and patted Dorothy on the head, dismissing her the way she did her little students. Dorothy was astounded. She inherited her height from a great uncle, a turn-of-the century actor traveling about the country and performing his one-man show as Abraham Lincoln. He threw himself whole heartedly into the role, persuading the theater goers who flocked to see him and eventually even himself that he was the Great

Emancipator, and died in an insane asylum screaming he'd been assassinated by John Booth. The considerable wealth he accumulated on his tours passed to Dorothy's Aunt, also Lincolnesque in height, and when she died in 1967, Dorothy received a wardrobe of pre-Depression flapper clothes that fit her nearly six foot body, as well as the money she and Billy used to purchase the old Berkeley house. Only Rosa dared patronize a woman with the ghostly penumbra of Lincoln.

"Mom, I took the bus to Rosa's house. Would you mind picking me up?" Max asked on the telephone.

She parked down the road and came up to Rosa's house, finding the wild tangle of vegetation in front the same as before, when Max took lessons. Inside sat a new flock of children, but the clutter of upright black cases, the line of cellos on their sides beneath the grand piano, and the coffee can on top into which pupils casually stuffed bills or checks for lessons were familiar too. Photographs of former students hung on the walls.

"Dorothy!" Rosa cried and rushed to embrace her. Rose was not s tall as her, but Dorothy felt the force of her size. She evoked a visceral memory of childhood and mother towering over one's small helpless self. Unlike Rosa, she'd never been able to command the power of her height.

"I hear Max's doing well."

"How do you know?"

"I have my sources," Rosa replied mysteriously. "What are you doing these days?"

Nothing much. I have a little job. I bake in the mornings and sell what I make to a posh restaurant in San Francisco. That way I can be around when Jack comes home from school." Billy had purchased ample life insurance and the annuity and the already paid for house, freed her from financial cares. She loved the morning baking, the smell of yeast and the soft, rising dough. After, she could dawdle in the garden, read and take nature photographs, developing her pictures in a closet transformed to a dark room. Not that she intended to exhibit or even share the prints with friends. Hers was a private pleasure. Locked away in the tiny dark room, she thrilled as her shadowy images emerged, a bee, a thistle, and a humming bird.

A subdued Max waited to one side. "Let's go," he said in an undertone.

Dorothy hardly kept up with him as he raced to the car.

"I'll drive, Mom."

"I don't mind."

"Please, I'd like to."

She gave him the key and he drove quickly, making her nervous as the car spun down the spiraling road. Magnolia trees, expanses of lawn, red tiled roofs gleaming on stucco houses, views of San Francisco's skyline, the Marin hills and the Golden Gate bridge, passed in a whirl.

Max told her, "I dreaded seeing Rosa. I should have broken away from her and switched teachers my last year. The relationship was too intense. My teacher at the conservatory doesn't give a shit about me. I like it a lot better."

His anger intimidated Dorothy, making her fearful he harbored dissatisfactions against her. When he fell into silence, she said nothing, although she yearned for his companionship. Since he had told her how stressful he found the conservatory, she wanted to continue the discussion, to say she understood about 'soloists.' It wasn't only a question of talent but temperament. Her father and Billy were soloists in their lives, daring, careless and self-absorbed. She wasn't. She spent her time pleasing and appeasing people or day dreaming the way she did those summer days when her father had dressed her in a prim dress with a high collar and made her sit perfectly still and pose for him and his students. "Look...look," he'd say, appraising the curve of her shoulders, the length of her neck, the way the light splashed over her face. The attention flattered even though it focused on her flesh and not on her, but she hated the long, enforced stillness. If she squirmed her father scolded, "Why can't you hold still?" "I'm tired," she complained. "Stop whining," he answered, annoyed that she interrupted artistic creation. When a modeling session ended, he patted her on the head and told her to run off.

Yet she adored him even more after her mother died when she was five. Her mother had been one of his students, but when he remarried it wasn't another artist from his rarified community, but a strict Christian Scientist, whose endless lectures on love made Dorothy yearn for the lighter yoke of child-model. Dorothy thought of this second marriage to a woman who prayed over him and insisted he refuse medical assistance in what, untreated, proved to be a fatal illness, as an aberration similar to the madness of the Abraham Lincoln impersonator. Like the great uncle, her father determinedly followed his own path, and when she met Billy, she saw the same light shining in his eyes. Slow moving and cautious, she surprised her friends when she married after only two weeks, but she might have married him after two days, so strongly did her impulse overwhelm her.

Max interrupted her ruminations. "Mom, I'm going back to New York."

She barely brought herself to speak. "When?"

"Right after the recital. I called a friend last night. He's going to let me use his apartment."

"Right after?"

"The morning after."

"Isn't that too rushed? You'll be tired the morning after. So will I, and we'll have to get over to the airport. Just one more day would be better," she pleaded.

He interrupted her, "I'm leaving the morning after." Then regretting his abruptness, added, "It's better for me in New York. There aren't any distractions. I know how to work there."

Jack ate quickly and retreated to watch television while they lingered over coffee, the dirty dinner dishes with their debris of chicken skin and bones and baked potato skins, still on the table. So many meals she'd cooked, offerings like the rice and raisons left for Hindu gods. The sight of the dishes saddened her. Max toyed with a spoon and Dorothy rose to clear the table.

"Don't go, Mom."

She sank back into her chair.

"How was your day?"

O.K." She had visited the gynecologist for a pap smear that morning and he had told her a fibroid the size of a three-month fetus had grown in her uterus. Perhaps she'd need a hysterectomy. "Not to worry. It's not serious, not cancerous, just an unpleasant experience. You'll survive," the doctor said when he noticed her eyes film with tears. His reassurances didn't take the pain away, her grief gathering for other losses.

She told Max, "I went for a pap smear."

"How was that?"

She felt tempted to tell him about the fibroid, but then realized it was only to evoke his guilt and pity and get him to stay. Restraining herself, she said only, "Fine. Routine."

"You look sad."

"I'll miss you, Max."

"I know. I'll miss you too. I wish you understood how it was. I didn't tell you a lot of things. Like about the promotional."

In June he'd played for a jury of conservatory teachers who evaluated his progress for the year. "Didn't it go well?" she asked anxiously.

Impatiently, he snapped, "It went O.K. That wasn't what I was talking about." He picked at a spot on the wood table Jack had burned there, trying to learn to light matches. Even now, two years later, she felt a frisson of fear at the danger he'd escaped. Max talked about the conservatory, the square concrete building like a prison, the guard at the door in a maroon uniform to whom he had to show identification, the long corridors he'd walk through, glancing in the glass windowed doors to insulated cubicles where his fellow students practiced piano, violin, oboe, drums, giving off into the hallways a constant blurred cacophony of tension and competition. When he settled into his own cubicle, when he tuned his own instrument, he found it difficult to free himself from the practicing of the others, particularly the other cellists. Almost always he picked out the strains of cello music and agonizingly compared his own talent.

"But sometimes, I forgot everything. As I was preparing for the promotional—I was going to play Dvorak's cello concerto—I had an evening like that. I really lost myself in my playing. Another student, Enrico, slipped into the room. He had originally been a pianist, but then switched to the cello. I was so absorbed that I barely noticed him, and it seemed natural when he sat down at the piano, just running his fingers over the keys without depressing them, then accompanying me. Having him come in with the piano just at that point, I played better than ever before. We were both really hot. It was a perfect performance that, unfortunately, had no audience but us. When I look back on it, I think he came that night despite himself. He was drawn from his practice room because he heard another cellist doing something he wanted to do. The music swept him up and he helped me and submitted to being only an accompanist. When we finished playing together, I felt excited and asked him if he'd accompany me for the promotional and he agreed. But the practice sessions were different. Stiffer. I kept hoping we'd catch the same free spirit again, but he worked against me. It was too late to get another accompanist. One day I was warming up on the cello and waiting for Enrico. He didn't come and it made me uneasy. I heard some tittering in the hall and then I heard someone playing the cello part of the Dvorak concerto in exactly the way I did. I walked outside and I saw Enrico surrounded by a big crowd, doing the little nervous mannerisms I have when I perform, tossing his head and chewing his lip while he played, pretending to be me. The others loved it."

"What did they do when they saw you?"

"They didn't. I just slipped out for a moment and then back to the practice room. I felt like vomiting, but I had the presence of mind to sit down and start practicing again, so when Enrico came in I could pretend nothing happened."

"You should have told him off."

"What good would it have done? The next day was the promotional."

"And did he try to trick you up in front of your teachers?"

"Oh no. That was too dangerous. He didn't dare do that."

"You should have told him off, after."

"Why? What was the point? It was over. I don't even think he could help himself. That's just the way it is. Don't you see? That's why I can't stay here."

"Tell me, what did I do wrong? Did I do something wrong?" she asked.

"You didn't do anything wrong. I have things too good here."

"I don't understand."

"I'm sorry," he said, his face veiling over. "I have to go practice."

"Well, are you coming to Max's recital?" she asked Jack. "I hate music. I'd never study an instrument like Max," he said and shook his head that he wasn't.

"I won't make you, but maybe you'll change your mind. I'm going to shower."

After the shower, Dorothy stood on the bedroom carpet and studied her naked body in the full-length mirror. A rosy hue tinted her skin and with her large breasts and round belly, and her long silver hair loose   over her shoulders, she looked voluptuous. She slipped on a silky bra and underpants because she wanted to feel dressed up from the skin. In the closet, she gazed with boredom at her neutral colored shirts and dresses.

When she unzipped the long untouched garment bag with her Aunt's clothes, the smell of naphtha erupted. Dorothy ran her fingers lightly along the bright silk and beaded dresses and the fur coats from the 1920's and drank in their expressiveness and beauty. She tried several gowns and they all fit perfectly.

Gazing in the mirror at her body sheathed in a clinging salmon colored silk, an ostrich feather boa wrapped about her neck, she saw the ghostly presence of her Aunt. A box of jewelry had been bequeathed too, and she arrayed herself in heavy silver rings, bracelets and a necklace. She wished for nail polish and a less meager supply of makeup; she needed blue and gray eye shadow. With her limited palette she painted her face as if it were her father's hand on a blank canvas, rubbing a touch of lipstick onto her forehead and even the tip of the nose. Taking a final glance in the mirror, she thought how Billy would have liked the sexy dress.

She stood in the doorway to Max's bedroom. Reading one of Jack's comics, he sat on the edge of his bed but looked up.

"What's up, Mom?"

"Nothing. Shouldn't you get ready soon?"

"You're not going like that?"

"Well...I guess not." She laughed to cover her embarrassment, not knowing exactly what she'd intended. Putting the dress away, she thought how she might model it again when she was alone and photograph herself. It would bring her Aunt to life. The idea excited her. Hastily, she changed into a shirtwaist dress and sturdy sandals, and then loaded the car with the refreshments of wine, cheese, crackers and home baked cakes she'd prepared for the reception after the concert. Freshly showered too and in a navy suit, Max came down with his cello, music stand and a backpack loaded with music.

While she set up the extra chairs, Max stood in the corner, cracking his knuckles, pale with terror. Jack walked about the perimeter of the wood paneled Quaker meeting room, munching on a cookie, a look of virtue and heroism on his face for what he would have to endure. Rosa arrived with her protégés, as well as church members who recalled Max from high school when he occasionally played for services. They sought Dorothy out to compliment her on Max's ability. Out of gratitude to him for these past favors, the church waived the rental fee for the evening. She greeted the friends and neighbors who came, and Paul, Max's accompanist who calmly chatted with Dorothy and then Rosa and a few others he recognized. Max remained frozen, staring blindly out as people seated themselves. Dorothy suffered along with him, impatient for the evening to be over.

The room blacked out and in that moment Max and Paul disappeared. Then a spotlight shone on a small podium with its grand piano, a carved, antique instrument of rich dark wood. Beside it stood a chair for Max, eloquent in anticipation of its occupant. Trembling feelings of pride and love for her son, swept through Dorothy as the audience burst into applause. Paul dipped his tousled head, but Max bowed deeply. On stage they appeared transformed, no longer familiar but distant performers and making each movement with priestly precision, the way they sat down, the way Max gripped the cello between his knees and tuned it by bringing his ear close to the pegs. They exchanged a glance, nodded, and then their music filled the hall, first Dvorak, then Stravinsky and Bach.

Max's violence shocked her, the way he used his bow like a saber, stabbing it through the air and slashing against the strings. During the lyrical parts his face contorted in an agony of care. Paul's slender, curled fingers flitted swiftly over the keys, his face impassive in contrast to Max's. The music washed the high windows, the walls, and seeped into the people as if they were sponges, and into herself. Poorly played, with memory lapses and errors, it would have forced an agony of attention, but the smooth performance allowed her mind to listen and to wander too. The music's passion stirred memories of Billy. She thought of Billy's joy at Max's birth, his saying to his father, "Don't worry, he's kosher according to the communist party. His name is only one letter away from Marx." She thought of his high laugh and the dazed way he meandered down a street. Once he went to a convention in Europe, but on the airplane his shaving cream bomb exploded all over his shirts and pants. "It's an emergency, a disaster," he told her excitedly through the static of a trans-Atlantic telephone call. "I can't handle it. You'll have to fly over immediately." She'd flown out, knowing the absurdity of the request, that he simply wanted her by his side. How absurd too for Billy to die from a careless, generous impulse. He picked up the hitchhiker and the man stabbed him for a few dollars. If only he'd asked, Billy would have said, "Oh, you need money," and emptied his wallet. But maybe it wasn't the money the hitchhiker craved but to terrorize and hurt. In her imagination, she'd gone through the possibilities in those moments before he was killed over and over and prayed it happened swiftly.

Beside her, Jack squirmed with impatience. "It's almost over," she whispered and squeezed his hand. When it finally did end, he clapped frantically, not for Max's playing but for Max, who bowed his crisp bows while long waves of applause greeted him.

Through the airport's plate glass windows, Dorothy saw luggage floating on conveyor belt into an airplane cargo hold. Beyond, silver painted airplanes taxied along the ground, while others roared into the air. Passengers and uniformed stewardess hurried to their destinations. Dorothy stood beside Max on the slow moving line of people waiting to board the airplane to New York. After the blue-suited attendant checked Max's ticket, Dorothy hugged him and blurted out, "Not enough time." It struck her there never would be again. Now there would be quick visits and airport goodbyes like this one. "You'd better go," she said but he lingered and would not release her from his burdened look. "I understand," she whispered and his face lit with relief. "Thanks, Mom." They embraced again and he disappeared into the tube, like a birth tunnel, leading to the airplane, and she ran off to the parking lot.

She drove back through the thick of traffic on the lower deck of the East Bay bridge, past the industrial city of Emeryville, off at University Avenue, stopping for milk and bread at the supermarket, and then back home. As usual, several neighborhood boys played ball in the street and she expected to see Jack among them, but found him perched on a pillow like an owl, watching television in the dark den.

"Why aren't you outside with your friends?"
"I don't feel like it. Where you been?"

A few feet away stood his discarded bowl, sticky with uneaten dry cereal and milk. She considered asking him to put it in the sink, but afraid to irritate his present mood, decided to do it herself. "You know where. The airport," she said and swooped down to pick the bowl up. At her reminder of Max's departure, he jerked away and angrily twisted the television volume up, and then as she left to rinse out the dish, slammed the door shut after her. Sighing, she took the newspaper into the living room and sank into a chair. Jack crept in too and implored shyly from across the room, "Can you talk to me?"

"What's the matter, Jack?"

"Nothing."

She folded the paper and put it aside. "Why don't you come and sit on my lap?"

Jack looked startled and unbelieving.

"No, I mean it. You're not too big yet." She patted her thighs and smiled.

Her heart rose high in her chest as he rushed to her like a huge infant and wound his arms about her neck and hugged her tightly.

A Final Gift

I went up to the land of Israel, to Jerusalem so ancient, the oldest of the oldest. It seems one should be ancient to walk its stones. And I had become old. I wanted the dust in my mouth, the burning heat and the cemetery with French names, the Tunisian Jews who write *"Je t'aitne toujours."*

I rented one large room with a small balcony where I could sit and write. First I thought I would go back to writing with simply a pencil and notebook and then I realized that I could not do it. I am an artist of many drafts. First there are simply colors and hidden shapes--the sketch. Then forms become clearer, then details, and so on. I bought an old typewriter. It did not work with the efficiency of the electric one I once had, and my fingers were stiff.

I was determined to break old patterns, old ways of thought. I read the Song of Songs "You Are My Beloved." How haunting. Even an old woman's heart is tender and perhaps most of all. Now is the time to read the Old Testament. I bought one that is used and stained. Everything is old. I lave a fanaticism about this now,

I walk a great deal. The Arabs have indifferent, veiled eyes. In the afternoons they sit outdoors and smoke the hookahs, suck-on the snake-dike tubes from glass bottles, like babies. It is good to be old and sexless, to feel safe to walk the streets. One is so inconspicuous in one's old age. After death, there is no longer the body to hinder. Perhaps other barriers break down as well, like the old hates. Yes, even now I begin to feel how insignificant they were, that the only thing of importance were the things that I scarcely noticed, the rhythms and faithfulness of the days, my husband and my child.

A tourist asks me directions, a woman in a pink Dacron dress and sunglasses. My voice has deepened, husky from disuse. I don't study the language, want a pristine silence. Still I try to answer patiently and then move on to buy some grapes and sesame covered bagels with a handful of salt, to eat not as breakfast or lunch, and yet it is a meal. I will have nothing until evening but a cup of tea. I will sit on the balcony and try to work.

In the mailbox is a letter from my son. I break the seal with trembling hand. He is playing a concerto in a concert here and is coming. The date he will come is today. I try to find the postmark on the envelope, scarcely put the sheet of paper down when the bell rings and it is him. He is thirty years of age, handsome with his dark curly hair, devastatingly handsome. We embrace. He has always been so intelligent takes everything in at once, that my skin is brown like a nut and wrinkled. "I've aged.,, I've taken to wearing an Arab robe.,,so much looser, freer and cooler,,,and,.and..,come we'll go to a nearby cafe...I have nothing in the house,,.,there's no place to sit,,,come,.... the letter just came.,.I'm not prepared,,, I want to be in movement...come...We'll walk….I walk and walk just like when I was pregnant with you...the days are long for me and I must walk or won't sleep at night. My neighbors are working people, need to sleep and they resent me with my pacing...come.."

We climb the hill, go to the cafe, and look out at brilliant white square buildings, at mountains and hills and ruins. We drink fruit juice and people glance at us from other tables at the odd sight of the old woman in an Arab gown and the handsome young American. Of course he's always invited stares, that god-like aura about my son, like Dionysus, or like a young ardent Rabbi.

"So in the end you became a great, great musician."

166

He's amused. He puts on his sunglasses. When we finish our drinks he asks me to show him the city. "Come let us go."

Now our feet are wearing out the ancient stones of Jerusalem.

"You know I always think of you as I wander these narrow streets and alleys. "

Our eyes meet and I see he's pleased.

"And you a musician.1ike David with his harp...exactly."

He pauses, tilts his head and smiles a moment, and then that intent focus so typical of him returns.

"Surprised at the cats, aren't you? Their curling bodies, their tails brushing your legs. Gray smoke. They're distasteful at night when you tumble over them, ...Yes, I do go out at night,,, and yes,.yes...I admit, sometimes I'm afraid, have terrible, sudden vision of my body with a gaping hole, that some mad, angry Arab has blown me up,..,and I rush home to the balcony and my insomnia, to sleep,.and in the morning the donkeys wake me up as they jig along the path with their belled harnesses, leave behind their shit and blue-green flies buzzing over it..."

We come to the Damascus gate and I see these Bagdad beggars and their wounds distress him. Spare you that, just give a few coins and then on to the vendors with their grapes, figs, Saint John's bread and other fruits of the oasis. Let's buy some and feel the juices in our throats. So dry this land and we must conserve water. What a treat to swim, to feel fresh water.

"I fell in love with Jerusalem, the little gardens with the fountains, the hot streets, the mosques, the Arabs, the Hassidim with waist length *peyes*. What excesses. If one lives alone, at least the streets ought to be interesting.

Yes, I still write and on an old typewriter. Whatever I write, it's never good enough. I write and write and work, work, and it's never good enough. Always a sense of darkness. That the mind is below the surface of a sewer and can't get to the fresh air, the secret, sweet place. You understand, don't you? You who work so hard,"

He nods abruptly, his expression complex and almost pained, I wonder if as an old man he shall live in Jerusalem like me.

I'm suddenly terribly tired and we go home to my room. "Play for me..,you won't be hurt if I don't come to the concert,,,I want you to play for me here, in my large, cool room with no furniture... I don't even have a chair for you to sit on. I'll knock on the door of the neighbor woman."

She's short, squat with dyed black hair.,,Her mouth falls open in surprise. She nods, tries to be helpful and gives me the chair.

My son sits down near the open door to the balcony, tunes his instrument and begins to play. I can scarcely keep from crying. So close we once were, held to my heart, but then like a dove with strong, fluttering wings he was set into the air. Moved, I cry, as he sings in his strange language. There in his music is Israel. The true Israel is yearning.

"I must go," he says. Oh yes, children always must go. Myself in a new flesh is standing there in the arch of the door. I won't walk you down. Part and part quickly. Press my hand but do not kiss me with your wide mouth and do not press me to your strong, hard muscled body. You look at me with pity, never thought I would be so thin, would discipline myself with fasts. My last words, "There's a little plot below. I'm going to dig, become familiar with the earth, start a garden...go, go."

He is gone. One hour, two. I sit. First out on the balcony, then the brilliant stars come out and impel me to the dark streets, I intuit that this is my end. Soon I will be in my catafalque. What an odd name like my 'long dress' or my 'fur coat,',,,The stars are serene, and off somewhere he is playing music and I can hear it now, suddenly have telepathy.

I walk into the desert; I fall on the soft, drifting sand. I knew I would not die until he came, that I would give him that, my beloved child.

Daddy Helps

A little girl was afraid of her first day of school. Nervous about being separate from her mother, of making friends, and things seemed to be working out, when the teacher gave them crayons and asked them to draw their families. Excited when said draw, but then feeling upset, didn't know whether to put daddy in, an angel, sick in his bed as she remembered—only saw photos of him playing his violin, swimming, barely remembered—blank piece of paper while everyone drew—finally drew only herself and her mother—and the other kids asked where was he—didn't she have a father? Were her parents divorced? She didn't want to say and burst into tears and said he died—and a boy told her you don't have a daddy—made her feel terrible—then remembered something her daddy had told her, walk away, don't have to listen to a mean person—so just ignored him, and in the recess, saw a lot of the other kids mad at him too, wouldn't play with him no matter how he begged—he came up to her and said, "I'm sorry." She was still angry with him, but she remembered another thing her father said, "forgive" said, ok, and as soon as she said it, could forget about it, big black cloud went away, and felt better—her teacher wanted to put her picture on the wall, told her wanted to work on it more—and this time put her dad in—she was standing right in between her mom and dad—he was still part of her family.

Went home that day, wasn't until she was going to sleep told her mother what had happened—daddy helped me today—I'm glad he helps me too

I still don't know how to do this.

Sara thought the steps going up to the big door of Public School 153 were like a mountain. She held Mama's hand, and the big door opened wide for her and all the other children. It was the first day of kindergarten. Mama had to leave along with all the other parents. Sara was left on her own and was afraid she might cry.

"Everyone take a seat," Miss Gardner said.

There were small tables and chairs, just the right size for children. Sara sat down at a table along with Sam who wore a baseball cap, and with Mary and Jean who were twins and looked exactly alike. The girls asked Sara to be their friend, and Sam wanted her to be his friend too. That made Sara feel better. "I'll be friends with all of you," she told them with a smile.

They played together the rest of the morning, painted pictures, looked at story books, and sat next to each other at circle time while Miss Gardener strummed her guitar and sang 'Old McDonald' with the class. Later, they went outside to the playground. Sara felt happy when she saw the swings, the slide and the green jungle gym. There was even a wooden box was full of balls, jump ropes and a couple of bats. She wanted to try everything. First, she swung high in the air.

Then she zipped down the slide. There wasn't time to try out the jungle gym because the bell rang. That meant it was time to go home.

Miss Gardner said, "Class you have homework. I want you to draw a picture of your family and bring it in tomorrow to share at circle time."

Sara chattered excitedly to Mama, the entire way home about all the things she'd done on her first day of school. She'd painted, played with clay, climbed on a jungle gym and zipped down a slide. Best of all, she'd made friends with Sam, and the twins, Mary and Jean. "I have homework," Sara boasted. It made her feel like a big kid to have homework.

"What is it?" Mama asked.

"I have to draw a picture and bring it in tomorrow."

"That's nice, Sara. You love to draw, and you're a good artist."

At home, Sara sat down at the little desk in her room with a pad of paper and crayons, and was ready to draw. Except, she had a problem. She didn't know whether to include her daddy in the picture. Most people don't die until they are old, but her daddy became sick and died when he was young. Sara was only three and a half years old at the time. It was hard for her to remember what he looked like except for the photos Mama showed her.

Sara decided to draw just her mother and herself, and she did a picture of the two of them walking home from school earlier, past a park with trees and flowers. In one corner she put the sun. It hadn't been raining, but she added a rainbow.

The next day at school when she showed her picture, one of the other children called out, "Where's your daddy?"

Another asked, "Is your Mommy divorced?"

Tears welled up in Sara's eyes. She would have burst into tears, except that her teacher, Miss Gardner, said, "Sara has drawn a beautiful picture. Now, it's time for someone else's turn. Come up to the front of the room, Jimmy and show us your picture."

At recess—gets goaded—and remembered something about her father, that should walk away, and then about forgiveness—went home that day, did a new picture. This time her father was in it—didn't know if she'd take it to school or if it was just for her to look at—Her mother had told her father played the cello in an orchestra—had him playing music—made her feel good to have him in the picture, he was part of her family—him, sometimes when she looked at pictured, she was crying, still missed him, felt like she'd been too little to miss him, to know how to miss him—but now as she was older he was here and she was getting to know him. That was the picture she took in the next day to school.

In the pictures he had a beard and glasses, and he looked handsome. Mama had told her that he played the cello in an orchestra, and that he'd loved her.

Nose

I dressed carefully for my doctor's appointment. I wanted to look my best, wanted to look as if there was hope. As I stared into the mirror I took my finger to the top of my nose and pushed it ups so that I looked like a pug dog. Then I got out my compact mirror and held it high up so that I could see in the opposite bathroom mirror how I looked on the diagonal and could see my profile. The nose wasn't bad. So it was long? So it was hooked? I placed my hand over my face to see how I looked with no nose--not so terrible either. The face was fine. That nose, that face--it was the conjunction of the two that made me shrivel up inside. One day[5]when I was fourteen years old and wanting very much to be admired by the opposite sex, I was walking down the street and some boys shouted, "Hey, look at that nose. You better do something about that nose, girly." At last I was heeding their wisdom. At thirty- four years of age I finally realized that I went to a dance no one was going to ask me to be their partner. Maybe my big nose was too competitive for men to endure. When I called the doctor for an appointment I thought, "Why challenge the Gods with excesses? I'm no Prometheus." From hitherto on, in mind and face, I would follow moderation.

The waiting room was California gold rush saloon style. On a red plush couch with antique gold wood legs sat

three identical women. Yellow hair, blue faces--it was not that
so much that surprised me as the fact that it was the first time
I had met triplets. When I thought about it I realized I had met
baby twins, but never grown-up twins together because by the
time they grew up they usually went their own ways. But here
was the strange phenomenon of grown-up identical triplets on
a red velvet couch with splints on their noses. Cecelia had
decided to get a nose job and the other two had followed suit
because they were so used to looking alike--or had the
decision sprung up in one Xeroxed, triplicated thought.
Cecelia, Cecily and Ceil.

The doctor's name was Bernie Fleece. He had a
large pompadour hair-do slicked back with vaseline, a
high forehead and black horn rimmed glasses--sort of an
intellectual hairdresser. I was telling him, "The first
words from my first boyfriend were 'Who broke your
nose?' Now how do you think that makes a girl feel? To
make it clearer Doctor, when I was nine years old my
best friend's mother told me 'not to worry, that maybe it
would be with me like the case of the ugly duckling and
I'd be beautiful when I grew up.' I ran home crying and
my mother held me in her arms and tried to comfort me
saying, 'But you are beautiful. .. .on the INSIDE.' Doctor,
have you ever heard the expression, 'Only a mother
could love that, face?' My own mother thought I was
ugly. She was president of the Debbie Reynolds fan club.
I forgive her now. You know, Doctor, people are very

conservative. They read **Seventeen, The Wall Street Journal**, and adore Twiggy, the model with no breasts. They like understatement; they prefer nothing to something. My nose is a bit hooked you see, but not really so big. I measured it and it's an inch shorter than Jimmy Durante's."

The doctor was very understanding. He got out his tape measure so that we could know precisely how long it was. "It looks bigger when you smile," he smiled at me. I wiped the answering smile off my own face.

Dr. Fleece's office is on the fifth floor of a glass and concrete building on top of a high hill. Unlike the waiting room, the theme of the office was Hawaiian, with appropriate furniture and flowered curtains. The window looked out on San Francisco bay and the beautiful Marin hills. There was a small bird perched on a ledge outside Dr. Fleece's window and he sang and chirped something that sounded like this:

> Ring around a
> rosy
> Get rid of that
> nosey
> A nose is not
> for breathing
> A nose is not
> for smelling

A-choo, a-

choo--away it

all goes-y.

The bird was a mynah bird in a golden cage, bred and trained by Dr. Fleece's wife Goldy. Above the doctor's head hung a blown-up picture of Greta Garbo in profile as usual.

"How much will your surfaces.. " I slipped. "I mean services cost Dr. Fleece?" I asked demurely and shyly.

"My secretary has taken a financial statement?"

"Why yes....but she would not say..."

"Oh must we speak of ugly lucre?" said Bernie emphasizing the word 'ugly' with an extravagant gesture of his hand and a shake of his head that brought down his pompadour.

Although all my life a shy, ugly woman, I managed to insist, "We must talk about money if a lot of it is involved." In fact I was determined to talk about money with Bernie. My job in Danville as a teacher of high school English left me closer to destitution than millionaire hood. Money was as important to me as it was to Bernie.

Hearing the determination in my voice. Dr. Fleece's face hardened- granite rock. The smile slipped off like wet paste. "Ugly people come to me and they bring along pictures from a movie magazine. They think I can make them gorgeous. They think their whole life is going to change. People come to me when their marriage is failing and they think a nose job will patch it up. Some

178

people I won't operate on--I just tell them 'no.' You see," he said silkily, "'it' is a luxury operation. We in the profession, figure if anyone wants the operation, they'll manage to scratch up the fees...and if my secretary looked at your credit rating, at a certain modest rate of interest I am willing to let you extend payment over a number of years. It's all for **beauty,"** he wheedled.

He knew when to be soft, when to be hard. He had gone through this a million times; he knew he had me where he wanted and that I would pay anything he wanted. I was fighting a race with time. Better to have the operation now then when I was too old for it to do any good. Do not hesitate, act. At 34 I figured I had about five years left to catch a man. I was like a junky willing to steal, beg or borrow for Dr. Fleece. "Dr. Fleeces,"...another dam slip. Dr. Fleece, are you free on Thursday? Would that be a good time for you to operate?"

When I left Dr. Fleece I went to the Ladies' room in the hall. All the tension and excitement I had felt had stimulated my kidneys into over-activity as usual. It was soothing to sit down in seclusion. My hand moved down there to the secret place. I felt I'd give anything for a man--Tom, Dick or Harry, I did not care. But I was thinking about Jack-- Jack the other English teacher at Danville High. I was always thinking about him. Oh God, when would I forget him. Jack, Jack, Jack. The name escaped my lips in a scream. It was never good in the toilet. For a young girl maybe it was okay, but I felt too old for these lonely lavatory sessions. I wanted something real. I left the stall dejectedly and then followed the directions on the white container above the sink to "Wet hands and release;" a stinging orange powder dusted my hands. I looked into the mirror and for a moment instead of my big nose I saw Jack's face. Now I was hallucinating about him.

Last summer I had joined a thirty-day SAS tour specifically for spinster schoolteachers—although the title of the tour was euphemistically kinder to our little group. It was called Singles See Scandinavia or S.S.S. Henry James is my favorite author. I had administered to myself the old-time, traditional Jamesian cure. I went to Europe to fix-up my broken heart'. It was impossible with Jack. A home breaker I was not. I could not go through the rest of my life with that on my conscience. I had to forget him or I'd go crazy. Actually, I was going crazy. The only thing Europe did for me was that I met Elsa, an English teacher from East Lansing, Michigan whom I correspond with now.

An image of my colleague Elsa Fleegler came to mind. Ah Elsa, irresistible Elsa, fat body, encasing fat brain. Elsa was 5'4" and 225 pounds of shivering fat. I looked at the container of powdered soap, "Wet hands and release." "Drink me"...Alice in Wonderland, drink this magic potion and you will be two inches high. Here, drink this Elsa and you will be svelte, slim, shining, superior, super. And at the same time Elsa, Dr. Fleece will take care of me.

I sat on a wooden chair in the waiting room to the laboratory. It was like railroad station, and I studied everyone's nose as I always do in waiting rooms. In my pocketbook was the requisition Dr. Fleece had written out for a urinalysis, blood-clotting time and iron tests that I needed before the surgery. The magazine rack was empty. With nothing to distract me, Jack burned clearly within me as he did day and night. Jack with his virtuous wife and five darling children. When we meet he stares at me so hard; through his eyes he reaches my guts and poisons them with desire. Love comes in through the eyes. People think it is so safe to be ugly. No one wants you. But it is dangerous, like being poised on a high cliff. Jack doesn't really want me; he stares at all the women. He wants them all. He is notorious for his women. But all he had to do was glance at me and I flung myself over the edge into infatuation, hopeless infatuation with a married Don Juan. It was degrading. We ugly ones are proud. Yet, "We ugly ones cannot resist being wanted." It was fat Elsa who had come up with that bit of wisdom.

S.S.S. had toured Tivoli in Copenhagen, the Kontiki museum in Oslo, the Volvo factory in Gothenburg and now we had reached the Stockholm part of the tour. A boat had been rented to take the group of schoolteachers out to Gotland, an island in the Baltic. It was to be a picnic, and swimming for those who were brave. Elsa came over to sit with me. She was interested in the Swede who acted as our guide. "A chance encounter," "a one night stand"--she did not

ask much. "What do you think of Hagge?" she asked and did
not wait for an answer. "Red moustache, bald head--doesn't he
look like a bull without cows for a month?" (Elsa had grown
up on a farm and also admired Henry Miller). The motor of
the boat roared and it was hard to be heard. We went out on
the deck and watched the tail of foam behind us and the black
skerries in the distance that jutted up like sea monsters. So
many little, identical islands. How could the navigator tell the
difference I wondered? Hagge had told us that in the winter
the Swedes ice-skated on the Baltic. At last we reached the
island. We could see a castle in the distance and its walls were
covered with roses. Everyone spread out to picnic or hike. Elsa
and I climbed a hill to change into our swimsuits behind the
slender privacy of some rocks. All around the blue seas, and
on the plain below, Hagge the bull kicking about a soccer ball.
"Oh, I've gained weight," sighed Elsa, "I can barely get into
this suit." In her black tank suit and with her swim cap on, she
looked like molded jello. "Do you think Hagge will think less
of me when he sees me in a swim suit?" She had said before
on the boat, "Hagges looks at me like he would like to sink
into me. Europeans have different values than Americans."
Was she losing her cross-cultural courage? her flimsy faith
that Hagge would look at her and love what everyone else
disparaged? A slight breeze blew through my hair and my
hawk-like face stared into the deep infinity and I thought with
bitter- sorrow, "We who are ugly know the other side of
ourselves, the invisible, phantom positive. Our ugliness has

sharpened our imaginations. We carry ourselves as if we were surrounded by flattering shadows--exotic shadows, or corrective shadows. The concrete reality, the electrons spinning around the nuclei are merely a suggestion that the loving eye must enlarge upon. Elsa and I pray every night, "Oh loving eye carry my image to the zenith of its possibilities and you shall see such beauty as never before."

I looked at impossibly fat Elsa who wanted Hagge to want to sink into her and gently said, "Elsa try being conceited instead of vain, it hurts less. The disappointments are fewer." With a wonderful noble charm, Elsa cast her head up in pride and said, "0 no my dear, I am committed to both." Elsa sashayed down the hill past Hagge into the cold water.

The water was so cold it made me gasp but Elsa swam out, and cavorted like a young whale. Water is her natural element I think. It's a mistake, a tragedy for her to be on the land. She danced in circles by herself so happily and then lightly came close and blew a blast of water at me through her nose. "Ah Elsa," I thought, "If I was a man I would want you. How beautiful you are. If I were a lesbian I would court you. But I am what I am, trailing on my stomach like a worm after that miserable species with the 'thing' swinging between their legs."

But for all her charms Hagge gave her not a glance. Does it matter if she wears her suit which discloses without a doubt the vast fleshy truth or not; he never turns his head, never, never.

Drink come in through the mouth and loves comes in through the eye. W.B. Yeats said that.

On the boat back, in a most casual way Elsa glances at Hagge and quickly away again. "Oh he likes the doe eyed school teacher with the black hair. It's understandable is it not?" Silence. Then bitterly, "Soon she'll grow old. I'm so glad for decay, the one compensation in my life." Then with infinite sadness she says, "God, we who are ugly cannot resist being wanted. Do you understand?"

The other day I saw Jack leaving a restaurant with a young girl with long blonde hair. What a gambler I am. What slim psychological chance do I have that a new nose will give me the strength to forget Jack? And yet I am desperate, so desperate. Thank you God that it is a bad nose, and not a fat body that I have; a bad nose can be corrected much more easily. I am waiting for the woman behind the desk to call my name for the tests and inside the great whirlwind of Jack spinning around until it hurts too much and tears squirt out of my eyes like blood out of a wound.

A nurse's aide in a grey uniform with frizzy hair comes over and says kindly in her southern drawl, "What's the matter honey." Everyone else sits there reading a magazine or looking at the ceiling. "Nothing," and then I feel badly that I am so cold to her, so with semi-honesty I tell her, "I'm going to have my nose fixed and I'm afraid of being black and blue later, of having my eyes blow up to little slits." I figure that will satisfy her curiosity and motherly instincts. "Don't do it honey, ain't nothing wrong with your nose." I smile a little, bitter smile. She sees it and with her low-down astuteness that black lady gives me a blow beneath the belt. "They tell me black is beautiful...but if you think there's something wrong with your nose, try being black for a week." Which is worse black, or black and blue, I am forced to wonder. Guilt, horrible guilt. If I have my nose fixed she will be even blacker and I will be more Anglo-Saxon, and never the twain shall meet. She compels me to see her point. I wonder if Dr. Fleece could do anything for this woman who carries the bedpans? Surely a little bleach would do the trick.

So with red eyes from crying I go into to have my blood and urine tests. When I get home I re-read Elsa's last letter. She starts off by telling me about Punjab, the Indian student. "With the wisdom of the Orient he chose me. He had the Kama sutra at his fingertips," and then there is a page on Leslie the Australian rabbit rancher whom she met at the Great Lakes Conference and three pages on Wayne the motorcycle mechanic who picked her up in a bakery where she was eating five whipped cream tarts. Story after story. The adventures of Elsa of Michigan, whose imagination has been sharpened by rejection.

"Dear Elsa," I write, "the other day I was at the grocery store and I was selecting Winesap, organically grown apples. Are you conscious about pesticides? I hope you are.

There was a large fellow all in green with a big moustache by my side that was looking at the kumquats. Suddenly he turned and saw me and dropped the bag from his hand. "Oh my God," he cried, "It's you lass. It's you that I've been looking for me whole life." "What are you talking about you Irish zany," I managed to gasp. "Listen I'm a big man and me whole life I've been looking for a gel with a big nose, likes yours, sweet rose. I'm telling you, I love you. It's not ever before that I've said such a thing, but when I saw you, the words came dropping from my lips." His moustache sizzled. He reached out his long, lanky hands and lifted me into the air and then dropped me in his shopping cart as if I was a little baby. He tried to wheel me through the checkout line with his groceries. It's then Elsa, that I decided to get my nose fixed because I decided it was too much a burden to me to have people love me for my nose, and not for myself."

Dear Elsa, adorable girl, I thought as I licked the envelope, not only have I a long nose, but a tall tongue. Maybe it will get shorter too after the operation. Who knows what I am sacrificing?

Nancy stared at the linoleum of her room. It was pink, white and blue with nursery rhyme designs. She had never liked it, considering it too babyish'—but now she liked it. Maybe it was because people kept telling her how grown-up she was supposed to be. Everything was changing too fast.

There was a big crowd of people in the living room and her father came for her and insisted that she go in and be with them. It made her a little sick to be in

that hot crowded room with all her Aunts, Uncles, cousins, friends, neighbors and even her teacher from the fifth grade. They all brought candy, flowers and a pat on the head for her. She sat on a small stool in a far corner of the room and did not want to smell the flowers or taste the sweets.

She had to answer the door every few minutes. It was not locked but no one felt comfortable about just walking inside as they might. Nancy could tell how peculiar people felt when they first came in the apartment. They did not know what to do, whether to smile or have a long face, and would just say to her anything that came into, their heads. "Your mother suffered a lot, so it's for the best...You're a big girl, you should help your father...he's the only one you have now..." They all wanted to touch her, to hug her, to muss her all up. They acted so strangely. One lady with bleached blonde hair and a wrinkled face who had worked with her mother at the elementary school took Nancy aside to say, "I want you to

187

know what good friends your mother and I were..." It embarrassed Nancy because she knew nearly everything about her mother, and her mother had told her that Nancy was the only friend she had. "The rest are fair weather. It's too depressing for them to come around, and anyway I don't want anyone to see me when I'm like this." Then a certain pained expression would come into her eyes and Nancy knew she was thinking about Nancy's father and how Ben had left.

The condolence visits would last a week and had keen going on several days already. In the beginning Nancy had liked the attention, had sat still and gravely in her corner and been occupied with thoughts of what it would be like later when she could go in the street again and be with her friends. She would pin the button with the slashed black ribbon to her blouse and she would walk around looking at her shoes, at her iron-arched Rosenwafter oxfords with the scuffed toes. Everyone would be envious; all of the other children would be for sure.

As the days passed she began to miss her mother and became ashamed of those first feelings. The grown-ups sipped their coffee, chatted and would forget about her and she closed her eyes and pretended her mother was invisible and sitting beside her. She thought of the happy times like when they had gone walking on the boardwalk. It was the middle of the winter when no one went to Coney Island. Only her mother thought of things like that. Her mother began to run with her "We're free... we're free. we're free..." The wind was

188

so fresh in their faces, so cold and wild like the blue-green ocean pounding hard against the shore. Her mother was like a bird with great wings.

Something or someone was always interrupting her thoughts like now, her Uncle Nathan asked her father if he could give Nancy a quarter. Ben puffed out his cheeks and then said I guess it's all right" and smiled at Nancy. Her Uncle took her limp hand in his fat and hot one and pressed the coin to her palm and closed her hand into a fist.

"Thank you."

"Such a polite child," he teased.

Stupid, stupid, stupid Uncle Nathan with the pale, sad face and chipped front tooth. She did not know why but she felt enraged. As soon as no one was looking
Nancy swept her hand along the side of her chair and then a little lower and as if by accident let the coin drop onto the green rug without a sound.

"Have a chocolate covered cherry Nancy," Uncle Nathan said a few minutes later.

"No thank you." Her Uncle's face looked so perplexed and she felt how sullen she was. She felt all stiff and everything was twisting up tighter and tighter
in her. She thought of that awful night when her mother did not know what she was doing and she kept screaming at Nancy "Give me my nightmare pills."

Just as she felt herself in danger of bursting into tears in front of everybody her Aunt Jeanette made her happy. She had brought some photographs of her mother in her purse and she took Nancy in the kitchen and spread them out on the table. "Anna was the life of the party; if you knew her then..." Nancy saw her mother as a young woman dressed in a fringed dress or in another photograph dressed in shorts and a halter, surrounded by a group of people and playing a ukulele. "She was just the cutest little thing, and she would put on these plays at grandpa's in the country." Nancy was eager for every word. "What else do you remember? I wish I could have been there. I wish I could have seen her then."

Her Aunt had given her an idea. One morning while her father was still asleep she had gone to the secretary in the alcove of the living room, opened the heavy bottom draw and taken out the photograph albums and ripped out every single picture of her mother from the black pages. There was a manila envelope in the same drawer and she put the stack of pictures in it and then put it in her own dresser in her room beneath her undershirts. The thing that was awful was that her father would never think about those "dusty old albums" and would never even realize or care that something was missing. When he had come back from Chicago he had said to Nancy "I want you to know it was because of the sickness that mother and I started to fight——but we didn't know she was sick then, did we? There was no way of knowing—and now I'm back, I can help you Nan. I missed you." She had let him press her to him; his hands pushing her head against his chest hurt. She had thought, "Did you miss mother?" Something astonishing happened because she was certain she did not say the words and yet he answered "Yes, of course."

Twenty days later her mother died. When the week of mourning was over her father said "Well that's finished. Thank God. I'm glad I don't have to entertain anymore."

"Are you?"

"Well life has to go on...and we have each other. We can start a whole new life together. I want you to know how very much your daddy loves you..."

To this Nancy answered "Please could you sleep on the couch tonight?"

"But why Nancy?"

"Please Dad, don't sleep in the bedroom."

"You know I have to crunch myself up. It's too short for me. I'm going to work tomorrow honey and.,"

"You're going to work?" she said wondrously.

"Well life has to start again. My boss has been great, but I can't stay out any longer or I'll be looking for a new job. Oh Nancy you know I don't want to leave you alone...I'll tell you what I'll sleep on the couch, I did it all those weeks mother was sick, so one more night won't hurt."

"Thank you Dad."

She looked down at the coffee table with the little mill ashtray and the one her father had gotten in the war from

Belgium of the small boy peeing. Her eyes were burning and she felt unsteady as if everything inside of her was being rocked back and forth. "All those weeks" he had said when it was only twenty days he had been with her mother. "I don't want to leave you alone" he had said, when he had left them alone for six months.

Her father watched television. The late show and the late, late show. The door to her bedroom was glass and covered with white gauze curtains and Nancy could see the flickering black and white light through them. He had the volume nearly off and she wondered how he could hear. She knew he was drinking beer—he always drank a lot of beer in the summer when it was hot. He was munching on chocolate from the boxes of candy that were condolence gifts.

Her father's restlessness disturbed her and she kept falling asleep and waking up all night. She supposed she was mean to ask him to sleep on the couch. If only they could go back in time and start again. If only her father never left. If only her mother never got sick. If only she was about five years old now and they could start again. She would never be mean then.

Her father was snoring and she went into the living room and turned off the television and then in the darkness groped her way back to her bedroom. The linoleum, in spite of the heat, was cold against the bare soles of her feet. She dreamt of her mother being kidnapped by men with red and yellow scarves over their faces.

Her father interrupted her dream by shaking her shoulder. He had eased himself onto the mattress so it swayed to one side and she felt like she was going to fall out of bed. He stopped shaking and whispered "Nancy.. Nancy.." She could smell the clean odor of his shirt, but also he did not smell good. There was something stale mixing in with the laundry soap smell. She decided to pretend to be asleep. Somehow she just did not want to talk to him. She wanted him to go. She needed to be alone. He stood up and the bed went back to being straight and she shifted her position a little to adjust to that. Her father had gone over to the window and she heard the blind open with a snap. Hot, humid air, bright light, the sounds of the street, all rushed into her from the open window. She became aware of the sound of cars passing, children shouting, women talking and a garbage lid clanking shut. Her eyelids fluttered and she saw her father was staring out the window with his back to her.

"You could fry an egg on the pavement. Whew, August in New York. I'd like to just stay home in my underwear with a beer. You have to be nuts to go out there.

She kept staring at his back and she felt something towards him in that moment that she had never felt before. It was horrible as it swept over her. She hated him, with all her heart, with all her soul. She hated him. It brought tears to her eyes. What an awful child she was to hate her own father.

Herb, an orthodox Rabbi lived nearby and each morning while she watched her daughters play outside, Fran noticed him descending the stairs of his house. She knew he saw her too, but in the few months since he and his family had moved in, he had kept his face averted, refusing to signal across the chasm between his belief and her falling away from Judaism. Then one spring morning he surprised her with a greeting. Earthquake tremors the night before jolted him into friendliness. Skull cap on his head, short sleeved white shirt exposing stubby, muscular arms, his cheeks darkened by a new grown beard, he approached calling out, "I heard it was five on the Richter scale." He talked about how the windows shook in their frames the night before, his fears of ricocheting glass and his sons' panic. When this subject exhausted itself, he pointed to the shoots sprouting on the slopes in front of their houses and said, "The elm roots are bad aren't they? You can break your back getting them out." His efforts to extend the conversation surprised Fran. "A miracle," she'd tell Rob later, "the Rabbi deigned to talk to me." Why? She remembered one early morning, looking up towards his living room's large picture window and catching a glimpse of him praying in *tallis* and *tzvilan*. Angrily, he snapped the blinds, as if she were a *voyeur*. She held that insult against him as well as his fiery temper that exploded in frequent squabbles with his wife, Naomi. Often shouts flew from the Rabbi's kitchen across the yards that separated their houses.

"Your husband teaches at the University, doesn't he?" Herb asked amiably.

Yes, History," Fran replied, watching her girls pedal rain-rusted, squeaking tricycles down the street. Four-year-old Jane sat dignified and upright while Elly, a year younger, crouched down over the handlebars like a motorcycle racer and roared, "Brrooom."

"History. I see." Herb raised his eyebrows. "I'm interested in history too. What period does he specialize in?" he asked, glancing towards his house and wondering whether Naomi, who was suffering a severe postpartum depression, had gotten out of bed. Sometimes when he was at the *shul*, frightening images streaked through his mind of his sons, Avi and Judah playing with matches or knives, or of the baby wailing, while Naomi lay shivering beneath the blankets. Even if he had just phoned home the hour before, he would telephone again, his heart pounding with each ring. What if she had killed herself? Finally, he heard Naomi's reproachful voice, "I'm still here. You don't have to check up on me." He felt ashamed. No matter how dark her moods, he ought to know that she wouldn't neglect or injure the children or herself.

Doves cooing on the overhead telephone wires recalled him to the present moment. Across the street, the alcoholic neighbor staggered out to buy her bottle of gin at the corner grocery. Another neighbor, the one who recoiled so strongly from the new feminist ideology she saw growing week-to-week like a fungus, had installed herself on hands and knees with a bucket and brush to scrub the pavement in front of her house. Expecting confirmation from a Rabbi, she once confided to Herb her disgust with working mothers, even single mothers, demanding, "If they need money, why don't they take in washing? Why do they have to go out of the home?" He distrusted feminism too and fought congregants in the *shul* who objected to the *mechitza*, the curtain separating men and women while they prayed. In life there had to be a *mechitza*, a recognition of profound differences between the sexes. Still he felt irritated by the woman's strident tone and had asked, "Is that practical?"

The green Fitzgerald's milk truck drove sedately past the street's brown shingle and stucco houses. Dressed in white, his bottles clinking in a wire basket, the driver climbed down and greeted Fran. "Leave them on the porch," she called.

Three-year-old Elly, cycling up the street, wondered, why mommy talked so long to Avi and Judah's father? Mommy better talk to her and look at her. Everyone looked at Jane and said, 'What pretty yellow hair." They didn't like her brown hair. A man came down the street with a big, black dog. She felt scared and jumped off her tricycle and pulled on Fran's mini-skirt and wailed, "I want milk."

Fran flinched. Why did she still need to cuddle like a baby and suck on her bottle? "In a little while. Wait until I

197

finish talking to the Rabbi." Hoping to distract Elly, she picked her up on her hip and kissed her forehead. Elly twisted a strand of her dark hair about her finger. Her lips parted slightly and her face relaxed.

"Mom, I want to watch T.V.," Jane said, reminding Fran she needed attention too.

"We should all get together sometime," Herb suggested and felt relief to finally come to the point of the conversation. Naomi's postpartum depression fed on isolation and loneliness. But in her present state she couldn't make friends. He had to do it for her. "Your girls are the same ages as Avi and Judah, aren't they? The kids would enjoy an outing together. "

"Oh yes, they've played together on the street. They introduced themselves the first day you moved in, while you and Naomi were busy with the movers."

"I know my wife would enjoy getting to know you better," Herb interjected, and then added in a blander tone, "We could all get to know each other."

Fran nodded, placated by this friendliness but also suspicious. Was he proselytizing for new converts like the beautifully groomed Jehovah's Witnesses who came to the door? Did he expect Rob to pay due and contribute money to Israel, and for her to join the Ladies' Auxiliary and supervise a booth at a carnival? Judaism meant little more than such memories from her childhood. Rob's associations with religion were of brutal compulsions. Neither his mother nor the Rabbi

spared the rod. She beat him to force him to go to a Hebrew
School, and when he got there, the Rabbi beat him some more.

"Mommy, milk...bot...tie."

"Baby....baby Elly," Jane taunted, dancing just out of her
little sister's reach. She hated that whiney voice. Always
getting mommy to pick her up and make a fuss about her.

"Dummy, doo doo."

Tears smarted in Jane's eyes when she heard the word
'dummy.' Everyone said Elly was so smart even though she
was just a baby.

"Coo-koo, coo-koo, baby."

"Girls!"

"I have to be off." Herb said, turning walking towards
his van. Behind him he heard the girls bickering. "I'm not a
'doo doo,' am I mommy? "No." "See, I'm not." "You are." He
felt relief as he dispensed with the smile pasted to his face. He
had to meet with his women's study group and then with his
Board of Directors. A few congregants would linger and
approach him after the meetings and insist on his personal
attention as if it conferred blessing-"Rabbi, just a moment of
your time." "Rabbi, please listen..." "Rabbi, let me tell you
about my grandchildren." Others, not even members of his
congregation, milled about the shul and then followed him
into his office. Berkeley was a lighting rod for the cataclysmic
changes occurring in the country and he wasn't surprised
when approached by a woman in work boots, overalls and
with a crew cut, a bearded man in a dress, a drug addict or

199

someone who wanted to confess the sin of participating in a sexual orgy. All the time he would be worrying about Naomi. Last night she had said, "I wish the earthquake killed us all. Then it would be all over."

As he came up to the van he noticed once again how its beige paint had cracked and rusted. Black electrical tape sealed a jagged crack in a side window. Naomi drove an equally old sedan while he used this one for events like funerals because it looked more official. Often he drove the Hebrew school children on day outings or took them on camping trips. Then a dozen children packed into the van, while sleeping bags, tents and suitcases loaded down the roof. Herb waved to Fran and drove off with an explosion of smoke and a blasting roar from the broken muffler.

Naomi spent half the afternoon getting up her nerve for the visit. Finally, she dressed in the red kaftan that concealed the weight she had gained, put on the heavy, dangling earrings from Yemen and covered her head with a scarf. Her mirror reflected a beautiful Old Testament woman. When they first came to Berkeley, she had expected to make friends with the women in the congregation. It was Herb's first appointment and she had not realized how conspicuous her every action would be as the Rabbi's wife. In *shul* people gazed at her and whispered, "That's the new *Rebbitzen*." How was she to know who belonged to which faction and who felt ignored if she befriended someone else? Her youth and inexperience made her particularly sensitive to the gossip and backbiting. Finally, instead of making friends, she held herself aloof.

At home the phone rang all the time interrupting her cooking, cleaning and taking care of the children. Many people, not necessarily Jewish, wanted to pour their troubles out to the Rabbi. If he was at the *shul* or cosseted in his study, then Naomi sufficed. She listened to the loneliness of the recently bereaved, the details of medical operations and the desperation of those contemplating suicide. Seeing nothing outside their own agony, her callers had no curiosity about her. She was simply an ear to them. Her own thoughts abided with the child growing within her. And when Sharon was born, she felt ecstasy. She loved Avi and Judah but having a daughter made her feel as if her mother had come alive again. She named her Sharon, which evoked the pure delight of the *Song of Songs*. The first day, second and third day were so filled with joy that she thought she'd escape the months of mental illness that had followed the births of her sons. But no, when she returned from the hospital the old despair overtook her, a retribution for her excessive happiness. Every act, even stirring herself to get up and use the toilet became an intolerable chore.

Her heart beat quickly as she locked the door behind her. Sharon drooled onto her shoulder. Lithe, nervous Avi ran ahead. Her younger son, round faced, sturdy Judah, scampered devotedly after his brother. "Wait for me," he cried, adjusting his blue velvet *keepah* on his short-cropped hair.

Already at the top of the steps, Avi rang the bell like Joshua blowing down the walls. "Where's Jane and Elly?" he cried when Fran opened the door. Naomi called up, "Hello. My husband talked to you yesterday."

"Yes, the Rabbi and I talked. What a surprise. Come in."

Avi darted into the den where the girls watched cartoons. The television blared, "Here he comes. Here comes speed racer." On the couch Elly sucked her thumb and wound the ripped binding of her blanket through her fingers, while Jane sat so close to the screen, that if she reached out she could touch it.

Judah tugged on Naomi's free hand and shyly hid his face in her skirt.

"What's the matter? Do you want to go with Avi?"

"Uh-huh," he nodded, gazing at the thick, orange carpeting in the hall.

"It's all right. Go ahead."

"Mom-my!"

"You don't have to have me come with you."

Avi, the protective big brother came to the door and called out, "Come on Judah," and Judah rushed to join the other children.

Hello Moodah-Cootah," Elly greeted him ebulliently.

Good natured Judah smiled with enchanting dimples and plopped down next to her, forgetful of his mother and baby sister.

"His name's Judah," Avi announced. "Call him by his right name," and felt the same satisfying rectitude he saw in his father when corrected someone.

Jane broke free from her mesmerized state and seconded, "That's right, call him by his right name. You don't like it when people call you Belly." She got up and patted Judah's arm in a motherly way. "Don't let her hurt your feelings." Although Judah was the same age as her sister Elly, she treated him as much younger. "Your feelings are hurt, aren't they Judah?" she crooned.

He shrugged and smiled, only wanting to please, while Elly threw her blanket over her head and thought with grief, "Everyone always picks on me. Nobody likes me. I'm bad."

"I've been meaning to get acquainted," Naomi said.

Fran watched her take in the white walls and nearly empty room. Rob had insisted upon a few pieces of furniture, a couch, a single easy chair as "a place to sit," compromising her ascetic preference for space. "Would you like some tea?" Fran asked politely.

"No, thanks." Naomi settled on the couch. She wouldn't allow herself food or drink in this *treif* household, and instead lit a cigarette. Her hand trembled slightly. "Where do you come from?" she inquired and discovered they had lived in the same neighborhood in Brooklyn. Fran's dark eyes, angular cheekbones and aquiline nose proclaimed her to be of Polish Jewish stock. Naomi had seen similar faces among her own relatives. "Do you know what *beshert* means? It's fated that our people should have come from Europe to Brooklyn and that now you and I live on the same street in Berkeley."

"*Beshert*"?" Fran shrugged doubtfully as she would have at the astrology report in the newspaper. "Do you like Berkeley?"

"Herb," she began, legitimizing her own opinion by her husband's authority, "Herb and I like Berkeley. The Congregation's less materialistic than the ones in New York, more intellectual, more spiritual. Of course, there's temple politics like there is all over." Sharon whimpered and Naomi held her high on her shoulder and massaged her back.

"Can I hold her?" Fran took the baby who stared at her with dark, Oriental-looking eyes which slanted upward like Naomi's. "She resembles you," Fran enthused. "I love them at this age, don't you?" Sharon's sudden smile revealed a tiny tooth glimmering on her lower gum. Uneasy, Naomi reached out to retrieve Sharon, so she could feel her weight against her like a tiny anchor.

Domesticity linked the two women and they talked about the older children whose chatter drifted in from the den. The children switched the television's volume to a blaring high and then just as Fran began to scream her disapproval, they turned it low and giggled. Avi bleated a whinnying laugh and then sang along with the television tuned to a new channel, "...on Ses-a-me Stre-eeet." In a moment Judah and Jane joined him, while Elly contrarily warbled, "Old McDonald had a farm, ee-i-ee--i--oh!"

Naomi asked, "Are your parents in Brooklyn?"

My mother died recently," Fran replied softly.

"Of what?" Naomi pressed.

"Cancer."

"I'm sorry. Mine did too. What about your father? Is he alive?"

"Yes."

"What does he do?"

"He's a lawyer for the city." Fran felt relieved the conversation had changed course from talk of her mother's cancer. Not that she cared to discuss her father either. His insistence on cremation, disregarding her mother's wish to be buried, still rankled. When Fran had accosted him, he defended himself by saying, "I'm not made of money and she won't know the difference." Fran even offered to pay, but he turned obstinate and refused her.

"Mine too! He got his law degree during the Depression years but couldn't find work, so he became a plumber. Then a few years ago, without a word to anyone, he took the bar examination, passed, and got a job with the city."

"You know my father had the same problem--but he wasn't as enterprising as yours. He was unemployed for a long time, and finally the city took him on. He never really got over the Depression and the helplessness he felt. To this day he thinks it's still going on."

"I told you *beshert*," Naomi exulted and felt glad she had listened to Herb and made herself come. He kept reassuring her she'd recover. "You need time," he said repeatedly, but only in this moment, awake to the beauty of ordinary things like the light coming zebra striped through the shutter slats and Sharon's warmth as she dozed in her arms, did she believe. Hadn't she climbed out of the chasm before, after the boys' births, and after a crisis her first year of college? She remembered how everything had gotten out of control. Her medical student boyfriend foisted the new birth control pills on her and pressured her into having sex. She felt so dirty and used. She could scarcely concentrate on her work and a professor humiliated her by mockingly reading aloud one of her poorly written papers. She didn't have the courage to go to the next class, then the next and finally saw she would flunk the course. Then she stopped going to her other classes as well. Instead she sat through doubles feature movies or rode the subway, longing to fling herself in front of the tracks. Nothing had meaning. Nothing mattered. One day she wandered into the college chaplain's office. Rabbi Bernstein had been a Messiah to her, showing her that what could be viewed as mental illness was really a spiritual crisis. "Like so many Jews, you've denied your history and loss more deeply," he had told her. "You'll feel whole when you discover who you are." But it had not been his words that uplifted her so much as the beauty in Judaism, the flickering white *shabbes* candles, and the raw emotionality of the cantor's singing.

A scrawny, black and white cat padded into the living room and sprang onto the mantle over the fireplace. "No you don't, Rocky," Fran pulled it down, carried it to the door and cast it out. As she returned the phone rang. "I'm sorry," Fran mumbled and disappeared into the dining room to get it.

Her sister-in-law's voice had its usual brittle cheerfulness, and Fran felt stiff with distrust. Anita always wanted something and wouldn't be offering to pass on a carton of her daughter Stacey's outgrown clothes for Jane or to cook a Memorial Day bar-b-que without an ulterior motive. The last time Anita and Rob's older brother Gary, dropped by, they asked would Fran mind watching Stacey for "a short while" and then returned five hours later, both laughing and flushed with pleasure, dismissing her objections with, "But, surely you didn't worry!" When they first moved to their suburban tract house, Rob had been expected to spend his week-ends as unpaid handyman helping to put in their new lawn, build their fence and to paint rooms. Now Anita revealed that they were planning a vacation in Mexico and needed a babysitter for two weeks.

Fran told her, "No, Anita, we can't come on Memorial Day."

"Too bad. I'm so sorry."

"And I can't do the babysitting either."

"But why not? Will you be away?"

"No."

"Then of course you can. You're our only family out here. Who else can we count on? I won't take no for an answer. Don't say another word. We'll let you know when our reservations are made. Goodbye now."

Shaken and angry, Fran slammed the receiver down. Would Anita and Gary just leave five-year-old Stacey on the doorstep and run off?

Naomi stood transfixed by the picture window, her feet padding up and down as if she were treading water. "Naomi." Fran's voice startled her. She turned and smiled, smoking a fresh cigarette and displaying the baby in her arms.

"You must have to get started on dinner. I should go. You're busy on Memorial Day? I couldn't help but hear. What a shame. The reason I came over was to invite you and Rob."

"No, we're not busy," Fran answered, flushing. "I just didn't want...." Her voice trailed off.

"No? Good! I'm so glad. Thanksgiving, Armistice Day, and Memorial Day—Herb can get away from the *shul* on the secular holidays. It's the only time we could get together with you. Why don't both our families go on a picnic to Stimson Beach on Monday?"

"Sure," Fran agreed, glad that her lie to Anita became the truth.

"It's all arranged. God willing we will have good weather. The children will love it and the men will enjoy talking." Her only fear was going back to the house. Herb planned to visit someone in the hospital and would come home late. She stubbed out the cigarette. When she got better, she'd give them up.

208

The hot brightness of the Memorial Day morning irritated Fran. She blinked against the light while the children danced about dressed in sandals, hats and sunglasses. "We're going to the beach," they sang gaily to every passerby. In a scholarly tone, Avi amended, "Stimson Beach." "Simps-son Beach," Judah lisped. The doors of Herb's van stood ajar while the men made innumerable trips to carry out blankets, towels, swimsuits, toys, playpen, an umbrella and an ice chest.

Rob's rubber thongs padded against the concrete steps as he strained under the burden of a heavy grill; the ones at the beach were not kosher. Thin, wiry, with bifocals perched on his nose, he looked older than his thirty years. His sensitive, slender hands with their knobby knuckles reminded Fran that he had considered being a surgeon before choosing History. He brushed by her without a word, the coals of a fight the night before still banked and glimmering.

Any conflict between them was unendurable and Fran felt sick remembering. If only she could have been silent, could have put the girls through their complicated nighttime rituals of stories, kisses and drinks of water, and then gone as usual and read a book or listened to music. Instead she sat down on the dark stairs, exhausted and brooding. Sometimes she felt like she could not breathe, not since Elly was born and she had two babies so close in age for whom to care. Rob came looking for her. "Anything the matter?" he asked and led her to the living room.

"I'm restless," she said, fatigue breaking her reticence, her need to protect him. "What's the matter with me? I feel so trapped. I wish we never bought the house. I want to feel we could get away. It's so tedious, so boring taking care of the girls. I love them, but I can't stand it."

"What would make you happy? Do you want to go back to school? Do you want to work?"

"I don't know what I want. I don't want to grow old. I don't want to be like my parents. When Anita phones me I feel old age crowding in on me. It's the phoniness of her voice, like everything has to become phony."

"Forget about Anita. She's not important. What about you and me? What can I do to help?"

"God Rob, it's not like you can fix it. I just want you to listen to me, to not have these feelings locked up in me. I feel guilty. I want to be a better mother. You know the girls will be in the back of the car bickering and I imagine myself driving up into the hills to the lake, leaving them on the shore and slowly wading in and drowning myself while they watch. It makes me happy to think that I can escape. Or I have fantasies about sex, that I'm a Go-go dancer in North Beach, that I'm the Playmate of the month. Am I crazy? What about you? Do you have thoughts like that?"

"No. I don't. I don't understand. What do you want? What can I give you?"

"I don't know. I want to join the Hari Krishna or a commune, or have free sex."

210

He blanched as if she had slapped him across the face.

Gently, she said, "We got married so young. Aren't you ever curious? Don't you ever want to know how someone else would be? Everyone else we know..."

"No. I don't care what other people do. You're enough."

His voice was so full of hurt, she felt ashamed. Why had she broken down the wall between them?

"But I guess I'm not enough for you?" he continued.

"I wish you wouldn't take it so personally."

"How else am I to take it?"

Passing her now with cold dignity, Rob handed Herb the grill. Herb sighed as he loaded it into the van, "We ought to stay there all day to make this worth it. Is there anything else?" He had to shove and rearrange the playpen and shopping bags to make room.

"No, we've got everything."

"O.K.--is everybody ready? Pile in."

"We're ready." Elly did a little dance.

"They better *pish* first," Naomi intervened and when Jane refused, she appealed to her in an irresistible way as the mature one. "Can't you try? Everyone can always make a little. You set an example." Dignified and responsible, each step Jane climbed to the house to visit the toilet, brought her a greater distance from baby Elly. Who knows? Elly might wet her pants.

A mood of adventure possessed them all when at last they climbed in the crowded van. Only Sharon remained oblivious to the excitement, sucking her thumb and curling up in her infant bed. Her tongue darted about her mouth touching the tender gum where another tooth was about to erupt.

Herb remembered the broken seal on the van's back window. He squeezed into the back and stuffed a towel in the crack to prevent the exhaust fumes from blowing into the car. Finally, he drove off. The children giggled and screamed piercingly and a piece of the towel slipped out from the window and fluttered like a flag.

Herb drove over the San Rafael bridge. In the distance white spots of sailboats bobbed on the bay. "You study Russian history?" he asked Rob who sat beside him, his arm out the open window and resting on the van's roof, his face impassive. "How did you get into that?"

"It just appealed to me," Rob said remembering his parents' grief when he had switched out of the premedical program. Medicine was a clear-cut profession they could comprehend, one that led to 'livelihood.' But he had discovered history by the chance of taking a liberal arts class and been drawn to the way it sorted through bias and ambiguity towards an objective truth. Late nineteenth and twentieth century Russian history-the fairness of even 'approximate' truth about his own history- countered his overbearing immigrant parents and older brother. He had chosen Fran for related reasons, because she was so much gentler and considerate than his mother, someone he expected not to hurt him. Yet last night she had wounded him, so that he could scarcely sleep and now his head ached.

"We have a lot of professors from the University in the *shul*." How could he reach him? Herb wondered. If he wouldn't come himself, maybe he'd send his girls to Hebrew School. That would be an achievement, particularly if Avi and Judah were going to be playing with them. He didn't want the boys enticed by their assimilated ways. Wasn't it bad enough they lived among *goyim*? The television set in their own home, displayed such allurements as elves dancing about the screen holding out bowls of *treif* food. That was the dirty secret of assimilation. You traded the brilliance of Moses for what? For cocoa puffs. Why did Jews let themselves be swindled? They gave away a treasure for trivialities. Like the American Indians they would eventually forfeit their heritage and peoplehood.

"There's San Quentin," Avi crowed as the van passed the low yellow buildings of the prison.

"What's San Quent...?" Judah asked.

"Where they lock up bad people!"

"Kids too?" Elly asked and looked worried.

"Yeah--they're gonna lock you up."

"Are they mommy?"

"Don't tease her, Avi," Fran said. She closed her eyes and imagined an escaped convict stopping the car and forcing everyone out, but saying to her, "Not you, broad; you're coming with me." Then the convict would force her to drive fast, running away, over the mountains, through the empty desert. She would have the same feeling of space she had had when they came from east to west across the country.

Naomi probed, "Does Rob have any family out here?"

"There's a brother. He and his wife followed a year after we came."

"How wonderful. You must see them often."

"No. We really aren't close. We don't keep up family contacts too much."

"How can that be? How can Rob not be close to a brother?"

Fran wondered if it had been a mistake to agree to the outing. Fair like Jane, Rob, burned easily and didn't care for the beach, and now he squirmed in the front seat while Herb sold him on the *shul*. She, in turn, had to endure Naomi's censure. It reminded her of her mother-in-law's recent long-distance phone call. "Anita told me you don't want to help out when they go on vacation. Why don't you like Anita and Gary? Is it because they've furnished a lovely home and you haven't yet?" Obeying demands to join the *shul*, to have furniture, to be friendly to an exploitive sister-in-law, reminded Fran of when she was in grade school and she was forced to queue up with the other students in straight lines.

"How can you not enjoy family?" Naomi persisted, but Fran made no effort to answer. She searched for a new topic of conversation and said the first thing that popped into her head. "Did you read the article on offended her sensibility, she

214

was bound to do the same to her. Not just Naomi, but Herb stopped speaking and sat frozen. Why, Herb wondered, was she so tasteless as to discuss something like homosexuality in front of the children? Next she would bring up open marriages, group living, flower children, LSD and sado-masochistic cults. He didn't want Sodom and Gomorrah dragged into his family.

Even Avi caught the broken mood and demanded, "What's going on, Dad?"

"Nothing, Avi," Herb replied.

Rob rescued the moment by flicking the radio on to the baseball game, the announcer's voice filling the void. 'Poor Fran,' Rob thought, automatically protective of her when she was in difficulties, 'she put her foot in it.' Last night, he had shut her up just like the Rabbi's disapproval did now. Did she want a divorce? If he had let her go on talking, would she have said that? Great truth seeker that he was, would he risk asking her? He couldn't bear to lose her.

Sharon woke from her infant bed and wailed as they came to the narrow winding highway leading to the beach. The car swerved from side to side and redwoods streaked by on the rollercoaster road. "Be careful, Dad. Don't get us killed," Avi shrieked. A taut line existed between Herb and his oldest son, and he replied through clenched teeth, "I know how to drive, Avi."

As the car swung past one curve to another, Naomi clenched the door handle, her knuckles turning white. 'Poor

215

Herb....poor Herb...poor Herb," kept sounding in her head. The way he was driving, the tension in his voice as he spoke to Avi, told her his resentment. Why did he have to be saddled with a nervous, crazy wife? He wanted the Board of Directors to give him tenure. What if someone saw her as she ran out of the house two nights before determined to join the Hell's Angels? Herb had to run down the street after her and bring her back. Why was she running away from him? In college she had found a cure to chaos of her psyche. When would she find it again? Perhaps if she practiced her religion more strictly? Perhaps she had to move to Israel. If they lived among observant Jews, she might not feel so restless. Jerusalem's holiness would confer serenity.

Fran felt clammy and sick and waited for the children to be afflicted. Shortly, Jane complained, "I'm nauseous," and put her hands over her mouth. "I'm gonna throw up," Elly chimed in, but knowing her resilience Fran reserved her concern for white-faced Judah. "Are you sick Judah?" He nodded, unable to speak while his baby sister cried louder than ever. "When are you gonna get there, Dad?" Avi moaned. Naomi attempted to comfort the baby with a pacifier and at the same time searched about in her bag. "Suck on this; it will help." Jane and Elly grabbed the candy with surreptitious glances at Fran who usually forbid sweets.

"Dad.."

"Shut up, Avi."

Herb drove recklessly fast.

The van pulled into the parking lot filled with people dressed in bathing suits and rubber shoes running by and carrying umbrellas, buckets, baskets and thermos bottles. "Well, we made it," Herb announced with a grin. "Only nine in the morning and already the lot's half full. In another hour we wouldn't have been able to get a spot." The oppressive mood of the drive gave way to celebration. "Hurray, we made it," Avi cried, exciting the other children. Even Sharon gurgled and kicked her feet as Naomi lifted her from her infant bed. Avi, Jane, Elly and Judah raced ahead to the beach, but Herb called, "Get back here and help carry stuff." Leading the children like the Pied Piper, he rushed across the hot, black tarmac to the sand to stake claim to a spot near the lightly lapping water. He fluttered a blanket, letting it catch the air like a parachute and then land on the sand. The children helped him weight the corners down while Naomi arranged the baby in the playpen beneath an umbrella. Then everyone changed into bathing suits.

Herb and Naomi were the last to go to the rest rooms. Soon they emerged with shockingly pale bodies as if they had not been exposed to the sun in years. Naomi wore a modest one-piece suit in contrast to Fran's bikini. Herb still wore his black skullcap and the fringes of his ritual undershirt hung down beneath the shirt he kept on. He blinked at the bright sun that reflected on the white sand and the humanity about him. How bewildering to be caught in this crowd, with ever-more people arriving, all stripping off their clothes. He longed

217

to be safe, back in his study instead of on this outing. The trivial chat required drained him. Slowly, he lost his energy and his capacity to concentrate on his inner thoughts. He lost himself.

The children ran splashing into the water and Herb and Rob, now in a blue baseball hat, followed. "Are you going to send your girls to the public school? They could start Hebrew School in the autumn too," Herb began, while Rob thought of the futility of Herb's efforts to persuade him and felt tempted to say, "I like to keep things simple." He didn't see himself as a Jew or identify with any larger group at all. He didn't care about anything, not even his work-only Fran. Why couldn't she understand that they needed each other?

"I love going to the seashore," Naomi addressed Fran. She sat on the blanket, knitting a red scarf, the motion concealing her trembling hands.

"I do too," Fran answered slipping her finger through the playpen's mesh into the baby's grip. A slight breeze blew. At the water's edge, the children jumped the waves ecstatically. The moment had a sisterly intimacy and Fran wished she could confide in Naomi, I'm so restless. I have strange fantasies,' but how could a Rabbi's wife understand such madness? Instead she and Naomi exchanged recipes and advice about child rearing, while they watched the sea and the constant flow of the mob. A man with his leg in a brace limped by, a radio on his shoulder blasting a news report concerning the Vietnam War. Hippies with feathered headbands and flowing long hair, pitched a blanket near the lifeguard's high chair. Several families brought dogs even though notices in the parking lot proclaimed, 'No dogs allowed,' and she could see Elly's uneasiness when one drew near. Occasionally the children ran shivering to the blanket. Fran found a towel and rubbed their shoulders and chests vigorously. "Don't drip...don't drip on the blanket," she warned, but they did. Then they ran back to the water. Rob seized one, then another and swung them through the waves, exhilarated by the physical action. He glanced back at the women talking together. If Fran had an affair, if she got it out of her system, would she return? Why did he keep focusing on the sexual angle? As if that was all she had said, the only thing he could hear because it hurt so much. If she dragged him to an encounter group he'd be universally condemned for feeling jealous and possessive.

"Were you raised in a very religious home?" Fran inquired of Naomi.

Naomi laughed. "No, not at all. My parents were typical Jews, making their American assimilation. The only time they went to *shul* was on the High Holidays. Occasionally they ate gefilte fish and hoped I'd marry a doctor. And it happens, I was dating a medical student."

"So how did you marry Herb?"

Sharon began to cry. Naomi lifted her from the playpen. The baby sucked noisily at a bottle of water, making a flow of bubbles. "There was a period at college when I was....upset. During this time, I was influenced by a Rabbi and became Orthodox. He showed me how beautiful it was to be Jewish. Later, he introduced me to Herb. One thing followed another and we got married."

"You gave up the medical student, eh?"

"Don't think my parents weren't heartbroken. It was hard for them. I couldn't eat the same foods as them. I couldn't go out for their Saturday drives. That was their relaxation, to drive around on the *shabbes*. Yes, they would have liked it if I married the doctor and all that meant. Not only that I would be well off, but I would be in the same world as them. For them," Naomi laughed, "it was unJewish of me to become Jewish." She balanced Sharon's wobbling head with one hand, and patted her to burp her. Then she put her in the playpen on her back and readjusted the umbrella to position against the rising sun. The baby blew a film of saliva across her tiny mouth.

Relaxed, realizing she didn't have to play the *Rebitzen* in front of Fran the way she did before the women in the Congregation, Naomi confided, "My sister's the opposite of me. I chose tradition and she became a feminist. I wish we got along better. I know she feels uncomfortable with Herb and me." Then repenting for the hypocrisy of her reprimanding Fran earlier for not possessing proper family feeling, she added, "We're not close even though she lives in Berkeley too."

"Is your sister married?"

"Oh no."

"Maybe she'll marry a doctor and fulfill your parents dreams."

"Charlotte's determined not to marry anyone!" Naomi shook her head. She had read the newspaper article Fran asked about earlier, drawn to it by a sisterly loyalty that conflicted with the religion she'd passionately embraced. No Ladies' Auxiliary for Charlotte. They had flung themselves in opposite directions, and secretly Naomi envied her sister's independence and daring.

At noon when the sun was high and blistering, everyone gathered at the blanket for lunch. Herb, Naomi and Avi murmured prayers while Judah peered about and shrugged as if bewildered by his relative's piety. Naomi distributed sandwiches from a large paper bag. They hungrily devoured the tuna and mayonnaise on soggy white bread, the sea and fresh air stimulating appetite. "This is de-li-cious," Elly said, filling oozing out onto her lap. Naomi restrained herself from reaching for a second sandwich. She had to get control over herself, not eat so much, not smoke, and not be depressed. How thin Fran was, and she was fat, a fat wife and mother. Her children would be ashamed of her one day. No, she'd get better. She'd have more control. She knew she would. If only life was as effortless as religion. Willingly she had given up *treif* food, had accepted the restrictions of *shabbes* and even now hoped for more sacrifices to make her purer.

"Do we get desert?" Judah asked shyly. "Ice cream is kosher," Herb noted. Rob took the hint and trotted off to buy popsicles, stepping gingerly over the sand. Fran saw his skin was already flushed pink. She smeared sun tan oil on blond Jane who pulled away against her urgency. "You'll be sorry Jane." Elly grabbed the bottle and spilled half of it accidentally. "It's expensive," Fran complained. "Do me," Judah begged. "I'll do you," Avi said. As he massaged the oil on his brother's shoulders he asked Fran, "You know why a lot of Jewish men are bald?" "Why?" "If you had so many brains you wouldn't want to hide them." Elly got down on her hands and knees and crawled around. So many dogs at the beach and not one bit her. She even petted one. Now she was a dog. Did they see? " Rrrrf... rrrfffff

Rob returned, popsicles balanced precariously in his hands. "Help, help," he cried to the children. "I need someone to eat this. Who's going to eat these?" Elly shot across the sand to him. "Dad, don't give to her first," Jane complained, but already Elly had a handful and with a proprietary air distributed them. "This one's for mom, and this one's for...,"she deliberately bypassed her older sister and handed it to Judah who sat patiently with a hopeful, outstretched hand. Herb shot him a warning glance, having taught him not to take a bite of food until after his parents had begun eating, a sign of respect. Finally receiving a pop, Jane sucked blissfully on the delicious cold ice cream and then held up the bare stick and said, "I'm going to build a sand castle and use this for a flag."

"Yeah," Judah seconded and the children ran off to the shore, Elly the last one.

Naomi took the baby off to nurse while Herb removed his skullcap, his shirt and *tzizis* and went for a swim. How free the buoyancy of the water and the wide horizon made him feel. Seagulls flew like letters of the Torah in the sky. Each day he longed to pray ardently and with all his soul, but was easily distracted. Something trivial, like Fran once glancing up from the street at him while he prayed, destroyed his concentration and made him furious with himself. He often preached about murmured and seemed drunk to the high priest, as a model for prayer. Turning over on his back, floating along and feeling unfettered in his near nakedness, it came to him that it was Naomi with her tormented passions that drew close to God. Yes, yes, he muttered and his limbs turned to jelly, not a care weighed on him and he felt stirred with love for his wife. A Jewish woman showed a reticence before the world that could make passion between husband and wife flare out all the more extravagantly. Seeking and just missing ecstasy, the profligates he met considered themselves on the vanguard of sexual freedom. They couldn't comprehend that self-restriction intensified passion. Before the *shabbes*, Naomi bathed, perfumed and dressed herself up. The candles, the soft challah like flesh in his mouth mixed with sweet wine, filled him with excitement. He was still her ardent lover. Looking about at the bathers bobbing in the sea about him, he thought how flesh to flesh, people really weren't different.

Naomi disappeared into the woods beyond the beach. It felt good to be secluded in the cool shade, to listen to the birdcalls and to feel Sharon hungrily suckling. She loved her babies so much. She looked at the ridges that ran from Sharon's nostrils to her mouth. Her rabbinic father-in-law had told her that was the thumbprint of the Angel Dumah whose touch forced each soul to forget heaven. What if Sharon had not received Dumah's touch? Remembering paradise, would she suffer less? Or would the contrast with the reality of this world be an agony?

Alone on the blanket, Fran and Rob stared at the swimmers bobbing in the sea. Rob kept running sand through his hand over and over.

Finally, he said, "Do you want a divorce?"

"Oh God, no. What's the matter? Do you?"

"No, I just want you to be happy."

"I'm not sure I know what happiness is."

"Do you love me?"

"Yes...I love you. Last night, I just wanted to talk, to not be so afraid of hurting you. I don't want lies between us. "Tears filmed her eyes.

"I'm glad you spoke to me. I don't want you to feel like you can't. I'll try not to be so fragile."

She kissed him lightly on the lips. "You taste of ice cream," she murmured and remembered the last time they had made love. He had just drunk coffee, and the delicious taste had felt as if it spread from his mouth to hers, and to every pore in her body. When they got home and put the children to bed, they would make love.

Fran stood by the edge of the icy water until some teenagers splashed her. Finally, she plunged in and swam. She felt delighted to be swept along by the waves, to go out further and further, daring her strength and skill. She treaded water in a peaceful spot beyond other swimmers and noticed on far-away cliffs young men with hang-gliders. They jumped from their steep ledge, floated above and landed dangerously on the crowded beach, forcing people to run out of their way to not be crushed. She felt so exhilarated, so free.

As she came dripping out of the sea, shivering, sand sticking to her feet, she met Herb who had been swimming too. "Did you enjoy your swim?" he asked, his voice gentle after the relaxation of the ocean. They began to walk along the shore. "I'm glad we all came. It's good to get away," he said. He had felt ill at ease not using the time to work on a sermon. His intellectual Berkeley congregation judged him by his sermons, wanting them to be scholarly even though many of the congregants were ignorant about the most basic aspects of their religion. To his surprise, while he swam, a few of the theological ideas he had been struggling with took shape. Taking pleasure in talking, he began to discuss how the rebelliousness of Judaism was expressed in the Old Testament in many of the stories concerning younger sons. "Jacob triumphs over Esau, overthrowing the legal precedents of inheritance. Joseph triumphs over his brothers. It's really a religion of younger sons and change...." His eyes shone and he spoke with excitement. New ideas came quickly.

Fran thought how charming he could be and felt a stirring towards what he knew. To her surprise she told him about her mother's cremation which was against Jewish law. He informed her simply and without recrimination of what she could do, that the ashes could be buried in a Jewish cemetery and the proper prayers said. She didn't know if she would do this even if she could persuade her father, but she felt grateful and more at peace. "People want to follow their religion only for death and
sickness, but don't see it has wisdom for the rest of life," Herb said, and she was not offended as she might have been earlier in the day, but glad to hit up against a steadfast vision.

Later, while Naomi grilled hamburgers at a picnic table near the parking lot, an elated, boyish Herb gathered the children to teach them a card game called, 'I doubt it.' The winner of the game was the most successful liar. He himself was inspired with a facility for perfect deceit. "I have an ace," he said, grinning.

Not just the children, but Rob too was fooled as he watched Herb's features. Rob sat beside Fran, his arm about her.

"You're burned, aren't you?" she asked.

226

He squeezed her shoulder and she felt his strength flowing through her.

From behind the sizzling, smoking grill, Naomi squinted at the hippies she had noticed earlier by the lifeguard. Surreptitiously, they passed about a joint, a few kicking up sand while dancing to a blaring radio. "Are you experienced?" came the teasing, insinuating song. She had heard it before. When Herb wasn't home she sometimes tuned in to Jimmy Hendrix, the Doors and the Beatles. "Are you experienced?" she unconsciously mouthed the words and one young man with wavy red hair to his waist, noticed and smiled at her. The sea glistened behind him with the pink calm of sunset. Swaying to the music, he held out his arms to Naomi. For the last hour she had been thinking about how she wanted to move to Jerusalem, how she wanted to become a purer person and yet she discovered her feet paddling up and down. She could scarcely keep from racing across the sand into his embrace.

Patience

Waiting for the sound of the car. My son, my husband bringing our guest from the San Francisco airport, whom I invited mostly out of guilt. I know they had to reserve a wheelchair to take her the long walk from the gate. My ancient Aunt, an octogenarian. I have not seen her in six years, and then only for a short hour, passing through New York. A concession. I didn't want to see her at all. Not with what was so firmly lodged within me——all that hate. And now too, palpably, fluttering in my butterfly stomach, while I wait.

Sound of car. Feel myself choking. Peer out picture window. No not them yet...not them. Too nervous to turn on hi-fi. Back to sprawl on couch. Wait. I was silent those child years I lived with her. That was right after my parents were killed in the car crash. And then later I was silent. Once for two years not writing her at all, so finally my silence had a message. So finally loud and cruel as those insults she had heaped upon me while I sat limply in her steaming kitchen, blood pounding in my ears. She chopped liver, ground fish, dropped lumps of egg and matzo meal into soup. "What you did," she began. "I won't tell Mara. I don't want to upset her. Such an angel. Wait, quiet,"

"But I didn't, I swear I didn't."

"So now you lie. My poor sister to have a rotten child like you. She'd still be alive if not for you. But I don't tell Mara; I don't want to upset her. Such an angel. Wait, quiet,"

I hear, coming up the stairs, with a swish of petticoats, with a pervasive perfume, In comes Mara—one of five grown children, the best loved. She bears a green Lord and Taylor bag with a new skirt, a new dress to stuff into the already bulging closets of her possessions. Mara is on a diet and is served a special meal of steak. Mara is a spinster with bleached peroxide hair. Immediately she is told the alleged crime--that I answer back or went without my coat being buttoned and might catch a cold, or was late home even though I have a watch. And it begins, or rather continues to the clink of knife against plate, while Mara pushes tiny pieces of steak with her pinky. While I clear the dishes and wash them with kosher soap, pink striped for dairy and blue striped for meat dishes, "You're rotten," I sponge the table. I spill Ajax on the porcelain of the sink.

"You know ma, she really deserves nothing. What did Mrs. Geneva give her that five-dollar birthday present for? It makes me sick. She really deserves nothing," "All she cares about is books... doesn't even care about herself. You know you deserve nothing. Nothing. You are nothing." "Everyone thinks so. We talked to the neighbors about you. Don't think people don't know, They know what an awful person you are," "Look Mara, all we do for her? Does she appreciate? Nothing." "Are you crying? Good. You didn't cry enough for your parents, a rock, a stone would have cried more. What kind of daughter, ten years old, you're old enough to understand," "Yeah, you should have cried more after their car accident, but not you..."

Sound of car. Rush to window. My son stands to one side, my husband is helping her out. Force myself to run down. Choked by what I see, death sitting on her bent, shriveled form like a halo. Oh, she's changed. And before I can get to her she is struggling up the stairs, and even though I am by her side now, she says nothing, does not greet me, only comes slowly, cautiously up. "Our house is high on a hill," I wrote to her. "I'll send you the airplane ticket, I want the trip to be my gift. I hope you can come, but must warn you we have a lot of steps." And she wrote back, "Little by little, I'll climb them, and I prayed to God that I would see you and your family."

"There's no railing by this part. Hold my hand." "Not on this side. Hold the other hand."

She comes up cautiously, she kisses me cautiously, I am to be feared, as perilous as the heights she has ascended, and I lead her into the living room. "Is this a study?" she asks. "My Phil has a study, my Alex has a study, my Mara, God bless her," "Are you tired?" "No, no," She gets her bearings. "Sit down." "I've been sitting." She admires the carpeting.

"Here's your bedroom." "Oh I have the baby's room." "See the roses by your bed: white, yellow, orange." "But where's the bathroom? Never before it used to happen. Just recently I have to get up. And once at my Alex' there was no light and I got lost. Everywhere I went was a window or a closet and I almost peed in my pants." "I'll leave a light on." "I never thought I would live to see your house, to come here, never thought..." Silence. "I don't deserve," she says, fishing for the compliment. I say nothing. Silence. I won't say it, won't say thank you for that time she took me. Don't fish like that. Don't force what you want, but take what you can get, "Good night." I leave her among the teddy bears.

The first morning. Oh endless week. Will it end? "Today I'll take you on a tour of the city, but first I must go to the grocery," I rush to shop, an excuse for going out. We must have food. As I drive I am haunted by the horrible thought of her death. Selfishly I want her to live, to live, not die at my house, live and go on to her next stop where my responsibilities stop. Air-conditioned store. My responses slow and tired. Whirring sound. Kept awake by her rambles to the bathroom. Old people fighting incontinence.

Return and her voice goes on, as before. She judges. Royalty. "This is a palace; your husband is good; your son is a prince; the baby is adorable; everyone is good; you're a darling, an angel-princess." Recognition of her fear. I scream so she'll hear...I hear her humanity. The silences-all her flattery poured into the gall of memory. I feel the blast of her loneliness, talk to me, talk to me, "In Meeami..,I have no...no one, make some friends, but not the same as family." Talk to me...talk to me., whispering can't escape. Seven more days, six more days, five more, four. Each day I fear the onus of it, like babysitting, am responsible for her happiness. Quick, take her places, to the beauty parlor, the theater, feed her. Elegant restaurants. She forgets her glasses. Read to her expensive dishes from the menus. Bathing her in money. I was unaware until now how money cleans and brings relief. Money and love, always knew they were related. Give it away and it acts as cleanser, keep it and it turns to dirt, "In Meeami I don't even go in the water. I can't swim and the waves make me dizzy. But my feet hurt. They say the water would help."

"In Meeami there are people at the *shul*. Women talk, but I go to pray. Every Saturday, for all my children, and you too. I consider you my daughter. The daughter -in California. And this is how I spend the other days. I walk, walk all day. Before it was with a cane, I walk slowly like a snail. The others play cards. I'm not interested. Anyway my fingers are too twisted to hold the cards. I get 171 a month social security. For lunch I have one roll. I don't eat too much and have lost a lot of weight. I gave everything away. Don't even have pots and pans, hut at least I had the pleasure of giving a few things away. Nathan got a lot. Remember the secretary, a genuine antique. Remember the painting of a deer. Alex didn't need. Phil's wife got the sewing machine. And I made out a will. I don't have money. But there are a few things, a little jewelry I want to make sure they go where I want before I'm under the ground. Here take this necklace."

Her hand is trembling as she gives it to me. She whispers, "Did my sister tell you I tried to put you in an orphanage? She said she'd turn you against me... She..." So I receive from her for the first time the jewel of acknowledgement, an apology in gold, and begin to forgive. Before she died she did give to me! I wanted that, not the too-glittering title "angel-princess" and her saying "I'll never forget, I'll tell everyone all you did for me this week. I don't deserve." And I stared ahead, would it end? I never wanted flattery from her. Then somehow the flattery stops, and the last vestige of my anger that burned white so long begins to wither like a withered hand I held as I helped her up the stairs and down,

"I feel healthier here," she says."

"A burden. Never wanted to be a burden. Should I turn my children's home into a hospital?" She spoke of her broken hip, the convalescent home, the wheelchair, the walker, and the cane. And like Othello telling stories to Desdemona, she won me. Because she returned from the place from which there was no return. Pour years before they had taken her in an ambulance to the old age home. And she wouldn't eat in the dining room where they dropped food on the floor from lifeless hands. And people were rotting and really stank. And Medicare paid. They had given up and the children wanted them there, out of the way. And the beauty parlor dyed the old women's' hair, one week red and another yellow, and billed Medicare fifteen dollars for each color. And the children said "At least her hair is clean; she gets her hair done once a week."

She left the old age home the same way she came, in an ambulance. She forced herself to learn to walk. She used the walker. And then the cane with four wheels. She went shopping and cooked. And when someone stole the cane she struggled home without it and never got a new one. She said it was a sign from God that she could do without. She moved to Miami. Such obstacles she overcame with patience.

The week goes. Short really. Petals falling. In the end, speaking quietly in the kitchen about trivial things. Just talking about the weather, the taste of water, the airplane ride. Just a simple evening, the light gradually fading. And from my own head too goes the clutter of, "she is my mother's sister; this is my duty, obligation." Fades like her hoarse voice saying, I had a nice evening." And I say, "So did I."

The Silence of Dishes

Crumpled newspapers littered the Miami airport. Young men in undershirts clearly not travelers, hung about an arcade of jangling pinball machines. I overheard a frantic woman saying her plane was delayed two hours because officials were searching the crew for drugs smuggled from South America. The filth, the air of lawless disorder surprised me. Those years after my mother's death when I lived with Ruchel, I had absorbed her paradisiacal vision of Miami. More affluent schoolmates had returned from Christmas vacations transformed by golden tans. We heard talk of ballrooms, chandeliers and fountains. But I could see that Miami had fallen from its previous glory, and the change made me feel as if I were walking on a slippery surface.

I had come only because Ruchel's daughter-in-law Brenda wrote, "She's old and she'll die soon. You better come." So I booked a flight from San Francisco for the same week Ruchel's youngest son Simon and his wife Janet were flying from New York.

The cab driver that picked me up at the airport, a former Iranian general, reminisced as he drove about the drivers he had had, of long black limousine with flags streaming above the fenders and how a lengthy entourage followed. The only entourage now was senile drivers oblivious to all rules, who tailgated and cut in front of us.

"Where's the Bass Museum?" I asked. In my purse was a newspaper article about the Jewish Legacy exhibit, a collection of torahs, silver candelabras and other booty plundered by the Nazis. I figured if Ruchel could spare me, I'd make a side-trip to the museum.

As we turned onto Collins Avenue, I noticed an old woman totter and fall on the sidewalk. I wanted to help her, but my driver said, "Do you want to stop on every street?" Ambulance sirens shrieked, the noise twisting above the scruffy palm trees and dilapidated buildings.

We passed small bodegas and a store called Torah Treasures. A heavy-set, white-bearded man with a skullcap lounged in the doorway. Old people, as if on ship deck, sat in front of the small hotels. We pulled up in front of the Sea Breeze, a narrow three-story building. Pink flamingos and palm trees adorned its plate glass front. There was no verandah. The residents sat on folding chairs directly on the sidewalk. Just a glance at the men in their straw panama hats and the women in sundresses and rolled stockings, and I knew they were Eastern European immigrants like my aunt.

The general palmed the fare and shook my hand as if we were friends and he had driven me as a favor. Then he drove off and left me to face the line-up. A dozen old people turned to me in one perfect, synchronized motion of expectation as I made my way into the lobby. I wondered if Ruchel had any friends among them. Thirty years ago when I was ten, I had gone to live with her. I stayed seven years, and during that time no friend ever phoned or visited her.

Hers was a third-floor corner room. She had written to me in her broken English of her scheming and waiting to get this new room and gain the advantage of two windows. Shortly after this, she had stopped writing completely, and I couldn't phone her because she was too hard of hearing. Finally, Brenda had responded to my unanswered letters with her summons. I went up in the tiny elevator and knocked on the door of 307. Simon had told me she had two paid companions, both Haitian boat people who were illegal immigrants. One of these black women answered my knock. She smiled and whispered, "Ruchel is tired. Couldn't stay up."

Behind her I glimpsed the small room stuffed to the brim with twin beds, a sink, tiny Formica table, television, dresser and metal utility cabinet. These were the remnants of Aunt Ruchel's life, the kosher dishes and pots and pans, the photographs and knick-knacks, and she herself was a kind of a remnant. The eldest of four sisters, she had outlived everyone despite constant complaints about her health. After my mother's death, she was always promising the drama of hers.

I remembered her waking up in the early morning and over lumpy oatmeal, telling me, "I almost died last night." Yet here she was, ninety-two years old, shrunken, stiff, barely able to walk, her no-neck head like a turtle's emerging from a shell, her skin deeply lined. It startled me to see her small as a child as she lay asleep beneath her cover. She hardly seemed the person who used to rage at me. Now she looked pathetic, and my brave plans to confront her with the past disappeared.

"Tell her I was here, and that I'll come back in the morning," I whispered and ran out.

The woman at the desk gave me a key to a room on the floor below my aunt's. Like Ruchel's, this room was crowded with twin beds, a dresser and tiny table, and against one wall a counter with a built-in refrigerator, burner and sink. All that was missing were the family photographs, but the nails on which they had hung still studded the discolored green walls. It was such a cramped, dismal room that the pink plastic wastebasket decorated with a Mickey Mouse decal struck the only cheerful note. A loudspeaker was shouting out numbers outside, "twenty-six, five, thirteen. "The bingo game in the adjoining hotel was already in full swing.

Restless, I went out and walked the few blocks to the flat, monotonous beach, so different from the craggy cliffs that met the Pacific in California. Even the gray ocean lay dead and listless. I meandered along a wooden boardwalk sunk into the sand and tried to untangle, one more time, why I had come. I wished I wasn't there, but knew I had to see Ruchel again one final time. My father, who had deserted my mother and me, was no more to me than a speck of sand. It was Ruchel who gave me a home.

But when she took me in, it was as a servant. The sight of the kosher dishes brought it all back, the endless dishes I had to wash, the poorer food I was served, the stingier servings, and the lectures I received as I ate. "You don't deserve," my aunt pronounced, taking the joy out of any good fortune that came my way. I was accused of having broken a chair, a stepladder, and the television; on other occasions, of having stolen missing photographs, a handkerchief, her corset, and chocolates. "I didn't!" I cried, and Ruchel spurted out, "So you're a liar too!" Hers was a niggling assault, a slow paring away of who I was, until I learned to sit with hanging head as her accusations sharpened to the final knife to the heart, "If you weren't such a spoiled brat your mother never would have died."

The sea looked thick, viscous, as if suddenly it could erupt and spill into the streets, bringing along a flood of sharp rocks, a force cutting down everyone in its way, and I wanted it to, the way I had wanted destruction thirty years before. I still felt the same despair. If my mother had lived I would have been a different per son. I yearned for this other mysterious self with all the grief of a mother mourning a dead infant. Seeking lights and noise to distract me from my thoughts, I fled the isolated beach.

"Twenty dollars," a young Cuban on Collins Avenue shouted to me. He was sitting on a stoop with his friends, but at my approach jumped up and swaggered half way across the street to me. I saw this was a performance for the other boys and speeded up. Another dark-eyed boy who looked no older than thirteen, smiled ingratiatingly. His approach confused me, but I automatically shook my head and walked further along. By the time a third boy called out mockingly, "twenty dollars," with a gasp I understood. Did I look that desperate? that old and undesirable? Although I had scarcely been gone a day, I felt stripped of my identity and missed my family. I ran back to the Sea Breeze where the desk clerk rebuked me for leaving a track of black oil which had stuck to my shoes from the beach. I had to take them off and walk along in stocking feet like a mourner. There was no phone in my room, and I called from a suffocating booth.

"I miss you," I told my husband, and then not wanting to worry Jim, recovered myself enough to banter, "Not much to do here but play bingo."

"Did you see Ruchel?"

"Yes and no. She was sleeping. Tomorrow's the big reunion."

"It's good you went. She's the last of a generation."

"Yes, yes."

"Susan can handle it."

"Of course, of course. How are the girls?"

"I picked up Joanie at the nursery school and she called me 'Mommy.' She went around telling everyone I was 'Mommy.'"

"Did she? The little devil."

I spun the conversation out for as long as I could. As long as I held Jim on the phone, I was part of the ordered, reassuring life I had with him, and my violently confused attachment to my aunt dimmed. But we said good-bye. Then I phoned the Holiday Inn to see if my cousin Simon and his wife had arrived yet from New York.

Simon, the youngest of Ruchel's five children, was the one I liked best. I remembered terrible scenes between the three eldest sons, particularly one at the cemetery with Ruchel

240

trying to reconcile them at their father's grave. The Goldstein family possessed a flair for drama. While the sons exchanged insults and nearly came to blows, Ruchel wrung her hands and her daughter Marilyn raced among the headstones shrieking, "Look what you're doing to mother." As the receptionist rang Simon's room, I twisted around and saw the elderly hotel residents gathering in the lobby. The television hung from the ceiling the way it would have in a hospital room. "Susan? Is that you?" came Simon's deep voice. "Do you want to meet for a drink? Janet went to bed early. Just wait where you are and I'll come get you."

With a quarter of an hour to spare before Simon would come and nothing else to do, I phoned Ruchel's eldest son, Sam. He spoke to me briefly and then put Brenda on. We had not seen each other in years, but I remembered this twenty-years-older cousin as a bleached blonde wearing a long chiffon scarf and rhinestone- studded wooden platform shoes who urged me to follow her example and have a nose j ob. Within seconds she was criticizing Sam's brothers and Marilyn for trying to foist Ruchel off on Sam and herself. "I didn't retire to Miami to take care of my mother-in-law." When I put down the receiver I felt drained. Brenda had worked herself into such a state of indignation that there hadn't been even a word of getting together.

A pale blue Ford drew up in front of the Sea Breeze. I jumped into Simon's rental car and he took me to a hotel bar, a dark place of chrome and black marble that made me realize that not all of Miami was run down. A decade older than I,

241

Simon lacked the self-pity and bitterness I detected in his brothers. Despite having gained a few extra pounds, he was still resilient and energetic. He had bristling hair, a pug nose, and alert black eyes. 'Whad'ya want?"he asked. He was having a Bloody Mary and I asked for plain tomato juice. Turning to the waitress, he said, "And a Virgin Mary" and gave his snorting- through-the-nose laugh. She retreated to the bar and Simon peppered me with rapid-fire questions. "Now give me the run-down. How's Jim? How's Dana? The other kid? Any pictures?" I asked him about his three grown children and his factory. He manufactured generators and sold them all over the world. "Good, everything's good." He'd made a considerable profit in the Iraqi war.

When our drinks arrived, he asked the waitress, "How about a few extra cocktail onions?"

She was middle-aged with a ruddled face. "Sorry. They don't like giving extras."

"Oh come on. I know you can pull it off. Just for me. OK?"

She trotted off, and when she returned it wasn't with one or two for the drink but a whole plateful of onions.

"Now that's terrific." He popped one into his mouth and sucked on it with enjoyment. "Mom's very excited about your coming. She can't believe it. I can't believe I'm seeing you either. How long has it been? It must be ten years."

His voice was loud and commanding. He used to frighten me as a little girl. "My motto's live with dignity and die with dignity," Simon announced as he sipped his second drink. "Sam's right here in Miami, and he could take some trouble with Mom, but Brenda won't let him. For every little thing now, the doctor throws Mom in the hospital. He can't take any risks. A month ago she got diarrhea. Sam was furious he had to sign her into the hospital land check her out. If he and Brenda helped, it would be a different thing. Meanwhile, Marilyn can't do much, she's so far away. Harry was ready to warehouse Mom fifteen years ago. Ernie doesn't care where she goes, just so long as he doesn't have to put out any effort. If Mom was willing to come back to New York I could look after her, but she hates the cold weather."

Listening to him discuss Aunt Ruchel's fate, I remembered when he and his family had argued mine. No one wanted Ruchel to take me in except for Simon. He told the others, "Oh, come off it. It's not going to cost any of you anything. Aunt Stella left some insurance. It will take care of Susan's expenses. "Then he turned to his mother and teasingly asked, "Look Mrs. Goldstein, you're not going to put her out on the street, are you? What will the neighbors think? Here's your chance to be a saint." Simon told me matter-of-factly, "The upshot is Sam refuses to help any more. I f she has to go into the hospital again, he won't sign her in. I have to put her in a home. I want you to come look at the places with Janet and me, and persuade her this is the best thing for her." Ruchel had five children, but Simon was alone in his concern and grabbed the only branch nearby. "All right," I said, smiling and hoping I didn't show my disappointment at being involved. The black oil stuck to my shoes.

A thin, young black woman answered Ruchel's door, the other Haitian immigrant who looked after her. She had short frizzy hair pulled back in a ponytail and wore rubber thonged zoris and shorts and a white shirt decorated with streamers of sewed-on pink ribbons. "Susan," Aunt Ruchel cried. When I hugged her, she grabbed my hands and kissed them. It was a self-abasing, feudal gesture. I could not keep from pulling away. Slyly observing the effect on me, she told her companion "This is my daughter." I flinched at this pretense and wondered if I could make myself stay in the room. The attendant gazed at me curiously. "I didn't know Ruchel had two daughters." She spoke with a Creole accent; the't' sounds made tiny explosions. Her name was Angelina Ostah, but Ruchel had taken to calling her Esther. She told me, "Esther's better than the other one who comes at night. Esther's very good to me." Angelina sat on the edge of a straight back chair, feet together, hands primly folded on her lap. "Yes, Ruchel," she said indulgently.

"Did you eat breakfast?" Ruchel asked. I'd gotten up early and gone for a run along the ocean. The smell of breakfast sweet rolls had drifted tantalizingly from the hotels lining the beach. Now I said I was hungry. Angelina rose to make tea and brought out a tin of biscuits.

It was odd for me to be waited upon as Ruchel's guest of honor. I could see the Passover dishes in the cabinet, pink-tinted glass dairy and pale yellow meat dishes with forget-me-nots painted on the rims. The night before the Seder I would carry cartons up from the basement and spend all night

244

unwrapping dishes from their newspaper coverings. The next day the guests arrived. Once the meal began I was exiled to the kitchen. Ruchel and her family feasted at the dining-room table, while I stood washing course after course of dishes and longing for the Passovers I had spent with my mother. Only Simon's wife, Janet, had looked in on me.

"All my life I kept kosher. Not a bite of treif passed my bps," Ruchel said, proud she had kept this faith amid other contusions. "My girl knows how to do it right. I don't have to worry," she nodded towards Angelina who gave her a cup of steaming tea. Ruchel held the handle with her little finger extended, a refinement clouded by the stains down the front of her dress.

I told he about my children: mischievous Joanie and serious Dana, only nine, but practicing her violin with fervor. She longed to wear nylons and put on jewelry. We looked through Ruchel's albums and I begged for photos of Sara, the first sister to die, the aunt I had never met. She was tall and blonde, a big-boned woman. Although it was a black-and-white photo I could tell her eyes were a very pale blue. Her son was ten when like me he lost his mother. He had been sent to an orphanage.

"What happened to Barry?" I asked.

"I don't know. I never heard from him. He just forgot everybody."

"What was he like?"

"Such a temper. After my sister died, I sewed a jacket for him. He came in and grabbed it and ran out."

The room was like a ship becalmed. We soon sat silently. I sipped my tea and nibbled on a cookie. My sweat-stained dress stuck to my sides, and in the wall mirror I saw my thin face, so much like my mother's with its high cheekbones, dark hair and the uneven nose that Brenda had wanted put to the knife. Outside I could hear the roar of traffic on Collins Avenue and the ever-present ambulance sirens. "Maybe you'd like to nap," I suggested. The remark hurt Ruchel. "I'll sleep at night," she answered.

Angelina rescued the moment with, "Ruchel, your television program." She turned on the set and Aunt Ruchel laughed and enjoyed herself watching a man talking to an old woman puppet, white-haired and bejeweled, but full of Punch and Judy mischief. Angelina sat painting her nails red and laughed with my aunt at the puppet's triumphant antics.

When the program was over, Angelina snapped it off and turned to my aunt. "Ruchel, time to do your nails. Come. Sit by the light." Gently, she helped her over to a chair by the window. Angelina slowly rubbed off the previous day's polish with a cotton ball soaked in sharp-smelling remover. I watched, fascinated by her smile and my aunt's responding delight. The sunlight illuminated the white and black heads and surrounded them with a private penumbra. "It's hot today," Angelina said. Her face glistened with sweat. She blew on my aunt's nails and asked tenderly, "Would you like a bath?" "Yes, Esther," my aunt replied with a child's simplicity.

I felt left out. I couldn't keep away from those familiar dishes and picked up a plate that was faintly veined like a Chinese Ming vase. As Angelina ran the bath, I was remembering how, as I ate, Ruchel would count the chits she received for each collar she had sewed at the local clothing factory. "*Eynsz, tsvey,dray,fier,finef, zex,...*" My mouth used to grow dry knowing she'd soon count herself into, "You didn't cry enough after your mother died. You never loved her."

For the first time I understood she was talking about herself, not my mother. It was a vicious circle, Ruchel punishing me for not loving her and turning me further against her. Angelina was more her daughter than I was.

"Susan! When was the last time we met?" Janet, tall and slender, her straight hair in a smooth pageboy, was dressed in a tailored skirt and beige blouse. She sat in the back of Simon's car. I was carefully helping Ruchel in beside the driver's seat. After I loaded her walker in the trunk, I squeezed in the back next to Janet while Simon drove off to the first residence home. On the other side of Janet sat her mother, Gertrude, a pretty woman with thick spectacles perched on a tiny turned-up nose. She was all pink and ruffled. Her frilly sun umbrella made me feel as if the packed car was a steamboat with paddle wheels and that we were drifting down the Mississippi.

After Simon parked in front of a tall brick building, we made slow progress—Ruchel with her walker and nearly blind Gertrude needing to be led—into a luxurious lounge with chandeliers, red and black rugs and soft leather armchairs. A woman in her forties, wearing a powder-blue suit, had been waiting for us. She whisked us up to an elegantly furnished model apartment. Each room had a wall cord that Ruchel could pull for help. Janet whispered to me, "If she's sprawled on the floor, how will she reach the string on the wall?" Downstairs we viewed a spacious dining room. The tables were covered with stiff damask cloths and bore vases of fresh flowers.

Then, while the rest of us were left sunk in the deep chairs of the lounge, Simon proceeded to the manager's office to talk about "business details." The four of us attracted attention, and several of the elderly residents gathered around, discussing us in loud voices.

A sunken-cheeked man in plaid trousers called out, "Which one wants to come here?" I nodded towards Ruchel. "That one! Who does she think she is?"

Strange how much of life is about who is in and who is out, whether it was myself as an orphan, Angelina as an illegal immigrant or Ruchel in her helplessness.

His boldness encouraged the plump woman beside him. Her face was heavily made up and her fingers sparkled with rings. "You have to be able to walk to come here. They won't let her in with a walker."

Another woman, cried, "How old is she anyway?" Stooped and deeply wrinkled, she must have been in her eighties herself, but was indignant to hear Ruchel was a nonagenarian. Hard of hearing, Ruchel only smiled as she was discussed.

Simon returned with a jaunty air and led us away. Janet accompanied her mother and I helped Ruchel. At a snail's pace we moved past the plaid-trousered man and his cronies. As we got into the car Ruchel complained, "My tooth hurts. It hurt me last night. Now it hurts worse." The next residence was smaller, but there the residents got more care. We walked under a navy awning into a one-story building, down along blue hall, past blue rooms, to a windowed lounge looking out onto the blueness of a canal and sky. Here and there, nursing aides asked who wanted Cokes. The manager, a short, pot-bellied man with thick eyebrows, discreetly indicated a senator's mother, who wandered about with an aide following after her. "She just keeps pacing. Even at night. She has to be watched every second or she'll walk out and get lost." He took Simon and Janet away and I was left on a couch sandwiched between Ruchel and Gertrude. Nearby, a short woman with a broad face and protuberant eyes kept flipping her skirt up and down, and another resident, a thin, neatly dressed woman, looked very pained.

I asked, "How long have you been here?" "Three months. They sold my daughter a bushel of hay, and I'm the horse."

Simon and Janet returned saying, "This is the place. What do you think Mom?" Ruchel smiled weakly. "My tooth hurts." As we left, I noticed a room with a few tables. An aide was setting up for the next meal, putting out the plastic cutlery and paper plates to which Ruchel would have to accustom herself.

Later that afternoon, I promised Simon I would take his mother to the dentist. When I phoned, the receptionist said Ruchel would have to get there by five on the dot or else the office would be closed. It was four thirty when I tried to hail a cab in front of the Sea Breeze. There just did not seem to be any. I wasted a precious five minutes peering into the traffic and praying for my Iranian General to come along. Finally, since the dentist was only a few blocks away, we decided to walk. Angelina proved a poor guide. "I think ... I think this way," she said, and leading Aunt Ruchel with her walker, we inched along following Angelina's vague navigation. At five minutes to five we arrived at the office but had to maneuver Ruchel up a flight of steps. Groaning and giggling we took the stairs. It was a great triumph to enter the office at the stroke of five. Ruchel went into the treatment room where she took out her dental plates. The dentist decided he would pull her last remaining tooth.

In the waiting room, I flipped through the Miami Herald. Angelina fidgeted beside me. She tapped her foot and cleared her throat. As I was about to turn the page, the brush of her hand on my wrist stopped me. I looked up.

"I have a three-year-old boy. He's in Haiti."

"Who is he with now?"

"My sister ..." She paused, unable to speak, but then went on. "No good there. I want him with me in Miami."

Her eyes were wide and she had the look of an animal caught in a trap. Run-down Miami was paradise after Haiti if only she could get her little boy back. She didn't ask me to help, but it was clear she wanted me to get involved. I had been only ten when I was foisted on an unwilling aunt, but Angelina's son was much younger. For a dizzying moment I considered hiring lawyers and fighting the immigration service, and then it seemed a mad thing to do. Bringing Angelina to the attention of the authorities might just get her deported. I knew nothing about these matters and very little about her. Not only that, but at home a husband and small children awaited me and I was leaving the next day. "I'm sorry," I told her and tumbled in my purse for a twenty-dollar bill that I pressed into her hand. It was better than doing nothing.

The dentist called me into the cubicle where he had been working on Aunt Ruchel. She was still sitting in the dental chair with a paper bib on. "Are you in pain?" She shook her head. Without her dental plates her mouth was collapsed over her gums and it was difficult for her to speak. The dentist, a tall gray-haired man, stood at his work counter. "With patients this age, "he lowered his voice, "they die, or move suddenly and it turns out I don't get paid. I have to take precautions. Will you write a check now?"
"I think her son ..."

He raised his voice and addressed Ruchel, "Didn't you say this was your daughter?"

"I'll take care of it." I snapped and wrote out the check. "Can I have a receipt?"

"Yes, yes, I'll do it myself. My receptionist's already gone home." He went off and Ruchel tried to say something to me. Her numbed mouth was so stiff that it took a while to get the words out. "Should I move? Is it the right thing?"

I thought she and Angelina ought to be together. Now at the end of her life, my aunt had found a friend who made her happy. But Sam and Brenda weren't going to act as back-ups and so it was impossible for Ruchel to remain at the Sea Breeze. I answered vaguely, "It's a big decision."

Earlier I had asked Simon, "Does Angelina know she's going to lose her job?" "She can guess," he answered. His attention was on his mother and he had no concern to spare for Angelina. "Could Angelina get a job at the retirement home? It would mean a lot to your mother." "My mother would like it, but I doubt it. She doesn't have a green card." Angelina would probably find another employer at the Sea Breeze. The Sea Breeze was a free zone. Angelina and Ruchel could not get into the posher places. Not together.

I glanced outside the dentist's window to see the street with its little shops was dark already and the street lamps on. How much I owed other people was ambiguous, as hard to decipher as the shadowed alleys below.

"Here you are," the dentist popped into the room and handed me the receipt. "Let her take some aspirin when she gets home. She might not want to wear her dentures for a day or two." He gave me his instructions briskly, removed

Ruchel's paper bib, and then disappeared. Ruchel struggled out of the dental chair and I stretched my hand out to help her. "Should I do it? Should I go in the Home?" she asked again.

I wasn't going to move to Miami and sign her in and out of hospitals. Nor would I invite her to come live with me in Califomia, begrudging her a place as she had done to me. Aunt Ruchel trusted me; I didn't know how to help either her or Angelina. I couldn't look at her when I said, "yes." She trusted me.

"I'll have to throw my things away. Do you want anything?" She was speaking more easily now as we moved down a long hallway towards the waiting room where Angelina sat. "Take my dishes."

"No," I said more firmly than I needed to, and then in a softer tone, "I don't need them."

"I'll give to the girl."

"Yes, do that."

At the door to the waiting room, she stopped short, grabbed my hand and squeezed it. Tears filmed her eyes. There was a long pause and then to my amazement, she told me something that must have percolated into her mind during those long afternoons with Angelina, "Those things I said to you when you lived with me. I didn't mean them."

I glanced away from her. My heart was pounding. It was as if she had put her hand deep inside me and touched all the soft, vulnerable organs. Angelina looked up with curiosity. "We can go," I cried. The bright sound of my voice surprised me. Angelina reached for the folded walker, but I grabbed it, saying, "You help Ruchel on the steps. "The walker was heavy, but I strained my arms to keep it aloft and raced down ahead of them. I needed a few moments alone to compose myself. Outside, it had begun to drizzle.

People ran into doorways. Cars glided by. Like church bells rung to summon the faithful, I heard the peal of ambulance sirens. "Didn't mean them ... didn't mean them...didn't she said of the poison she had dripped in my ears.

Across the street I saw the blinking neon sign of another bingo parlor. The night before, I lay awake listening to the numbers echoing over the adjacent hotel's loudspeaker. I hadn't expected to win the jackpot. The payoff had come late and much devalued but better than nothing.

In the morning while Janet and Simon packed Ruchel's belongings, I managed to steal a visit to the Bass Museum for the Jewish Legacy exhibit. The crowd wandering from room to room was hushed and reverent. Elaborately embroidered velvet torah curtains hung in high-ceilinged, dimly lit rooms. I felt like I was stepping into a synagogue. In one chamber there was a table set with mourning dishes, white platters with black trim used for the meals of lentils and hard-boiled eggs served following a funeral.

I thought of Angelina making her meal that night and perhaps eating on Aunt Ruchel's dishes. Maybe she would preserve those dishes for the time when her son came.

Or maybe she would politely accept them, walk out the door and dump them one by one into the first garbage pail she came across. I couldn't blame her if she did. Who wanted to eat off someone else's plate?

Stair Words

As Eva put down the phone receiver, the expression *l'espirit de l'escalier* rose into her consciousness. It described perfectly what she was feeling. She was choking on words she'd wished she'd said long ago. Now, it was too late. Her aunt and cousin were dead. More importantly, Herbert was dead! If only she'd tracked him down while he was alive!

Her only opportunity for revenge was to soil his daughter's memory of him. Most likely, he'd wronged Susan too. In that case, could she and Susan reach out and comfort each other as only two good women could?

Sitting at the computer she kept on the desk in her bedroom, she composed a letter. With each new sentence, a voice in her head warned her to stop. Herbert's misdeeds had occurred more than a half-century ago. Well, perhaps she wouldn't send the note, but she needed the outlet of writing it.

Dear Susan,

My cousin Karen phoned last night and said you wanted to hear from me. Two weeks ago, she met you while she was in New York, attending a *bar mitzvah*. At the reception, the two of you talked. You landed up telling her that your happiest childhood memories were of visiting your grandmother at 18_ _ East 10th Street in Brooklyn.

I was astonished. My Aunt Betty and cousin Mara had lived in the same apartment building! I remember well East 10th Street, particularly the apartment house that belonged to your grandmother, Mrs. Glickstein. My aunt lived in the flat across from her on the top floor. (Your parents lived on the first floor; your cousin Judy and your aunt and uncle on the second.

I know this because I lived there too after my parents died in a car accident. I was ten when I moved to East 10th to live with my aunt. There were three girls my age in the building Judy and I were the same age, as was Sarah, another girl in the building. You were a baby. We three girls used to take you for walks in your stroller, or play with you in your home. (Your father was usually in the bedroom, busy studying for the bar exam.) I got to know your mother. Sandy was a lovely woman. I was sorry to hear she died. I knew your father too.

With you in New York, and myself in California, I suppose it's unlikely we'll meet in person. However, I hope we can speak on the phone or exchange a few e-mails and share our memories.

Best wishes,

Eva

The letter was innocuous, yet Eva hesitated about sending it. Would she and Susan exchange a few e-mails, hinting, but never expressing what they needed to say? Or would they admit it wasn't nostalgia that caused them to reestablish contact? She felt curious, and clicked the mouse on 'send.'

Eva's Aunt worked as an operator in a dress factory. She had two sons, and a spinster daughter, twenty years older than Eva, whom she doted upon. Mara was a short, pretty woman with peroxide blonde hair. She never washed a dish, made her bed, or did her laundry. In the outside world, she labored as a bookkeeper. But at home, her mother did everything for her. Once Eva moved in, she too was obliged to wait upon Mara.

The top of Mara's dresser was covered with jars and tubes of makeup, cold cream, perfumes, and sponges, as well as a tweezers, and eyelash curler. Each morning, a fascinated, Eva would watch as Mara unfurled a bib, tied it about her neck, and proceeded to create the face she presented to the world.

Mara's clothes were beautiful. At least once a week, she bustled in after work with her arms filled with bags of 'resort wear' she'd bought at Lord and Taylor's. The outfits were packed into two large suitcases she took to weekend vacations at Catskill hotels like Grossingers or the Concord. "Wish me luck, " she'd say, as Eva handed over the suitcases she'd lugged to the train station for her cousin. Eva was glad to help. She hoped Mara would be grateful. But she received only a cold look as they parted.

Nor was there a warm greeting from Aunt Betty when she returned home. As they ate their evening meal together, Betty launched into the familiar monologue that poisoned every bite Eva took. "You don't care about anyone, not me, not Mara. You're selfish. No one wants to come here because of you. Mara suffers because of it. Why do you think she's still single? If not for you and all she does for you, she'd have her only family now." Two days later when Mara returned, she added her voice to the attack.

"You don't deserve," was repeated to Eva over and over. The one who deserved was Mara! She wanted to marry a professional, deserved a doctor, or a lawyer, but not even a lowly stock boy came along to court her. Someone had to be at fault.

Two breast bumps appeared on Eva's previously flat chest during her second year of life at Betty's. She felt ashamed when Mara's brothers Abe and Howard noted that she was taller and filling out. The brothers teased Mara, "Eva will be married before you." After they left, Mara turned on Eva wrathfully. "They're my brothers. Why do you have to hang around when they're here? Do you think they want to talk to you? They came to visit me and my mother."

Wanting to escape the criticism her presence evoked, Eva spent more and more of her time with Sarah and Judy. The girls called themselves the three musketeers. Herbert was Judy's uncle. He played the concerned uncle to them all. When Sarah left her new bicycle outside, it disappeared. Herbert had taken it to teach her a lesson. Returning the bike an hour later, he told her that she must be more careful with her things. Judy and Eva learned the same lesson. They left their schoolbooks in the back garden, returned ten minutes later, and found them gone. Herbert had confiscated them. Later, he returned the books with a lecture.

On the way to visit Judy or Sarah, Eva often saw Herbert glide out of the shadows of the dim hallway. He stood before her, blocking her way. His round, pale face was topped by tight coils of dark hair. He smirked as if they shared some secret. Eva recoiled, hated the way he was always popping up in dark corners.

One evening, Herbert paid an unexpected visit to Aunt Betty's. She made him a cup of tea. Mara gave him cookies from her private stock. She'd never considered Eva worthy of receiving a single one. Settling into a chair in the kitchen, Herbert nibbled, and sipped, while Betty and Mara looked on. They didn't dare to ask why he'd come. Not only was Herbert on the way to becoming a lawyer, he was also the landlady's son-in-law. Betty and Mara meekly waited for him to say why he'd honored them with his presence.

With a flick of his tongue, he removed cookie crumbs from his teeth and lips, then drawled, "The neighbors are complaining. Things are missing from the basement, some clothes, a lamp…I'm sorry to say this, but I believe that Eva must have stolen them."

"I didn't!" Eva cried. "What would I want with a lamp? Search my room for it."

"Who else would have taken them?" Mara stated, automatically siding with Herbert, and ignoring Eva's invitation to search her things.

The accusation made Eva frantic. She blurted, "Herbert's the one always sneaking around. He took Judy and my schoolbooks. He took Sarah's bike. Probably he took the lamp, and doesn't want anyone to blame him."

"Be quiet!" a furious Mara hissed. She turned to placate Herbert. "If she steals anything else, we'll send her away."

Herbert's lips pursed with satisfaction. With a nod to Aunt Betty and Mara, he rose and left.

Eva ran off to her room, threw herself on her bed and wept bitterly.

One afternoon a month later, Eva was doing homework at Judy's kitchen table. She needed an encyclopedia. Her junior high geography class was studying Africa. She must find out the names of countries, their populations, natural resources, and geographical features.

"My Aunt Sandy and Uncle Herbert have encyclopedias," Judy declared.

"I don't want to bother them. I can use the library at school," Eva demurred. Lately, the only sign of Herbert was the occasional flutter of a curtain in his bedroom window. The girls knew he was watching them.

"They won't mind. Why wait? Isn't your project due tomorrow? Come on," Judy cried. She was an eager, blue-eyed, generous girl, blue-eyed, her hair pulled back in a ponytail, braces shining on her teeth. "Mom…Dad…we're going down to Sandy's" she cried to her parents and hurried out the door.

It was easier for Eva to accompany her than to explain why she didn't want to see Herbert. She assumed Sandy and Susan were in their apartment. But once she and Judy had knocked on the door, she found Herbert alone. His wife and little daughter were off staying with another of Mrs. Glickstein's daughters. Ethel lived in Brighton Beach, a block from the ocean in which she swam in all-seasons.

"Be my guests," Herbert drawled, hearing Eva wanted to use the encyclopedia. He retreated to the living room to watch television—so much for his bar studying—while Eva and Judy seated themselves at the kitchen table with an oversized volume they'd taken from the bookcase in the vestibule.

Squinting at the text Judy said, "I forgot my glasses. I'll be right back." She jumped up, and with her ponytail bobbing, ran off, leaving Eva behind.

Eva's back was to the door to the kitchen. She was reading about Mount Kilimanjaro. Suddenly, she was grabbed from behind, and lifted to her feet. She couldn't move, scream or even speak. Herbert stood behind her, his arms encircling her, clasping her to him. He fondled her breasts and rubbed his penis against her back. His breath was hot in her ear as he rasped, "You need to get used to this. All the boys are going to be doing this to you in a year or two. So don't you tell anyone…"

A click of the door handle announced Judy's return. Herbert hurried to the sink, opened the tap and filled a glass with water. When Judy stepped into the kitchen, he was emptying his glass, as if to stay, 'the reason I'm in the kitchen is I'm thirsty.' Judy's glasses were perched on her small upturned nose. Her eyes grew bright with pleasure as she glanced at the open encyclopedia on the table. She was about to sit down when Eva murmured, "I have to go." Eva ran out. Judy followed, crying, "What's the matter?" Eva started up the staircase. Judy tugged on Eva's arm to stop her. "What's wrong? Tell me." Eva faced her friend, pointed to her breasts, and said, "Herbert was touching me here…And he was rubbing his thing against my back." She burst into tears and ran upstairs to her aunt's.

The next evening, Judy asked Eva to come to her apartment to watch television, something they did two or three evenings a week, sprawling on the couch, feasting on licorice, 'chicken corn,' and 'm and m' candies.

Halfway down the flight of steps to her apartment, Judy whispered to Eva, "I have to talk to you."

"Here?"

"Yes, here. I don't want your aunt and cousin to hear. I don't want my parents to either." They sat side by side on the steps.

"I told Sandy what happened. She's going to see to it that Herbert never touches you again. She begs you not to tell you aunt and cousin what he did."

Why would she confide in them? They always saw her as in the wrong. Eva promised. Her aunt and cousin would have said she was lying. They'd never dare accuse Herbert. But Sandy, who knew Herbert well, had believed her!

Two months later, a moving van appeared in front of the apartment building. Eva stood at her bedroom window, watching movers carry Herbert and Sandy's furniture from the building to the truck. Aunt Betty had said the would-be lawyer had purchased a tract home in one of the suburb communities sprouting up in Long Island. This one was called "Green Haven." Mara had breathed the name wistfully. She said that when she found her 'Prince Charming,' she hoped to move away and live in such a place.

Eva felt safe. Sandy was keeping her promise to protect her. Herbert was sent into exile. Eva kept checking the computer screen for new e-mails. She was disappointed a month passed with no reply from Susan. During this time, she'd begun to mull over news accounts of pedophiles--a coach on a university football team, teachers at private schools, Catholic priests. Those who'd been abused as children decades before spoke of 'needing closure.' They wanted financial compensation, and more importantly, apologies. Institutions had failed to protect them. The same was true of Aunt Betty and cousin Mara. Rather than protect, they appeared to have invited Herbert to injure her.

'I froze when he touched me,' appeared in the accounts of child molestation. The shock, the inability to move was a cliché, one that Eva knew kept playing itself out. So many times over the years of her long life, she'd been quiet when she should have spoken. Even in her sixth decade, the powerlessness of her childhood remained, the desperation to please.

She'd been telling herself to respect Susan's privacy, her sheltered world. But angry that she'd been ignored, she sat down at her computer and wrote a new letter.

Dear Susan, Why did you think of your grandmother's house as a safe, happy place? Were you escaping something horrible in your home? As I remember, your parents left that house in Flatbush in a hurry, one day there, the next, gone. I suspect that your mother had wanted a divorce. Your father probably got on his knees and begged her to not leave him. He'd have had to agree to move elsewhere, as well as make other promises. I wonder whether he kept them…Was Sandy an over-protective mother? Did you feel suffocated? In the end, was she vigilant enough? I believe you well know what I'm talking about.

She deleted this letter, wrote instead, "Your father molested me. Did he do the same to you?"

'This will lift her out of her chair,' Eva thought, typing her name at the end. As if with its own volition, her hand moved the mouse to 'send.' On the screen, a blue circle whirled round. The letter was on its way, irretrievable.

Susan, a woman a decade younger than herself, might this moment be bent towards the computer, reading. Perhaps, her hair coiled in tight curls like Herbert's. Was she heavy-set like him? Would her face go white as she read? A shovel had broken the earth of a grave, let loose stinking, suffocating gases.

As she rose, Eva's giddiness changed to panic. Her heart raced. She'd indulged a private passion, lost control, as if Herbert had guided her hand.

In a way, send a note to Mara—you invited it

She'd gotten off easily compared to the others, and yet she felt it was right that she speak out too…first inhibition about telling Susan—wouldn't she be like Herbert, all the arguments to silence…and after much struggle felt the truth must out—he mustn't be protected by either of them…and then more importantly, wrote to Mara

Transformation of self, no longer the victim—felt tired, been hard work, a lifetime's work to finally speak out.

Playing with it, see need to see the sunlight, that truth is important.

Dear Charlene

I am writing to you as a sister. That implies equality, when for you I've always been an intrusion on your family, an alien, a burden to be borne. Once I signed my name to a note, making my last name yours. You burst into rage saying, "Don't you ever use the Pressman name again. You're not a Pressman, and never will be."

What disgust I saw as you glared at me. Your hand was twitching, ready to slap. I was ten then, two decades younger than you. My mother had just died of cancer. Since my father was long out of the picture and wanted to remain so, I moved in with you and Aunt Rose. Many times you accused me of not loving my mother, of driving her to her deathbed, and said you wouldn't let me do the same to yours. Whom, I wonder, did you hold responsible for your father's death from cancer when you were a child?

Not yourself, the light of Aunt Rose's life, 'an angel.' She'd offer all her aches and pains to me—"my pressure's low...my heart's bad...I almost died last night," but when she heard your footstep, your coming home from your bookkeeper's job, she'd whisper, "Don't say a word to Charlene. Poor thing. Don't worry her." By the time you stepped in the door, there was a bright smile of greeting on her face, and she was busy cooking your special meal. We'd had macaroni or cheese, but you required steak.

After you finished eating you summoned me to clean up. As a child, you had a special place, the only girl among your five brothers. It fell to you to wash the dishes every night. The family was large. It took a long time. You described standing at the sink far into the night, and your eyes glassed over with tears. Although you hadn't been burdened this way since your brothers had married and moved out, you still saw me as a replacement drudge. Never again would you wash another dish or make your own bed. This was justice. I had to compensate you for how you'd suffered.

And how you continued to suffer. Your brothers made jokes at your expense. In the 1950's before the women's liberation movement, a spinster was ludicrous. "I have good news," your mother said to one of the 'boys.' I don't remember if it was Mo or Frank who was visiting and who shot back "What? Charlene's engaged?" But I do recall the snort of laughter that accompanied the remark, the whispers of your sister-in-laws behind your back, the frequent reference to you as 'Poor Charlene.'

Thursdays you were late because you went to the beauty parlor. One Thursday, you came home with a surprise. You'd bleached your hair and eyebrows blonde, and now you looked more like Doris Day, the clean-cut actress you admired most. Perhaps, you'd noticed a strand or two of gray in your hair. How frightening that would have been. A clear sign you were not meeting your destiny, to be the loved favorite to a man, as you were to Aunt Rose.

The two of you looked alike, the same short sturdy figure. But your mother wore faded housedresses and you dressed elegantly. I remember jeweled angora sweaters with pearl collars, wool skirts, suede shoes. Often, your arms were loaded with Lord and Taylor and Best & Co. shopping bags, booty from lunchtime and after work forays. You modeled your new clothes for us, the dresses, slacks and sandals you'd wear when you went to Catskill resorts like Grossingers or to the Caribbean on a cruise, hoping to meet a man.

Eager for affection, I didn't mind carrying your suitcases to the subway when you were on the way to your holiday. There was the big yellow one and the smaller blue, four blocks, then up a flight of steps to the train platform. You tipped me a dime. That dime hurt. There was no way you'd acknowledge I'd been kind. Of all the reasons to hate me, the most potent was I had time on my side. My opportunities lie ahead. And there you were on that wind-swept, winter-dark subway platform in Brooklyn, two suitcases full of futile magic. You snapped open your purse, gave me that dime and humiliated me. That put us on the same level.

In a few days, you came home in a fury of disappointment. "I'll see to it you go to a State Home," you threatened me, soon after you arrived. What was my crime? I'd forgotten to ask how you were feeling when you walked in the door. The phone rang. You rushed to get it with a musical, "Hell—ooo." Oh, you were so meek when you spoke to your brothers, so sweet if a man phoned for a date, but I was destined for the lash of your fury. Kick the dog. The moment

270

you put the phone receiver back in its cradle, you stormed into the living room where I sat watching television, snapped the set off and cried, "There's something wrong with you. I don't know what yet. But I'll tell you when I find out." Something wrong? *Everything* I did was wrong.

Each day, I looked more like my mother, her dark hair and eyes, her long, thin face. My up-turned childish nose became aquiline like hers. I'd hang my head, stare at my shoes, while you sang a litany of my evils. The crescendo came with my worst crime. "You don't love anyone, not even yourself."

You can't make a flower grow by lashing it. You have to water and nourish it properly. Not too much. Not too little. Similarly, love can't be bullied. I did love someone, Aunt Hannah. If only she'd taken me to live with her. She'd considered it, but she only had a tiny room, lived in a tough Williamsburg neighborhood, and I'd have had to change schools. For these reasons, I had moved across the street to live with Aunt Rose and you.

My visits to Hannah were the saving grace. I remember the first time she came for me, how she marked the occasion by wearing a bright red suit she'd sewed herself and black patent leather shoes. It was an hour's train ride all the way from Flatbush through the tunnel to Canal Street, the first stop at the other side of the East River. Swept along by the crowd, we hurried to another platform for a train over the bridge back to Brooklyn, to Williamsburg. The next time

271

Hannah met me at Canal Street. A third time she waited for me at the foot of the train steps near her house to guide me through streets full of Spanish music, the squawk of chickens from the butcher's, the screams of pushcart vendors, and the bustle of the fish and vegetable markets. It took me a month to learn to make the trip all by myself. She showed me there was an escape.

Not that I confused Hannah with my mother, but they were similar, both quiet kind women. It was like being with my mom again, because Hannah loved me with all her heart. Love is a simple thing. This is love: Hannah and I walking arm and arm, her stopping to introduce me to her neighbors, saying, "This is my niece. Isn't she something?"-- Hannah buying 'hal—vah' for me, treating herself to *The Mirror*, getting shampoo, lemons and beer to wash and rinse my hair; Hannah holding me against her, lathering my hair over the kitchen sink, warm water streaming over my head.

Oh, I know, she was a dreamer, not practical like Aunt Rose. On Saturdays, Hannah and I used to browse the narrow, hole-in-the-wall material stores with bolts of cloth up to the ceilings. She never looked at the cottons and wools but hurried to the silk, satin and taffeta. Eyes shut, she ran her fingertips over a bolt of gleaming cloth. "Touch it," she breathed. "When you get married I'll sew you a gown out of *peau de soie*." We'd go back to her place with new yardage. Pins in her mouth, she cut patterns in the high fashion styles from her 'operator' work, then sat down at her sewing machine to make me a 'trapeze,' 'bubble' or 'chemise.' These were party dresses. Even though I attended none, Hannah was hopeful.

The highlight of the weekend was our Sunday trip into Manhattan where we strolled up Fifth Avenue past Saint Patrick's Cathedral and the luxury shops to Rockefeller Center. There was the spired building, the black marble benches of the mall and the flags of different nations whipped by the wind. Noses red from the cold, eyes tearing, we squeezed in among the crowd of spectators, leaned against the concrete balustrade and looked down into the rink at the gliding skaters. Hannah loved the organ music and the couples that dipped and bent in synchronization, the young girls with hands bent across their chest, twirling round faster and faster with their flickering blades.

"Practice skating," she told me. "I'm going to make you a velvet ice skating outfit and you'll come here to skate. I'll watch you." She pointed to the rink-side cafe where people sat at small tables sipping coffee. "I'm going to treat myself. Won't I be a lady sitting there?"

At the subway, we parted, she to travel to Williamsburg and I back to Flatbush.

"Thank you," I told her.

"I don't need any thanks. Don't thank me," she cried and darted away.

I rode over the bridge, through the tunnel, back home.

You asked, "Did you enjoy yourself?"

"Yes."

273

Glancing at the bag I was carrying, you said, "I see she made you another *shmate*. There's no room in the closet." Turning to your mother, you remarked with disgust, "Of course she likes Hannah. She's just like her."

As the years slid by, you got used to me. Your hatred dulled but never disappeared. When I was seventeen, I got my scholarship to Williams College and was about to move out. In the midst of my emptying my drawer—the single drawer I'd been allotted--you came up to me said wistfully, "The time went by fast. You'll visit, won't you?"

It was too late. I left home and broke off contact. You let it be known to other family members you were hurt. Hadn't you been a sister to me? Frankly, Charlene, I'd have been content with a first cousin. Except the intensity of your feelings were not that of a mere cousin. You were and are a sister, a presence that will shadow me forever.

In my thirties, I phoned you one day—'out of the blue'—and said, "You were cruel."

"Me?" you asked incredulously. "You don't know me. I'm a good, unselfish person."

For all I know, except for those seven years of blunder, perhaps you were what you say. Another thirty years have passed. I've had breast cancer like my mother but survived. My eldest son died of melanoma five years ago. Every week, I visit the cemetery where his ashes are interred, reminding myself that soon I will follow where he has gone.

I am writing to you, my sister, because I believe its best to step into that unknown world with light baggage. The truth is that I too have been—how to put it—unenlightened? human? Humbly, I submit, that if just one person can wrench herself to embrace a sister, new beginnings can be made. A bracing breeze would ripple through our world

I still can't give you love. But forgiveness. Yes

A Death

"Nancy I'm leaving, I have to go to work today", her father said leaning over the ten year old child; she could smell the clean odor of his shirt, heard the concern in his voice. She shifted and pretended to sleep, pressing her cheek against the rough sheet; her thin little body, her buckteeth biting her lower lip, her shortly cropped thin hair falling over her face. She felt throughout herself how sullen
and unlovable she was. She knew her father left a bowl out and the cold cereal and a note on the wood table in the kitchen.

"It's not that I want to leave, but my boss expects me to come in." Then in a softer voice as if to himself, he said "It's hot as hell today. I wish I could just sit home in my underwear with a cold beer".

Go, go" her head pounded. She had been waiting to be alone all this time anyway. People had rushed about, visiting, bringing boxes of candies and cookies she would not taste, flowers that she would not smell, stroking her head, their touch making her flinch. They smiled at her father who stayed home from work, "Maybe it's for the best? Anna suffered so much. If you need something Ben, anything at all, don't hesitate. How sad, very sad to lose her mother so young, poor child, She's very sensitive...not taking it well, Anything at all, don't forget", and then always, the quick, flashing smile and her father smiling back in his friendly way, the door opening showing the yellow light of the hall, and then closing. In the narrow bed Nancy waited until she heard her father's footsteps on the wood floor and then the sound of the door closing again. She blinked her eyes.

She sat up; her small feet brushed the bare, cool floor. There was linoleum on the floor with a nursery rhyme design, "Too babyish" she had always thought before, but now it gave her pleasure. She did not want to grow; she wanted it always to be like now.

Her room was painted blue-green and the shades were drawn. She went over to one of the windows, opened the blind and looked out. An old man was standing in front of the apartment house opposite her looking up at her. Why was he staring she wandered.... had he heard her mother had died? She looked more intently and recognized Mr. Davis.

She would see him sometimes at the park and if she happened to walk by him he always began to mutter in a low growling way and once he had even reached out to touch her with his wrinkled hands for a moment, pulling her so close to him that she smelled his sour breath and saw the dirty spots all over the front of his pants. It disgusted her to remember it, especially the way he had laughed and laughed as if he enjoyed having frightened her. Now a strange, tingling thought passed through her mind as she looked down at him, and saw Hsu put his hand up over his eyes to shade them. He would never bother her again. She was above him, higher than he was. He would have heard what had happened to her mother and he would pity hen he would be afraid to bother her.

She pulled the shade down with a snap and ran to the closet. Impulsively she took out her only party dress that she was supposed to save. Then as she slipped it on shimmering about her, red and white striped silk with rhinestone buttons and puffed nylon sleeves, she felt light and free.

After eating breakfast and washing up she went into the living room sitting lightly and delicately on the couch, her heart beating like a clock with the quiet of the apartment, although outside cars beeped, people shouted in their guttural Brooklyn accents, children played, a clothesline squeaked on rusty pulleys and a sanitation department truck whirred along spraying steaming water on the pavement--nine in the morning and already a hot August. "I want to sit home with a beer". How could he forget as fast as he did? "They can fry eggs on the street," her father had said that the night before. She had glared at him, but he did not even notice the hatred in her eyes at him, that he could say that, what everyone said, that he did what everyone did, that he watched television. He acted as if nothing had happened, he said "Your mother..." when he said that she flinched. She said to him, her voice pleading, "You are not going to sleep in her bedroom, are you?" He had slept on the couch the last few months so as not to disturb his sick wife, even though he was so tall and he had to curl up and it hurt his back, "Jut why

Nancy?" he looked at her in surprise, not understanding. "Please don't, please, please don't sleep there", and she could not keep the anger out of her voice. "All right" he said finally and reached out to touch her and she had to keep herself from running away, to stand still because he was going to do what she wanted for her sake.

She got up and went into the other bedroom that her mother had used, large, white, mysterious, ghostly, and holy. She had her mother to herself, and greedily she sucked in the dry, clean feel of her, feeling exited. She did not think of her mother as a small body shriveling in that large bed, her hair tangled and white against the pillow, did not think of her mother saying "Give me my pills, my nightmare pills", always angry, furious with her husband, her child, her cheeks sunken, her arms swelling, little angry screams emitted by her throat, but as a wild, golden bird with green and blue spots on its wings, fluttering about the room, "Dear mother, dear mother" she prayed, the words coming naturally to her lips replacing God's name, a pink mist forming at the windows, spreading throughout the room and flowing over the mirror.

One time, they were going to see the ocean in the wintertime and her mother sat beside her on the trolley, absently playing with Nancy's hand, tracing each of her nails with her finger, and then holding her arm tight about her waist while they walked on the boardwalk, with the wind tearing at them and the ocean pounding beyond, green, white and furiously pounding up onto the grey sand. They walked together up and down the planking in quick steps, her mother shouting and laughing merrily above the sound of the wind "Now this is really refreshing". It felt like they were the only two people in the world.

So it was now. She could share nothing with anyone but her mother; they were all alone in the world. How she hated the woman at the funeral who had said, "You must accept. Adjust." She went over to the dresser and the draw squeaked as she opened it to take out a large, pink wool shawl.

After this she got her key from the cupboard in the kitchen and slipped the string to which it was attached about her neck. Downstairs she stood in the sun, wrapped in the warm shawl, her back to the brick wall of her house as her mother had so many times before at the beginning of cancer. She tilted her head back to the sun thinking a singsong of "I have been sick, I have been sick". She would not let herself notice the heat or that her cheeks were flushed. Her child's heart beat pure, cleansed. When she slept at night she tried to lie on her right side as her mother had because her mother's left side hurt; she tried to do everything her mother had* to recreate it all.

A neighbor came by, a large woman with a wrinkled face and a soft, fat hand with which she touched the child's shoulder. She said, "Are you all right Nancy?"
Taken by surprise, the girl felt terror. The woman said, "My husband and I feel so sorry". She was talking to her as if she

were an adult. All these weeks she had kept herself from grief and now this woman because she took her by surprise made it rise up oppressive and unbearable. The woman touched her on the shoulder again. "That is the way life is Nancy". She felt the tears welling up from deep within her. The shawl had dropped down and she left it behind in a heap.

"Nancy" the woman called. Some great energy coalesced run faster than she had ever run, her little feet pumping, her chest heaving, not knowing where she was going, wood and brick houses, sycamore trees whirling about her eyes dizzily. Blood was pounding in her ears and with great joy she thought she heard again the strong wings beating of that beautiful bird who was her mother above, deep in the white clouds, and yet close to her.

She saw the iron link fence of the park and then knew she was going to the park to play, to swing...the baseball field, the basketball court, and the playground. Some men from a nearby Italian neighborhood with thick black hair, hairy arms and chest were playing baseball in undershirts. She walked by carelessly not pressing to the fence as she usually did. A yellow bat was powerful and menacing as a man swung it round and round in his hands. Voices chanted " atta baby.,.o.k. baby,,", then changing "girly, watch out, watch out.,,", The hard, white ball bounced off the ground twice, losing some momentum and then hit her. She pressed her hand to her leg where she was hurt and her eyes filled with tears. "Hey are you all right?" She walked away, without looking back, numbly, anesthetized, confused, around the flagpole, the park house and to the playground.

At the swings she hopped up to sit on a canvas slung seat. She swung high with all her might, the chains jangled, her bones rattled in her skin, her protruding upper teeth bit into her lip. She was going to touch the sky, high, high, pumping, breathless, higher, everything swirled. A sky writer airplane wrote "Drink Coke," below mothers, children, some old men on a bench. With each swing she felt stronger, more excited; the pain in her leg throbbed only slightly. Nancy thought: my mother is home, my mother is cooking lamb chops,..back to the brick wall of the park house behind her...and fresh carrots and peas...to the clouds...scraping the carrots, getting out a glass into which to pour milk... Some younger girls cam over, three of them chewing bubble gum and wearing blue jeans. "Hey give us a turn on the swing....you're too big. Is there something wrong with you?" "I'm going on the slide now". She hopped down and walked away.

She happened to glance at the old men sitting on the bench-lax faces, rheumy eyes, silver hair, yellowed shirts, and baggy trousers. They whispered, stared at her, then called out "Come here...come here." They all tittered. "Me, you mean me?" Nancy wandered. She saw that one of them was Mr. Davis. She looked away and pretended not to hear when he called "Nancy" and instead walked towards the sand pit. A small, blonde haired boy was shoveling sand into a wagon and his mother said, "Don't get muddy". She wanted to play with the boy and for his mother to notice her and like her.

The old men continued to call to her. "Come on little girl, we're talking to you, you better come." Mr. Davis on the end cackled like a rooster taking flight under the shade of the tree, his face folding in wrinkles. She could not understand his anger at being old, lust for a child, lust like an amputated limb, old man's jokes, strange, devilish, must hurt, a weak hand rising will hit something weak. "Nancy" he crowed. She could not ignore it now. The mother of the small, blonde boy stared her in a puzzled way and forced to go. She ran over the black asphalt, mirror, porous like a sponge, obedient, be polite to old people. Anyway they would be nice to her? They had to.

The old men, four of them, rose from the bench, crowded about her, jostled each other in their excitement, locked her in the center. It was all the same to them, a mother's death (they were close to it themselves--Mr. Davis would die in two weeks of hardening of the arteries), or a fly buzzing nearby. They were no longer capable of making distinctions. Everything blended in their long hours of bored waiting and sitting.

"How is your mother?" Mr. Davis, the ring leader talked for them all, "She's fine", "Oh really?" She looked defiantly about. "She*s fine, she's fine" Nancy screamed at the top of her lungs for the whole world to hear. The four of them, led by Mr. Davis acted in unison. "Answer us, tell us the truth". "She's fine," the girl said again. Ha, ha, "Liar. Little liar,...she's dead...don't tell us different,

283

she's dead." They all broke into snorting laughter, wheezing, slapping their thighs, tottering about her. Above their grey and white heads and their stale smells she saw some clouds and blue sky. Empty.

Her mother was gone, lost to her. The blood drained from her face. She didn't know how it happened. She was just completely empty now. The old men shuffled back to their bench, sleep overcoming the triumphant grins on their wrinkled lips.

Pink Pants Blues

A few years ago I was on the way to my doctor's when a pair of pink pants in a shop window stopped me short in my tracks. The mannequin modeling them wore a tight white t-shirt, black high heels and huge sunglasses. The lycra pants clung to her hips and legs so they glowed and sizzled like flame. A woman noticed my rapt attention and tittered, "Who would wear those outrageous things?" "No one I know!" I agreed.

When she'd moved on, I went into the store and I couldn't resist trying them on. Alone in the dressing room, I felt as if I were pasting vivid life over my legs. Before I knew it I was doing a graceful dance. I glided and pirouetted about in the small booth. The pants evoked pink fluffy feathers, warm sun and blue-green waters. In my imagination, I was one of a flock of Florida flamingos. There was no question but I had to have those pants. By the time I made my purchase I was nearly late for my appointment. I ran along swinging my bag and headed towards the hospital.

I'd had a biopsy the week before. The doctor had asked me to come in to check how the scar was healing. He was a big burly, blond Irishman, son of a New York policeman, well intentioned, bumbling in manner, although other doctors I respected spoke highly of his surgical skill. He'd cut my lump out, peered at it and laughed, "Hey this is nothing. What was all the excitement about?"

This time, however, he walked into the examination room with a serious demeanor and said, "I've got good news and bad news." Dressed in a blue, paper gown, I was sitting on the examination table. My dangling feet made me feel childlike. "The good news?" I asked, smiling, disbelieving.

"We caught it early. We're going to treat it."

"The bad news goes without saying," I said, hoping that even now he would clear up a misunderstanding, but his head gave a quick jerk of acknowledgment. "You could have knocked me over with a feather," his voice trailed off. The pathology report had surprised him.

Legally bound to inform me of alternative treatments, he launched into his list like a Chinese restaurant waiter reciting the combination dinner menu. One could take off the entire breast or one could take off less flesh but add radiation, and so on.

"How am I going to tell my husband?"

"Just tell him you have good news and bad news," he said, suddenly tired, anxious to move on. "I have four other women to tell today.

"Maybe I should have a mastectomy," I said.

"I don't think so. I know you. You wouldn't do well."

David was gray faced but calm. He sat on a chair opposite while I lay beached on the couch. We'd married in college two decades before and yet we didn't really know how to talk. Everything was tact and indirection, so when he told me I couldn't take it; I thought he was talking about himself.

Later we were out at a Chinese restaurant with a doctor friend of ours. Nearby in a huge fish tank, white and golden koi swam round and round. Waiters brought out tureens of soup and platters of puffy white buns and steamed whole fish. There were Chinese families crowded around large round tables, toothless grandmothers gumming their food, toddlers grabbing chopsticks in their tiny hands and crying babies. Dishes clattered. Voices echoed off the tile walls.

David and our friend made an effort to talk gaily, but I was distracted wondering what should I do? By the end of the meal I was in tears. "I ought to call the surgeon and tell him I want a mastectomy," I said. "What if the cancer's multi-focal? What if there aren't clear margins?" By now I knew the terminology and that my case had certain puzzling peculiarities.

Both David and our friend looked helpless and leapt to assure me the lesser surgery was all right. I knew they wanted to tell me what I wanted to hear. Our doctor friend would have acted differently with a patient in his office than he did with me in the restaurant.

"There are women who go in for radiation who don't even know they are multi-focal," David said.

"And it doesn't work!" I replied.

"How do you know it doesn't work? It must work for a percentage of them," David insisted.

"I'm sure that's true," our friend said. "Let me pay the check," he added, at a loss, wanting to change the diagnosis and the treatments available to more humane ones. But taking the check was the only thing at hand.

In the days before the surgery, my sister-in-law, Thea, sent me a small, glass bell. The accompanying note said, "You can use it to ring for David."

I burst into tears when I read that note. Thea probably only intended to lighten the situation and cheer me up, but for me the bell was a symbol of helplessness and death. I felt terrible bitterness even to have her gift in the house and had to give it away immediately.

If not for that bell, I still might have phoned the surgeon and revised my plans. I was trying to save my life, but I'd sunk into an anxious delirium where all I could think of was Thea's bell. This craziness was stronger than my rationality.

"I have good news and bad news," the surgeon bustled into my hospital room with that sad formula once again. I lay in bed, my chest swathed in a pressure bandage. The shock of his words brought on a flow of menstrual blood.

288

"We didn't get all the cancer. I'll have to do a mastectomy after all," he said, "and a skin graft might be necessary." He spoke about the danger of the skin graft, of possible infections, of a long hospital stay. I watched a beam of light flash from the window and bounce off his front teeth— dentures, I realized. I felt miserable for my vain, trivial noticing, David, at the foot of the bed, reached for my hand. "What about my other breast?"

"It's hard to know. It may be full of cancer too, but none of it showing up on the mammogram."

"Take both my breasts off," I begged, swinging from desperation to preserve my body to a frantic urge for sacrifice.

"Now you're cooking," the doctor agreed.

"Let's take care of it once and for all," David said.

We smiled at each other, suddenly, reckless, exhilarated as if jumping off a high cliff.

My having been diagnosed with cancer may have saved several lives. People hearing about my misfortune, rushed to have the medical check-ups they'd been avoiding.

My mother-in-law phoned and told me, "I was telling my doctor about you. I said, 'I never had one of those mammogram things.' So he said, 'Well, why don't you?' So after I had one, I went in to talk to him again, and he got up on the table to sit next to me and put his arm around me. I knew this wasn't for romantic reasons, that he was going to tell me something really bad."

My heart pounded, but I made my voice calm as we talked. She too had to choose from the virtuoso treatments. I'd never heard her sounding so vulnerable. Years before, when David first took me home to meet her and his father, he'd warned, "My mother wears the pants in the family." I soon saw what he'd meant. Clara did wear pants that were unusual for women of her generation, and hers looked like army issue khakis. They kept her warm during freezing mid-western winters when she drove Sol to his grocery store. He'd had a stroke that left him partially paralyzed and needing her constantly at his side. Often he was clumsy and she'd glare or make some furious remark. Like an army captain, she barked orders at him. But Sol's disposition was so mild7 his gratitude so great, that he never complained. He died just before his fifty-ninth birthday and left her well off after their years of toil. Relieved of responsibilities, Clara moved to a warmer climate and exchanged the khaki pants for a wardrobe of frilly, pastel sundresses.

After talking with her about the treatments, I said, "Put Marty on." Her second husband was a plump, jolly old man who played endless gin rummy games at the Fort Lauderdale Senior Center.

"How're doing?" I asked5usually, he answered with a quip like, "I'm doing the laundry. What are you doing?" but this time he said dully, "I don't want to lose Clara." 'You won't! Do you think she'd leave and let go of a good catch like you?" I

290

wanted to infuse him with the strength to be a help and comfort. But it turns out, just like Clara, he wasn't good near sick people.

Two weeks later when she had her surgery, Marty told us, "I'm not visiting her at the hospital. She's crying all the time, and I don't want to baby her. It's better for her to just get used to it."

David acted far differently to me. He'd learned his gentle ways as a contrast to his mother's brusqueness to Sol.

For a long time my twenty-year-old son had had a mole on his back but even though it had bled several times, he'd let it go. It seemed, he told us later, "childish and unmasculine to go running to a doctor." Finding out about my cancer, he made an appointment at the university infirmary. A doctor did a biopsy then and there because he couldn't risk a moment's delay. My son's cancer had sunk deeply into him, and there was a terrible risk for his life.

I was heart-broken, nearly insane that summer, for myself, for my mother-in-law, but mostly for my son just embarking on life. It occurred to me it was fortunate I got cancer because it made my son go to the doctor. Even if I died, I might have saved his life that was exactly what I would have chosen to do.

We went to Ireland to celebrate a year of survival since the surgery. David and I visited Celt burial caves. We stood in a dark, cramped space in a crowd of tourists while the young guide glanced up and spoke admiringly of how the roof had not leaked once, not over hundreds of years. "You know what it's like in Ireland," she said. "The storms blow in from the Atlantic, do the worst to us, and then the weather moves on sweet and balmy to the rest of the Europe. We're the front-runners and it's shaped our characters."

David and I exchanged a glance. The fact was that our roof had been leaking for several years. Sometimes we just ignored it, or David climbed out on the roof's steep incline and dabbed at seams with black, sticky sealants. The patching helped for a while, but never for long. The roof kept leaking, here, there, then somewhere else. The roofers came, walked about noisily over our heads, then climbed down and talked with us. A year and a half ago, we'd even hired one company to replace a quarter of the roof. It didn't make any difference. This last winter, dark, damp splotches appeared on the walls and ceiling plaster.

One of the reasons we hadn't paid too much attention to this was because the cancer preoccupied us. Illness is a schoolmaster with a cane. It teaches so much and so quickly that there's scarcely time to learn one lesson before another blow strikes. It was in Dublin, at the tail end of our vacation, that I noticed the lump. I was dressing and caught sight of it from the corner of my eye. Oh yes, that, I thought. The faint pain, the itch, the red place. I'd had my suspicions and ignored them, the way I'd learned to ignore so much. Otherwise how could I live from moment to moment?

But that morning in the dimly lit bed and breakfast I let the world explode and looked. Oh God. Oh God. My head whirled. David returned from jogging, opened the door, and knew at once. "What?" He raced across the room to my side. Mute, I pulled down the collar of my t-shirt to show him.

That very morning we drove to Dun Laoghaire to take the ferry to Holyhead in Wales, and from there the train to London. A crowd streamed onto the boat. Two guards stood on either side looking for a terrorist to reveal him or herself in the curl of a lip, the flash of an eye, the tremor of a hand, the too-fast or the too-slow walk, the staring or averted eyes.

A guard pulled David aside and searched his suitcase, shaking out shirts, patting pants pockets. Then other guards gathered about. Two of them frisked David. The other passengers kept pushing by unheeded. In the end, with the greatest reluctance, they let David go. An inner radar told them he was carrying an explosive, but they hadn't known how to find it.

Cancer sprouted on my body. My doctors daubed at the tumors with this and that, trying with each treatment to buy me a year, maybe two years, trying to tease a whole life for me out of bits and pieces. Shortly before my fiftieth birthday, my doctor persuaded me to have a dangerous experimental treatment. I went into the hospital with the expectation of staying there two months, that is if I didn't die first. My body would be blasted with poisons.

The surgeon stuck tubing into a vein in my chest. Huge bags of fluids dripped into that tubing and the bags hung on a hat rack-looking stainless steel pole on wheels. I was shackled to that pole, had to walk with it, bring it into the toilet and even the shower. Through the tubing flowed the doctors' massive attack, the landing on the beach at Normandy. My doctors would nearly kill me in order to kill the cancer.

'My summer of drugs,' 'my summer of love,' I called it. I kept dreaming about Iranians. I thought I was in Paris, not San Francisco. The phone rang. I spoke with Tom, a friend. The nurse had told me he'd called before and was frantic to talk to me. "Let's talk about you. Let's talk about anything you want. You're the one in the hospital," he said in a slurred, fast voice. For once, he wouldn't say anything about his wife who like a yo-yo kept leaving and coming back.

Outside a window sealed against all microbes, steam shovels excavated a huge, yellow hole in the ground. The earth-moving machines, initially a fluorescent orange were soon covered with dust and looked as if the color was bleached out of them. Each day, they shrieked like vultures.

I got a bloody nose and the nurses raced for transfusions. My sense of smell was acute and the transfused blood dripping into my vein smelled sour and sickened me. I flung off the covers and rushed to throw-up in the bathroom. In the mirror, I saw the whites in my eyes had turned red, all the tiny blood vessels ruptured. The skin along my chest and legs had stained red too.

Brown moles sprouted on my face. When I opened my mouth, it was a dark hole, full of blisters. My bare scalp burned. I kept hearing the shrieks of the vulture machines outside.

The woman in the next room died.

In the middle of the night a young nurse found me crying and asked, "Shall I pray for you?" She held me in her arms like a mother. Like nuns, the nurses had modernized their dress in the last few years, some of them reducing their official uniform simply to a pin with their name and the designation, R.N. The one named Gay was older than the others, perhaps in her late thirties. Her blond hair was cut short and combed back. She had a bouncy walk, and she wore a shirt of orange and purple printed with chartreuse green parrots. The birds flickered about me as she made my bed. One midnight, she lingered, telling me about her hunger for life, that she'd worked as a bartender, saved up, went to nursing school, then she saved up again and went to a video dating service to find a sweetheart. With an impish smile, she said, "I found two possibilities. It's been hard to decide between them."

David was there when I woke in the morning, sitting on a chair in the corner of the room watching me as he would all day, as if his attention could keep me alive. He made a graph that showed my rising white blood count and showed it to the doctors when a group of them made the grand rounds. "What exactly is your profession?" a young intern, Dr. Turner, asked him. The graph was done with the precise draftsmanship of a research chemist. People scarcely give more than a glance to such charts in a textbook or a newspaper. No one stops to think a graph can be a stenographic notation of the heart.

Poor Doctor Turner. The only nourishment I could get down was an occasional lifesaver candy and a sip of Coke, but I looked up at his smooth face, into his innocent blue eyes and told him, "False rumors have taken root about me. People think I don't eat. You have to rectify this with the truth." The next morning the grand round stopped just outside my door so Dr. Turner could play his joke on me. He told the other doctors, "She just doesn't eat at all." Then he poked his head in the door winked and cried, "Pack your things up. We're getting rid of you."

The metal pole was unhooked and I was at liberty to dance and I did take a few jig steps, although not too many. I was sicker than I'd let on to Dr. Turner, except a sap was rising in me and I wanted to get out into the world again.

David brought a bag with fresh clothes for me to wear home. Inside I found a t-shirt and to my amazement, my pink pants. They still had their tags on as I'd never worn them. I held them up and asked, "Why these?" "I figured you earned the right," David said grinning. "Go ahead. Put them on." He wandered out into the hall to wait. When I was dressed I called him in. He looked me over, up and down. "Hubba, hubba," he pronounced and we burst out laughing. "Hey, where are you going," he called to me as I dashed out the door. "I want to show Robin." Robin was a patient who'd appeared in the hall with a furry cap on her baldhead. A raccoon tail hung down from the back of the hat, and deer's antlers adorned the top. I couldn't hope to match her splendor, but even so I hurried to her room. Just putting those pink pants on gave me vitality.

A few days after I got home, I heard the news about Tom. One evening he'd hooked up a pipe to the dryer in his garage, wrapped himself in a sheet, closed his eyes and turned his face to the wall while gas poured into the air and filled his lungs. He'd arranged things so his wife would discover him first.

When I heard the news I wished so much that she'd got to him in time. Then like me he'd have touched death. Not a fatal contact, but an electric jolt that might have revived him.

After a few months David and I had some house renovations done. We had the foundation bolted, the chimney strapped and fortified against earthquakes, and the roof stripped. There was a thunder of hammers. Rock and roll blasted from radios. Workers crawled everywhere, in the basement where some of the materials were stored, up scaffolding on the sides of the house, and on the roof to rip off all previous roofs.

Dust and hidden microbes flew into the air. The attic lay exposed like a body cut open to its bones. Dry rot was excised. Men crawled over the roof ribbing with hammers, with nails sucked between their lips as they unrolled and smoothed a blanket of black tar paper.

Huge stacks of metallic tiles arrived. They were imported from Australia, that pliable, masculine continent peopled with the descendants of convicts. The salesman had shown how the tiles locked together so they were impenetrable. "Like a locked safe," he said. We'd signed a long contract. It guaranteed against leaks, against hurricane and fire damage for the rest of our lives.

When she came outside Ruth felt a wave of pleasure from the bright light. Thank God she could still get around, she thought, not like Mrs. Dubrowsky who slipped on the ice in January and her hip never healed. Her sons had come for her and put her away in a convalescent home. No one sat in the little park now that separated her project building from the one across the way. Perhaps when Ruth returned from the store, if the sun would shine between the two high buildings, she would sit there for a while. Thank God, thank God, she thought, deciding to walk all the way over to Orchard Street for tie carton of milk she needed. It was a blessing she could get around. She was feeling well.

She had heard only last week that Mrs. Dubrowsky, who used to sit each day on the bench next to the concrete turtle, was dead. If she had known in time she would have gone to the funeral. She must try not to think about depressing things, not to think about Henry's visit last night. Why had her son-in-law come? She was so used to no one coming. She had not seen Edna, her daughter, for over a year. "What do you want to stay in the Project for? Some colored, some Puerto Rican will rob you, or do worse. Why don't you move out of this jungle?" Henry had asked. Also he had talked about her older sister Rose. Several times Rose had said "We're both alone now, come and live with me in Sheepshead." Rose (protected by her brood of five sons, her

299

ingratiating manner) she knew offered favors only when she was certain they would not be accepted. It was ridiculous, how could she and Rose live together when they could not get along? Now Henry told her last night, the five sons were sending Rose to Florida to live in a retirement hotel. "Why don't you go with her?" he had asked. It really made her feel sorry for Rose, for a woman like Rose—who did she know and what did she care about in Florida when her family was here? She would have to phone Rose, to go see her and say goodbye.

As Ruth approached the busy Avenue and the shops, pungent odors came down the street even before she stood in front of the delicatessen and saw the derma, kishke and cold cuts arranged on platters behind the plate glass window. Her mouth watered. On the next block there was nothing but bridal stores with wooden models in the windows wearing sweeping white gowns, followed by an entourage of bridesmaids, all standing behind the announcement *"Si habla espagnol."*

An old woman passed pulling a shopping cart. Ruth clutched her pocketbook. She saw her own reflection in a plate glass window. Her eyes, shrunken face, the hump on her back, and the loneliness of her eyes—and she thought, "I dress well." It meant, well, so much, going into the street with pride. The suit she wore was finely made with finished seams, fabric covered buttons and tailored buttonholes. She had been an expert seamstress, working thirty-five years in a sweatshop—a high fashion house. But it disturbed her that the suit was a little large and did not fit perfectly; she had lost weight this last year.

A gypsy woman with dangling gold earrings sat on a doorstep, laughing, suckling a child, her breast exposed over the top of her blouse. "Pig" Ruth muttered and looked away.   No one else seemed to notice the impropriety.

When she got to Orchard Street she went into one of the shops. Unsteady motes of light came from a hidden skylight, the only illumination. The walls were so narrow that they seemed to squeeze together. Material was piled in bolts that reached to the ceiling. "Good cloth. You couldn't get anything like the value anywhere else in the city." A young woman spoke to her in Yiddish. Ruth asked, "How's business?" "How could it be? Always bad." Somewhere in the back, three young children played and she caught sight of the thin, sickly husband, with his high forehead and white skin, drinking tea. Ruth did not stay long, had come in, not to buy, but simply to touch the material and to ask the girl, Chicky, about her mother and father. It was so unusual a young girl, still in Williamsburg, not running out to the suburbs like Edna. The woman asked about Edna. "Oh she's fine. She calls everyday. She looks after herself real well. She sees that everything is perfect. She's not afraid to talk to anyone. She has a mouth, my Edna..." She laughed, a sound like a curl of smoke in the dark store. Then she quivered thinking of Henry smiling at her. "Why don't you get out of here...move?" Edna's words-—she had sent him.

Then later in the evening last night, the phone began to ring. She let it ring several times, and then it stopped. She had already opened the couch with the usual difficulty up into a bed and began to climb beneath the covers. Almost at once the phone rang again. This time she picked up the receiver. "Ma, how are you?" Edna's voice grated. "Why are you fighting me ma? I've begged you a thousand times to get out of that lousy neighborhood. I thought maybe you'd listen to Henry....But no. Not you! You had to make a big dramatic scene with my husband."

Fury, the tap of Edna's fury to be opened and her desire to rule and be obeyed. "You're always this way ma, as long as I've known you, stubborn." and then swerving, "We're only interested in your own good ma.." She heard Edna was crying. For whom, she had wondered. Sometimes she thought she might have the phone taken out. What did she need it for? What?

"Well nice talking to you Chicky." She picked up her pocketbook that she had set down on a table. She hastened to go. She never wanted to impose herself and all her chance conversations were fleeting. It was strange that none of the sounds of the street penetrate the store, as if all the material absorbed it—-because when she came outside again she was startled for a moment at the way the driver in the large, white Oldsmobile pressed on his horn and bellowed at the man with the striped peddler's cap who had run out in front of him. All the cars moved slowly, stopping and starting.

From wooden wagons that lined both sides of the street, hawkers shouted urging passers-by to buy fruit, to buy pots and pans, shirts, buttons and vegetables. Ruth passed the kosher butcher and between the legs of matrons buying their dinner, a chicken escaped and danced out before her, ruffling its red feathers, bloody and headless, but still pulsing with life. The butcher's boy in a soiled white apron put out his hand and pulled it back. Jews, Chassids, in long gabardines (like her father) walked up and down the street with their hands in their pockets, staring at the pavement, their lips moving, their bodies rocking and swaying to the melodies they would chant at the afternoon prayer service.

Ruth stopped at a small grocery and waiting her turn behind several women, bought the carton of milk. She held it to her body as she moved along the street, and when a man bumped into her, the carton grazed her breast where the surgery had been and she gave a small cry of pain. Not that it ached after so long, but it made something within her hurt—a feeling of ugliness, a feeling of her husband abandoning her (never mind the heartache, she had put out a police warrant for him so he would be made to support her and the child—but it had been no use, he had not been found), A feeling of loss..loss.,.the surgeon in a green suit and cap leaning towards her and telling her not to be afraid and her thinking of those few people she cared for, becoming sick, dying....

But she had survived. She was dressed in a black silk suit that any lady who lived on Fifth Avenue would be glad to wear and walking along the street. She had survived and she did not like self-pity in herself. "I don't complain," she had said to Henry last night. "If I can't have my independence, I would rather be dead." The words had beat against the walls of her body she felt them so strongly. Even now as she passed the bridal shops again, they beat like swords within her and she could see in a mirror in one of the stores her jaw trembled as she moved it back and forth as if grinding her gums together. "If I can't have my independence, if I can't..." With each step she took she felt the import of those words and she made a movement of her whole body, of shaking and straightening her back and it reminded her just of that headless chicken that had run in front of her.

As she was coming closer to the Project she began to feel how tired she was. She stopped in front of an appliance store to watch television with a half dozen young boys with skullcaps and long corkscrew curled side-locks. Nowhere else is it like this, she thought, watching a man embrace a crying young woman on the soundless television beyond the plate glass-- while the elevator train rumbled overhead and darkened the street—and the fair faced boys with black, eyes and red lips raised soprano voices above the sound and chatted in Yiddish. They pushed each other and poked each other.

Ruth moved aside, her hand in front of her place where the surgeon had removed the cancer. All the people I care about are somehow in these streets} nowhere else is it like this, nowhere. And suddenly as the train had passed she felt a pang of sadness thinking of her sister Sarah who had jumped from the roof of a building and died. The young woman on the television was laughing now. "The beauty" Sarah had been called, much lovelier then the girl on the screen—just as Ruth had been considered "the ugly one." Whenever she thought of Sarah it bewildered Ruth that Sarah had given up. To be jilted was not so bad as cancer or being left with a child to raise yourself. How could a lover's betrayal matter so much if one was young and had golden hair and perfect features as Sarah did? She envisioned her sister's loveliness and a feeling of humility swept Ruth that she could not understand such beauty and its fragility.

Ruth moved towards the corner where at the foot of the stairway to the elevated train was a green kiosk. She bought a newspaper for a dime, the "Daily Tablet," the scandal sheet. There was a new man there now, with a goiter condition, a swelling of his neck, a ripped green sweater and dark sunglasses, who nodded to her as he took her money. "New here?" she asked. "Yeah, the other guy retired." "Oh really?"

A group of young colored men passed, all in caps, flashy shirts, tight pants. They congregated on the corner. A handsome Puerto Rican boy was with them and said to Ruth "Hello Mrs. Maloof" in a voice that was really charming. She recognized the son of the family that lived next door, and she felt more comfortable as she moved away from the kiosk. She slipped the newspaper into the paper bag with the milk carton. "The neighborhood's changing," she had thought, and the thought fluttered from her mind like the candy wrappers and scraps of newspaper discarded on the pavement about her. She wondered where the blind newspaper man had gone? Where had he retired? He had been always there in the kiosk since she could remember, steady, like some clock. Where?

Then she thought of Rose. She was leaving. It made her heart stop. Rose had always boasted about her children and all they did for her, phoning to describe stridently each scrap of affection she received. "My Phil asked me to dinner. He*s going to come and pick me up."

She and Rose had never gotten along, but she did not want her to go. When would they meet? Would Rose die down there, the way Mrs. Dubrowsky had died— an old plant pulled out of the soil. To move would be like being stripped naked. Here, she could walk along and say "I have my life," even if it meant just this walk and sitting in her one room apartment the rest of the afternoon. Somehow if she went away the emptiness would be louder.

A train going in the other direction clattered overhead again, making the street vibrate, making people stiffen and shout to each other. That was what it was, there was life here. She felt it as she moved slowly along, so exhausted that she had to stop for a few moments to catch her breath. She could see around the corner the looming presence of the Projects, the seven (windowed, but otherwise blank) rectangular buildings that climbed to the sky. She could not explain it to Henry, but there was life here. Her blood, her veins, her arteries, her flesh shaped these streets. Her brain danced with the sound of the train that finally passed.

Helen and Adele

The surgeon bustled into the tiny examination room, smiling so broadly that Helen noticed he had shiny false teeth. A big Irishman with a potbelly, he couldn't have been more than fifty, only a decade older than herself.

"I have good news and bad news. What do you want to hear?" he asked. His foot pressed the pedal beneath the sink and water whooshed over his hands as he soaped and scrubbed his fingers.

She was dressed in a paper gown and perched at the edge of the examining table in the windowless room. The walls, she noticed, were made of a perforated acoustic material. In the mirror over the doctor's shoulder, she saw a reflection of her straight blond hair and blue eyes. She looked washed out and thin. Her mouth was frozen into a smile like the doctor's. "The good news," she said.

"We caught it while it's small."

"I thought you said it wasn't cancer," she finally managed to utter. The word was uncertain in her mouth. Perhaps, she had misunderstood and he hadn't meant cancer. During the biopsy, he had examined the lump and told her, "It's nothing. You're fine."

"Well, you could have knocked me over with a feather when I got the report from path." He snapped a paper towel from the white metal dispenser, dried his hands and sat down in front of her on a small, wheeled stool. His hair was reddish gold and combed in a pompadour. He reminded her of a drake. While he nervously wheeled back and forth on the stool, he droned on and on about her options.

"You'll cut off the nipple too?"

"Uh-huh."

She began to cry.

He heaved himself up beside her and awkwardly put his arm about her shoulder. "I have four more women to tell today," he sighed.

Susan, her best friend phoned to say she had an acquaintance, a young woman who had been through the experience of breast cancer and who would be willing to talk about it and show her mastectomy. Would she like to meet her? Although dreading it, Helen agreed because she wanted to see a mastectomy, to absorb the shock before it happened to her.

Now as she nervously anticipated Adele's arrival, she scurried about straightening, picking up two-year-old Brent's toys. Since the doctor's visit, everything in her flat looked different to her, the white walls, the odd assortment of furniture, the cracked linoleum in the kitchen and the bright yellow cabinets she had once hired Hal to paint for her. Her father had been shocked when she had taken up with a "fly-by-night" who drifted from one odd job to another. He had told her, "If your mother was still alive, you'd have more self-respect." Probably he was right about that, but without Hal, she would never have had Brent.

From his bedroom came the peculiar puppy whimper which her son put himself to sleep with. She dared not look in on him. As quiet as she might be, Brent would hear and in a moment hoist himself up, stand there in his blue sleeper, his diaper bulging out, and one hand holding the spindle of the crib, the other his bottle. She was too tired to think of starting the bedtime routine again. As usual, she had been up before dawn, driving her van to the San Francisco flower market.

A wave of exhaustion swept over her and she sank onto the couch. In a moment she was asleep, dreaming of trying to pick up the cancerous lump with a tongs. Each time she tried, it scattered like quick silver. The ringing phone woke her, and she jerked the receiver to her ear. She assumed it must be Adele, but it was her eighty-year-old father who lived across the bay in an apartment in San Francisco. He said frantically, "Hello Helen...Helen." She had told him about the cancer two nights before.

Once again he wept, "Where's justice in this world? Why did this have to happen to you?" Although her parents had been separated, he said, "I'm glad your mother didn't live to see this."

"Don't cry, Dad. I'll be all right. Don't upset yourself."

Do you have a good doctor? Maybe you should go to Stanford. Don't they have the best there? Will you meet the anesthetist? That's the dangerous part. More than the surgery."

"I'm young. I can get through this."

"I'm scared they won't be able to wake you up."

She knew she had failed him. Her illness opened up his own terror of death. He always expected her to be around to help him. "How about a date for the week after my surgery?" she asked. "Will you take me to the Top of the Mark for a drink? I'm also going to ask you to buy me a new dress for my birthday."

"You bet I will," he told her, but in a little while he was back to crying, and she had to start calming him all over again. "Dad, I can handle this. Don't worry!"

"I know. You always had broad shoulders, sweetheart."

The doorbell buzzed, a blessed interruption because she didn't know how long she could keep going without bursting into tears herself. "Look Dad, someone's at the door. It's important. I'll get back to you. I love you."

Apparently Susan hadn't informed Adele that Helen was a florist. She came bearing a bouquet of roses. An athletic looking woman in her mid-thirties, she wore hiking boots, a low cut, bright orange blouse and a ring jangling with keys from her blue jeans. Wisps of purple feather earrings hung from her ear lobes. She had olive skin and dark eyes, but her hair was prematurely gray. "Helen?" she asked and seeing Helen's nod, hugged her tightly. Startled, Helen extricated herself with the mumbled

311

excuse, "the flowers." She had felt the hard unyieldingness of Adele's prosthesis.

Striding into the flat, Adele said, "Oh yes, I mustn't crush your flowers." She sniffed the roses before handing them over. "You know the chemotherapy smelled like roses." She added, "You look familiar."

"Do I?" Helen answered, although she too thought they had met before. She went to the kitchen to get a vase and as she cut the stems, recalled that her visitor had came into her shop the year before and extravagantly bought six dozen irises for a young woman dying of breast cancer. The memory made her uneasy about receiving these flowers.

"Don't they look beautiful," Adele exclaimed when Helen returned with the vase. "What a nice place you have." She looked about the living room with its high ceiling and gleaming oak floor, and furnished with the old fashioned pieces Helen inherited after her mother's death ten years before. At that time, Helen also received the legacy that enabled her to leave a detested bookkeeper's job and buy the flower store. "How are you managing?" Adele asked.

"I'm managing," Helen replied. Her father had worn her thin. She wanted Adele to undress quickly and show her mastectomy and leave, yet she felt guilty at her abruptness. After all, Adele was doing her a favor, and had even brought a gift. "Why don't you sit down?" she asked and pointed to the easy chair where she and Brent curled up together when she read to him. She could see the one about a fire engine half tucked behind the cushion, and Adele noticing too asked, "Do you have a child?"

"Yes, a little boy."

"How old is he? I've got a kid myself, but he's thirteen. You know one of those infamous teenagers. Tonight he told me he wanted to have junk food, potato chips and cokes like all his friends. He's sick of the healthy stuff I bring home from the health food restaurant where I work. I quote, 'Your puke makes me sick.'" Adele threw back her head and laughed. "Is your son sleeping? Can I peek in on him?"

"Brent's too light a sleeper."

"Can I see a photo?"

Helen got one from her wallet and found Adele endearing as she cooed and pressed her lips to Brent's image just as if he were there in her arms. Soon Brent's photograph was supplanted by ones of Adele's son. "There's my Marky," she beamed. He was a thin, spindly boy who lacked his mother's robustness. She took another photo out of her purse. It took Helen a moment to recognize Adele with dark black hair. "It's from before.... the chemotherapy turned my hair gray." Adele's voice was husky with feeling. Helen wondered if in the future she too would pass out pictures of what she had once been?

To ease the tension of the moment, she offered to make coffee. "Why don't I just help myself?" Adele marched off to the kitchen and Helen felt too exhausted to object. Soon Adele returned with steaming cups of peppermint tea. "Relax," she ordered. "You have to put your needs first now. Let other people take care of you. Who do you have to help you? I can drop in any time you need me."

"I'm okay. I'm trying to live the way I usually do. If I don't keep busy, I'm just going to fall into a pit I can't climb out of." She wasn't used to people helping her, but now felt she had to take care of other people more, her father and even Susan who was so worried. Yet with all her show of independence, she yearned for someone to tend her and make well this illness the way her mother used to do when she skinned a knee or felt feverish. Adele had been through it herself, the only one Helen knew who had, and she felt drawn to her.

"It's almost two years since it happened to me and every anniversary I know I've survived another year. You'll remember the date of your surgery; it'll be like your birthday. You know, when I look back to two years ago, I actually miss the way it was during the crisis."

"How could that be?"

"Everything was so clear and intense. It must sound strange to you, but I don't regret the cancer, not the changes it forced me to make inwardly and in my life. I meditate. I devote much of my time to helping women with cancer, women when they first get it, and women who are dying. What kind of support do you have? Brent's father?"

"We broke up before Brent was born."

"Could you contact him?"

With a mirthless laugh, Helen answered, "We didn't have much of a relationship."

"How so?"

"Just one of those things. He's gone."

"Doesn't he visit Brent?"

"He's never seen Brent. I've been alone these last two years, but I thought maybe things would change. Maybe when Brent was older, I'd meet someone. Now, with the cancer..." Helen shrugged, "I doubt there will be anyone else."

"Not necessarily. You think no one will want you because of your mastectomy? I've had lovers since mine. It would have been sad if the only one I had to fuck was Neil."

"Neil?"

"My husband."

"He doesn't mind?"

"We have an agreement. He doesn't tell me about his affairs, and I don't tell him about mine. There've been a lot of men," Adele laughed.

"Why keep a good thing to myself?"

"I want...I want to be around to raise my son," Helen blurted. When Adele put her arms about her, she clung to her and sobbed. She had felt so alone these last days.

"It's hard. I remember how hard it was," Adele said gently.

"Oh my God," Helen moaned. It was as if she was in that dream again trying to pick up the lump with the tongs. Everything was failing apart. She couldn't catch her breath and breathed like an asthmatic. Adele rubbed her back and offered her tissues. Her nose was clogged. When she was finally in control enough to say, "I'm all right," she had to laugh at her stuffed nose voice.

"Do you want to see now?" Adele asked.

Helen nodded. She stiffened as Adele unbuttoned her blouse and slipped the pink, silicon prosthesis out of her bra. Adele let it quiver in her hand and then tossed it into the air. "Do you want to hold it?"

The intimate offer, as if Adele had unscrewed her real breast and held it out, shocked Helen. "No."

Lifting her bra up, Helen revealed a flat whiteness and a horizontal scar. A smile played on her lips as she toured her surgery. "There's where the scar 'whited out;' there's the drain tube hole scar." Her eyes shut; Adele floated her finger over the scar, and murmured, "After the surgery, I stood naked before the mirror every day. I said to myself, 'That's me, that's me.'"

Almost every evening Adele stopped by Helen's apartment bringing macrobiotic offerings from the health food restaurant and once apricot pits. She wanted Helen to eat the seeds.

"Aren't they poisonous?"

Adele shrugged. "It's a natural laetrile."

When Helen visited Adele, she noticed shelves holding books about diet, vitamin therapy, visualization technique, I Ching, Buddhism, as well as oncology texts. Adele's kitchen counter was crowded with bottles of herbal mixtures and homeopathic pills; a twenty-pound sack of carrots stood on her floor and, Helen had watched Adele thrust carrots and cabbage into a juicer that instantly sucked them up and spewed forth juice and sprays of ground vegetables. She had grown accustomed to the drink's strong flavor but not the noxious smell or the diarrhea the concoction gave her.

"I eat apricot seeds all the time. It hasn't hurt me," Adele persisted, peeking in Helen's pot and inquiring if the broccoli she saw was organic. When Helen said no, she retorted, "You should see how they spray broccoli!" She refused the coffee Helen offered. "I used to drink coffee but then I realized I wouldn't have gotten cancer if I had lived my life differently."

Although Helen knew the glow in Adele's eyes was that of the zealous reformer, she was glad for the visits. She patiently listened to talk of coffee enemas, enzyme supplements, water purifiers, and every quack remedy. She repressed her urge to utter some sarcasm or laugh. She depended on Adele too much. If Adele knew how to live with the cancer, she needed to learn.

She regretted when her friend rushed off to her own family or to preside over the informal clinic she ran at her house. Often when Helen phoned, Adele told her, "I can't talk. I'm treating an ear ache," or "I'm treating cramps." She had no training beyond her passionate interest in the human body, and since she did not accept money for her ministrations, her closet folk healing practice was widespread.

Two days before the surgery, Adele taught Helen to meditate. She lit a candle and incense, rang a Buddhist bell, and while Helen sat cross-legged with her hands resting in her lap, she intoned, "Fire...earth...metal...water...wood." Helen concentrated on her breathing, growing aware of the air drawn into her nostrils and out, in and out; over and over the rhythm put her into a peaceful trance.

"Your face glowed," Adele told her after the meditation session, hugged her and kissed her hard on the lips with that overflow of animal spirits that drew so many people into her orbit. Helen had seen it when they went for walks and Adele called out boldly to men, women, children, and animals. Coming into Helen's flower shop, she even flirted with the plants, crooning to them and caressing the leaves. To a trio of policeman, she shouted, "Is anything wrong, you guys? Can I help out?" and enchanted by the lilt in her voice and her smile, the three of them looked ready to follow her down the street. Adele laughed to Helen, "I have too much power. Sometimes, it gets me into trouble."

In the darkened hospital room the night before the operation, Adele appeared with the Buddhist bell and her candle and meditated with Helen.

"Let light flow through the chaika, the opening, on the top of your head. Feel it fill you. Feel it go to the tips of your fingers and your toes. First white light which has all colors, then whatever colored light you need."

From the hallway Helen heard a rubber wheeled cart slide over the linoleum and the thick-soled squeak of a nurse's shoes. The noise faded as she followed Adele's mesmerizing voice.

"Each color heals in its own way. Let the light radiate off your skin."

Adele blew out the candle and sounded the bell to end the meditation. "There's a lot of spirituality here in the hospital. I didn't think there would be." Before she left she handed over an envelope of homeopathic pills. "Don't touch the arnica with your fingers, just shake the pellets into your mouth. Let them melt under your tongue. You'll see, you'll heal more quickly."

With Adele gone, Helen roamed the halls, peeking in one room, where a black preacher stood at a woman's bedside and prayed, "I'm pleading with you, the doctor who never lost a case...." Through a partially opened curtain in another room she saw a fat, immobile woman lying still, the ambitious two volumes of The Decline and Fall of the Roman Empire, on her

319

window ledge. Everyone, she thought, had her own magic, and she was relying on Adele's.

The next morning an orderly rolled her into the windowless operating room. The rough pull of the intern grabbing her arm to put it in a splint so she wouldn't move it when the lymph nodes in the armpit were removed, the bright Muzak tape playing, the chatter of the nurses, all made her aware of the routineness of the procedure. To the people in that room, he was only a body. When she asked the surgeon what they would do with her breast, he answered brusquely, "Burn it."

With a flick of her wrist, the woman anesthetist injected something into her arm and she felt herself go off. She woke hours later. Her throat was burning where the anesthetist had scraped it with the tube, and her chest was on fire and swollen with pain.

Boxes of chocolate, a basket of fruit, new nightgowns from Susan arrived at the Berkeley flat. Friends and relatives wrote kind letters and Helen cried reading them. She begged Susan to keep her father at bay. She just had to be alone, to get control and not show her vulnerability. Even as a child she had retreated to her room until she stopped crying.

She had sent Brent off to the babysitter's for the week while she got her strength back. At the hospital his photograph was taped above her she wept about him. Who would take care of her son if she died? The only place she felt safe was in the rocking chair, the one she had bought to sit in while she nursed. Now she used it to nurse herself.

Back and forth, she rocked, just like that time after Hal took off for Portland. He was white haired as an albino and with striking blue eyes. He had painted the kitchen cabinets gold as she instructed and then as if he couldn't keep his hands still, he had painted flowers all over them. "Got carried away," he grinned and shifted nervously on his feet. She decided she liked it, saying, "After all, I'm a florist." Before she knew it, he had cooked an omelet for the two of them and she was telling him about driving the van over to the flower market at dawn and how beautiful the fresh banks of flowers looked. There hadn't been many men in her life and she wanted a baby, so she persuaded herself there was a future for them. When she was seven months pregnant, she came home and found he was gone. She always suspected he would get restless, but she thought he'd at least see her through the labor.

Her pain pills put her in a trance and she didn't stir even though the phone kept ringing. Later, she was alarmed to hear someone at the door. The buzzer sounded, followed by knocking. "Helen, I know you're in there. You can't keep me out," came Adele's voice. Sheepish, Helen opened the door. Adele brought her a dish of brown rice and seaweed and Helen devoured every bit of it. She had thought she didn't want to see anyone, but was glad to see Adele, and confided the terrible dreams she had that she lost her other breast. Adele said she dreamt she found wasps in her bra. They laughed about their dreaming the same way.

It wasn't long before Adele asked, "Did you take the bandage off yet?" and Helen had to confess she hadn't had the courage. Adele did it for her, slowly peeling away the gauze and adhesive tape and then studying the red scar with its metal staples. "The ultimate punk," she joked. "You could get a job at an S and M sex emporium."

When Helen was ready for an excursion, Adele drove her to a discount store. Feeling a bit uncomfortable because she wished to please her friend more than she wanted the purchase, Helen bought a one hundred would return, she took all of the nostrums Adele dispensed.

She went to Adele's house to visit the attic studio where she meditated. As they were about to climb the steep stairs, Mark whined, "Where ya going, Mom? You're always running out." Adele threw her arms around him and crooned, "How can you say that Mark-y Wark-y? Don't I adore you? Tall, bearded Neil waved from the living room where he was listening to the stereo with earphones.

A huge poster of a bare chested woman with a mastectomy dominated one attic wall. A laughing woman ran on the beach with her arms held wide. A tattooed snake embellished her scar. Beneath the poster, Adele had arranged a shrine of rocks, shells, peacock feathers, candles and photographs.

Adele, it turned out, was a photographer. On a second wall were photographs of Mrs. Hayes, Adele's healer, an eighty-year-old Santa Rosa woman who claimed to be able to detect the presence of cancer by examining spittle. She was a small hale woman with white hair tied back in a bun. Adele had photographed her sitting in a slatted chair in the dappled light beneath an elm.

As Helen examined the portraits, the sounds of arguing rose from the floor below. Mark, shouted, "Fuck you! I hate both of you."

"Maybe I should go," Helen offered, uneasy to keep Adele from her son, but Adele answered firmly, "Neil will calm him down."

A door slammed and Adele flinched. "He must have run out. He'll jump on his bike and ride it out." She scrambled to her feet and ran to the window to watch, more deflated than Helen had ever seen her. "I don't really know what to do with him. He keeps getting in trouble. He's been in three different schools in the last two years. You know what he called me yesterday? He called me a 'fucking-one-tit-witch.' It was quite a scene. He threw a bread knife against the wall. I guess I'm lucky he didn't stab me. Later he apologized. He was really sorry." Adele laughed nervously, "They're really little buggers at that age. Wait you'll see."

She walked briskly to a dresser and pulled open a drawer. "Here, take a look." Adele handed Helen an envelope. Inside were photographs. They were nude portraits she had done of herself revealing the mastectomy. Helen remembered the photo of herself Adele had shown her at their first meeting. She closed her eyes trying to merge these images with that one.

"Can I photograph you, Helen?" Now Adele was smiling, her usual aplomb returned.

"Do you want to do me nude too? I'm not up to posing nude, you know.

"Too bad. It messes up my collection."

"My God, you're a mad woman." Months ago Helen would have been shocked. Not now. Adele had gotten her to the point where she could say something like "fuck" and not feel a priest looking over her shoulder. She knew if not for the cancer, she never would have let herself come so near to anyone, but now the barriers were down.

As if reading her thoughts, Adele remarked, "You're changing Helen, getting to be a mad woman yourself."

"I'll tell you what. I'll get a few white roses from my shop, wear my gold communion cross around my neck and hold Brent on my lap."

"Right. Madonna and child," Adele laughed, but she glanced out the window again.

"Do you want to look for Mark?"

"Neil went after him!" Straddling a round zafu meditation pillow on the floor, Adele closed her eyes and breathed deeply. The tension went out of her face and her eyelids fluttered open. "You have to keep all healing methods open--don't reject anything. Do you want to meet Mrs. Hayes?"

"I...don't know."

"Your reality changes with cancer." She took up a blue feather from her shrine and stroked her cheek with it, smiling. "This feather's magic. It brings back happy memories of the woods where I found it. Here you hold it. You'll see, it will make you happy too."

"What did your psychic tell you?"

"She said to visualize myself as whole as possible. One of the teachings of disease is that you create your own wholeness. Look at my poster. Don't you love her?"

The truth was, Helen recoiled from the poster. She found herself looking away from it and then drawn back. The woman's expression was exultant, as if she could triumph over any adversity. Adele possessed the same toughness. But Helen knew her own terror and wondered how she would be able to make herself feel safe. "I'm not used to it yet. I don't know how to accept myself," she said. Even after a month, when she'd begun working again and was 'back to normal,' she hated looking at the scar. Adele seemed to worship the mutilation, making it the ground for a sister and brotherhood. She had told Helen of wanting to accost a man in a wheel chair, unbutton her shirt and cry, "I'm like you!" Knowing Adele's spontaneity, Helen was surprised she hadn't done it.

"You have to create a new reality," Adele said. "Something that counters the big boobs culture. You could think of yourself as an Amazon warrior, if that helps you. The problem with cancer is you lose your confidence and become afraid to live. But you've got to believe you have the resources and imagination inside you. I see women with metastasized cancer who live more fully than most ordinary people. There's one I know who can barely sit up, and yet she's going to give a piano recital. You should come."

"It would be hard."

"Everything's new to you. You'll get used to it. Oh, this fucking disease makes me so angry. Come here." She stroked Helen's hair. "You're like a little girl." Adele began to talk about her love affairs and traveling to France on her own where she'd met two lovers and Helen listened raptly. "Get this," Adele laughed, "I met both of them on the train. Different occasions, of course. Both were named Martin. I spent a week with the second Martin and he asked me, 'Will you miss me when you go home?' 'Why should I miss you?' I told him, 'I don't even miss my husband and son.' I hate when someone tries to nail me down like that. I don't see myself being with Neil forever. I don't see myself as being with anyone forever."

"Will you abandon me too?"

"Maybe. No guarantees. How is the scar healing? Let me see." Adele unbuttoned Helen's blouse. "Does it hurt when I touch it?" Adele ran one finger lightly over the scar.

"No, it doesn't hurt." "What if I kiss it?" She bent her curly head to Helen's chest and kissed her gently. "Now it's healed."

The health food restaurant smelled of sautéed bean sprouts and miso, and was papered with political posters about El Salvador, Nicaragua and peace marches. Helen recognized Adele's touch in the charts on breast self-examination. They reminded her of the new demands, that she take ginseng, golden seal and purchase a water purifier like the one Adele just bought. In the beginning, when she had felt so terrified, she would have complied, but lately she bridled at being managed.

Not that she wasn't still attached to Adele. In fact, she had made a special trip to the restaurant because Adele hadn't answered her phone calls since getting involved with Lisa who was dying of breast cancer. At their last visit, Adele told Helen about the young woman's stroke and described the frightening details of Lisa's helplessness, the bedpan and the food dribbling down her chin. She felt in awe of Adele. To Helen, Lisa's dying would seem a frightening rehearsal of her own, and she knew she couldn't do it.

When she asked the waiter if she might speak with Adele, he told, her that it was her day off. "Can I leave my name?" she asked, scribbling a brief message on a napkin.

He startled her saying, "You one of her breast cancer patients? Most of the ones who come around here have breast cancer."

"I'm a friend," she said carefully. If not for his gaze on her, she would have run out of the restaurant. Crossing the street, she didn't notice the on-coming car, was too busy wondering, if Adele photographed Lisa too? Her jealousy surprised her. She was feeling the way Mark did. The screeching brakes distracted her for a moment. That was close. She climbed into her van and tried to calm herself before driving away.

The next evening, Adele phoned and spoke to her with concern. "I got your note. What's wrong? Have you had a recurrence?"

"No, not that. Not that. I just wondered. I hadn't heard from you so long."

"I did phone a few times and you weren't in."

"The phone machine...."

"I just didn't feel like leaving a message. How's Brent? How's that darling?

"Fine." "Thriving."

"Yes."

"You know, I really have to run, but I'll get back to you."

"Don't hang up," Helen pleaded. She wanted to tell Adele how much she missed her, how she waited for the phone to ring. "Please, give me a few more minutes. Better yet, come visit me." She paused but then blurted out the difficult words, "I need you."

"Fuck it, Lisa's dying. I'll come by after she's gone."

Helen flung down the phone. Adele was too busy sanctifying herself to see her. Not unless she had a recurrence.

"Just jump right in," Susan told her. She wore a frilly blouse and had just permed her red hair into tight ringlets, which reminded Helen of how she looked in parochial school when they were both practicing Catholics. "It's like when you're in a car accident. You have to start driving right away, or you'll never drive again."

Divorced after a brief marriage, Susan was eager as ever for Helen's company for "singles" events. She had different ideas from Adele's of healthful food and had brought over whipped cream tarts. Brent was ecstatically devouring his in his high chair. "Yum yum." Susan beamed at him, but looked askance at Helen's untouched treat. "Oh come on. Let's live it up. I figure if my number's up, it's up. I'm not going to change things by being miserable."

Helen forced herself to smile. She was still grieving about Adele. After the phone call, she felt so angry, even deciding Adel felt a secret frisson of delight when she heard someone was ill. She rushed right over. It gave her an opportunity to shine. Now,

Adele's abandonment brought back older losses, like when Hal left. She wasn't ready to go out and meet someone new.

She explained this to Susan, who said, "You're raising a child by yourself. You're running a business. You had the courage to go in and have a mastectomy. I don't see how you can be afraid of anything."

"I'm glad you reminded me. I keep forgetting, I'm superwoman."

On the weekend, she hired a babysitter and she and Susan went for a twilight hike with the Sierra Club in the Marin headlands where she walked along the cliffs and looked down at the crashing waves. Adele's charisma seemed to have rubbed off on her. She observed herself with astonishment, vivacious, getting into conversations with strangers. Karl, a divorced computer programmer, was intrigued that she was a florist. He told her he once took a course in Ikebana, Japanese flower arrangement. In his late forties, he talked proudly of his teenage daughter, Brenda, and she told him about Brent. They laughed at the similarity in names. He said he wanted to meet Brent.

In a few days, he phoned with an invitation to the theater. At the last minute, she tried to back out but couldn't reach him on the telephone. With each succeeding date, her nervousness grew. Was she letting herself grow fond of him? What with her experience with Hal and knowing that ultimately, she would have to tell him about the cancer, she couldn't put aside a creeping dread. Finally, one evening at a Thai restaurant, he asked, "When can we spend the night together?" He was like that, putting the question to her over dinner rather than waiting for a moment of passion.

"Let's see how well put together you are," Helen replied. The words were ones Susan had suggested, but the bravado was Adele's. Her heart pounded as she went on, "I've had a mastectomy."

Karl stared at her in surprise. He lifted his wine glass, but then put it down without taking a sip. "It really doesn't matter at all." She saw he was shocked and sorrowful for her. Her hand rested on the table and he reached out to hold it in his large, warm one.

The next day, she sent a basket of flowers to his office. In her ebullience, she felt like calling Adele and saying, "You were right. I can still be sexual!"

Then, after four months, Adele dropped by unexpectedly one night. Helen wasn't surprised. She knew Adele always acted on impulse. Adele said, "Lisa's dead." Helen tasted ashes at the sight of her friend. She wanted to blurt out, "You hurt me," but Adele held her mournful announcement in front of her like a shield. Trailing Helen to the kitchen, she continued, "I was with her all the time. It wasn't easy. I didn't think I'd make it and kept hoping she'd die sooner. At least I was there when she died, and I kept vigil with the body for an entire night. Lisa wanted that. She was a Buddhist, you know. I called her mother and asked her to come sit with me, and she wouldn't."

She paused for that to sink in, her charity greater than a mother's. Although, of course, Helen thought, she would have been neglecting Mark all this time she was outshining Lisa's mother.

Adele continued, "Now, it's over. I'm glad to be free again."

Helen knew Adele wanted her to ask for the details or at least to mumble, "I'm sorry," but she couldn't speak. She busied herself putting the kettle to boil and gathering mugs for tea. "I have chamomile. Is that all right?"

"Yes, yes. Like Peter Rabbit. Where is it? I'll get it?" Not waiting for an answer, Adele threw open the cabinets and noting the juicer now stored on a high shelf, threw Helen a reproachful glance. She began to rummage for the herbs and supplemental vitamins she had recommended.

Why aren't you taking vitamin C? Or Echinacea?"

Helen shrugged. "I gave them up."

"The cancer can always come back. Don't you want to fight? Have you stopped meditating too?"

"I just don't feel like living my life around cancer," Helen replied.

"Yes, I can understand that," Adele conceded.

Helen was astonished at the humble answer. But soon Adele rallied, smiling with the old charm. "Would you be interested in joining a support group? That's why I came over, to ask you tonight."

"For women with breast cancer?" Helen filled the teapot with steaming water and covered it with her mother's green and white crocheted cozy.

"What other kind of support group would it be? I've had a number of younger women I consider special in mind. I waited until there were enough for a group."

Helen filled the mugs and handed Adele one. "No. I'm sorry. I don't think I'll join." The words gave her satisfaction.

"Maybe you'll change your mind. You'll let me know. I always assumed you'd be in it."

Helen shook her head. She sipped her tea and gazed at Adele in her purple gossamer Indian dress, the fading light softening her features.

Adele pitched her voice low, as she inquired after Brent and other matters in Helen's life. She was making polite conversation so as not to break off in an abrupt way.

Out the window Helen saw a sliver of moon surrounded by a hazy aura and a few distant stars. She had to resist Adele's charm. Adele was too dangerous, wanting the drama of illness and death to give "clarity" to her days, and Helen wasn't willing to be one of the performers.

When Adele got up to leave, there was an awkward moment while both of them waited for the other to make the move towards a perfunctory embrace. But neither did. It made

Helen remember when they first met and she had recoiled at the hardness of Adele's prosthesis.

"Goodbye," Adele said, regarding her regretfully. She walked out and carelessly left the door open.

Helen had to close it after her.

She marked the seasons, the white dry summers, and the wild poppies and furze of spring by her runs in the hills, nature giving her health and bringing her to her forty-third year. When she returned to the silent large house, she prepared a bath. The water ran while she stripped off her clothes. In the mirror she saw a slender body, a thin, delicate face with dark eyes.

She slipped into the steaming bath and glided soapy hands over face, neck and arms. On her left breast she found a tiny pimple under the skin. Her hand lifted and returned. This time she could not feel the pimple. "Nothing," she thought, flooded with relief. It had disappeared. Then the small hardness rolled about between her fingers again. The bath water grew cold and her teeth chattered and the hair on her arms stood up straight, as she became experienced in locating it. She marked it off, three fingers above the nipple, on a fifty-five degree angle towards the breastbone. Over and over she returned, each time hoping she had just imagined it. Vaguely, she remembered months before her fingers stumbling upon an even tinier hardness that disappeared when she tried to refind it. She kept hoping that like the last time, this lump would vanish. But no, with the surety of a magnet, the growth drew her trembling touch.

Wearing a blue paper shower cap on her head and a blue hospital gown, she sat in a wheel chair leafing through the medical chart on her lap. The nurse practitioner had written, "very anxious," and the surgery clinic clerk had rubber stamped a picture of breasts onto the visit reports for the surgeon to draw in the tumor. Down the hall, she noticed a woman lying on a gurney as if dead, a jar filled with blackish blood on a stainless steel rack beneath.

A young Chicana nurse took the chart away and washed her chest with a cold yellow iodine solution. "Let's go," the surgeon said. He looked like a duck because of the sweep of blond pompadour hair and his way of shaking the water off his scrubbed hands before slipping them into the rubber gloves held open by the nurse. As she lay on the operating room table, a blue cloth called the ether screen stretched between her and the surgeon, named in another age when ether was used. "Ether screen," had a high-necked Victorian sound for her because now its only purpose was to keep her from seeing. Swathed by blueness, she could have pretended nothing was happening if the surgeon's elbow didn't keep banging through the cloth against her face while he cut. "The anesthetic's worn off," she whimpered. First he pretended not to hear as if the screen between them masked her voice, but when she insisted, he called to her tensely, "Yeah, can you just hold on a bit? I don't want to stiffen the tissue with more anesthetic." She panted the way she had during the birth of her child.

"Nothing," the surgeon said abruptly, sounding closer through the screen.

"Are you finished?

"I'm sewing you up."

"Can you tell if it was cancer?"

"I told you, it's nothing. I'm not even going to break it up. Just going to send it to the 'path' lab."

When propriety had been restored, the wound bandaged and her hospital gown pulled down, he ripped back the ether screen. His voice became casual, with a reassuring dismissiveness that told her she no longer needed his concern. "You're o.k. Come back in a week so I can see how you're healing.

The surgeon bustled into the tiny examination room, smiling so hard she noticed his porcelain teeth. "I have good news and bad news. What do you want to hear?" he asked. His foot pressed the pedal beneath the sink and water swooshed over his hands.

"The good news."

"We caught it while it's small." She stopped listening. His voice droned on and on about her options.

"You'll cut off the nipple too?" she asked.

"Yes."

Then she started crying. He heaved himself up beside her on the examination table, his feet dangling down and awkwardly put his arm about her shoulder. "I have four more women to tell today," he sighed.

Her husband sat across from her his face looking gray and old. He pretended to read, but she knew he continually stole glances at her. After she had told him about the cancer, they had not known what to do. How do you spend an afternoon? They had gone grocery shopping. In the evening he phoned her parents and then their daughter at a mid-western college. At her urging, her need to resume their ordinary routines-a way to pretend nothing had happened--he went back to work after the weekend, and then even went on a three-day business trip. She felt frantic by the time he returned. "I can't be alone," she sobbed and struggled to catch her breath. "I don't know how to go on from one moment to the next. There's no let up." "You can go on...you will...just this moment it seems hard." He drew near and she gazed at his face, as if at a stranger's. In a few days' time, everything had become foreign. His Adam's apple caught her attention, and she realized she had never looked at it before, the way it bobbed up and down as he swallowed nervously. "Do you feel better?" "What?" His voice sounded far aw

He stayed home now to watch after her, to answer the ever-ringing phone and to fend off people who wanted to visit. She didn't want to see anyone. At 'the second opinion doctors,' he asked questions and took notes, while she sat in forgetfulness wondering, whom was it he and the doctor talked about. One doctor was harried, answering his phone twice and scarcely looking at either of them; another, lugubrious as a funeral director, kept his pen poised over his prescription pad, eager to prescribe tranquilizers and sleeping pills. In his fumbling to help, the first doctor bullied, "What are you worried about? Is all your marriage based on is a breast?" After, walking down the brightly lit hall, she forced the words out, "Will you love me without a breast?" "I want you alive," he said, wrenching the words from himself too. He caught her hand in his.

At home she lay on the couch and listened to Gregorian chants, the only music that calmed her. She got up and paced back and forth, and then leafed through one of the newly purchased paperback books about cancer stacked on the coffee table. Her husband busied himself in the kitchen. He surprised her by stopping at Oakland's Chinatown and buying live crabs, blue and red ones, that crawled about in the stainless steel sink all afternoon. Occasionally, she went to look at them and laughed. "How are you going to bring yourself to kill them?" "I really don't know. But what else am I going to do with them? Do you want to keep them as pets?" The kitchen echoed with the thump of cleaver against chopping board andspatulascraping wok. The fragrance of ginger and onion drifted through the house. "Dinner," he called cheerfully, radiant with the gift of the meal. He set the dining room table, putting out chopsticks instead of silver. His excitement exhilarated her, and she seated herself happily but then felt of stomach knotting. Whenever she forgot the cancer, it reasserted itself all the more strongly.

She heard of a woman who had been treated for breast cancer and asked her to come to show her mastectomy. Thirty-five years old, Adele, dressed in work boots and denim trousers and shirt, worked in a collective health food restaurant. Her hair had turned gray from chemotherapy. She brought a bouquet of Persian lilies.

They sat side by side on the living room couch while Adele unbuttoned her shirt and unhooked a lace brassiere. Pulling out her prosthesis, she let it quiver on her palm like jelly.

"Do you want to hold it?"

"No."

"I find it comforting to just play with it like silly putty," she said kneading the pink latex with the tips of her fingers, then letting it shiver on the coffee table. She pushed the empty bra cup away and revealed her flat chest. "They lift the skin up and scrape out every bit of breast tissue. You'll be like a board when they're finished." Gently, lovingly, she ran her finger along the red scar. "See, it's faded in some places. The doctor calls it 'whiting out.' After the surgery, I used to stand in front of the mirror stripped and tell myself, 'That's me! That's me!' I couldn't believe it at first." Almost forgetful of her in her reverie, Adele now looked up, and said pityingly, "You look shaken. The first time's the hardest. It will get better for you."

A high priestess, an initiator into a secret sisterhood, Adele phoned and came again and again, detailing the lessons to be learned-hard lessons, written down no where.

Once the two of them drove up into the Berkeley hills. Each spring the city hired a shepherd with his herd of goats to clear the brush, and they joined the mothers and squealing youngsters watching the brown, white and piebald goats munching diligently at an overgrown hillside. A few had given birth and just beyond the fence, one goat nibbled at the membranes of the birth sack of her small, blind baby. "Look at the baby," one woman cooed. "Look at the one with a beard." The goats bleated. A young black one romped in a circle. Overhead fleecy clouds floated in a clear, blue sky.

Against this gaiety, Adele passed on her frightening knowledge.

"It's almost two years since it happened to me. I almost miss the way it was."

"How could that be?"

"Everything was so clear and intense."

The night before the surgery, her husband enclosed her in his embrace, unable to part from her.

"You know what scares me?" he blurted, "the anesthetic."

"Why? Don't you think I'll wake up?"

Tears filled his eyes. "I want you alive."

Adele's arrival allowed him to go. She brought a Buddhist bell and a candle and taught her to meditate. "Fire...earth...metal...water...wood," her voice intoned soothingly. She blew out the candle and sounded the bell to end the meditation. "There's a lot of spirituality here in the hospital. I didn't think there would be."

Then when Adele was gone too, she roamed the halls. She peeked in one woman's room to see a black preacher and hear him saying, "I'm praying to you, the doctor who never lost a case...." Through a partially opened curtain in another room she saw a fat, immobile woman lying still, the ambitious two volumes of *The Decline and Fall of the Roman Empire,* on her window ledge untouched. In another room an old man tossed about and screamed, "Oy, oy, oy," while he pulled the intravenous needle from his arm. "What's going on?" she asked a male nurse. He answered frantically, "He's senile, and he doesn't know what he's doing. We're going to have to tie him down or he'll kill himself. He's quiet during the day and then screams all night-that's how it is with this kind of senility. He's Armenian and doesn't speak English and I was so desperate, I even tried talking to him in Yiddish--not that I can really speak Yiddish."

She paced the glass walled hall that enclosed the ward, thinking how the hospital held the flow of life. Everyone ended up there. It had nearly the inevitability of death. Outside she saw the traffic of the busy streets and the lights of the freeway. A neon sign advertised a carwash-restaurant across from the hospital. Did people get their food at a drive-in window and then eat it as conveyor belts carried their car past twirling soapy brushes and spraying water? Then they could drive away onto the highway.

A student nurse waited in her room and asked shyly, "Can I take a medical history for my class? Do you want a back rub?"

The next morning early, her husband came. The surgery wasn't scheduled until the afternoon and they spent the endless time playing cards and watching television. She wasn't allowed to eat and he insisted on fasting with her. They strolled along the hall and like a tour guide she showed him the sights she had seen. A blonde woman and her husband stood in one doorway and invited them into his room. A metal disk in his throat, he had had his larynx removed and communicated on a small chalkboard. Nodding towards his wife, he hurriedly wrote and beckoned them to read the words, 'she stood by me.' Tears filled her eyes because she knew exactly what he meant. The nurse came looking for her and told her she better get ready.

Wheeled on the stretcher, she felt like an infant. She kept her eyes closed and held on to her husband's hand tightly, terrified when they made him go away. An orderly rolled her into the windowless operating room. The rough pull of the intern grabbing her arm to put it in a splint so she wouldn't move it when the lymph nodes in the armpit were removed, the bright Muzak tape playing, the chatter of the nurses made her sickeningly aware of the routineness of the procedure. When she asked the surgeon what they would do with her breast, he nodded his head brusquely, saying, "We burn it."

With a flick of her wrist, the woman anesthetist plunged her into oblivion and she became like the carcass she had seen in the hall before her biopsy. Later the oblivion didn't want to release her, but kept pulling her back. She felt smothered, as if behind another ether screen. In and out, in and out, she traveled, so she couldn't tell what was real, only knew her throat burned where the anesthetist had scraped the intubation tube, and her chest was on fire. It felt swollen as if the breast remained.

Then she felt herself being wheeled back to the ward. Although she couldn't rise to full consciousness, a part of her frantically sought to make contact. Drowning, struggling to catch a rope to pull her to shore, she strained to hear a voice that acknowledged her as alive and who she was. Her husband spoke to her. She felt him leaning his face close to hers. His hand grasped hers again. She knew from the moment she let go, he had held it in readiness.

Made in the USA
San Bernardino, CA
21 November 2015